HOW WE GOT
SWINDLED

BY WALL STREET GODFATHERS, GREED & FINANCIAL DARWINISM

The 30-Year War Against The American Dream

E. Henry Schoenberger

Foreword by David Satterfield, Pulitzer Prize-Winning financial journalist

ₚₚ riverrun press

HOW WE GOT SWINDLED
By Wall Street Godfathers, Greed & Financial Darwinism

Copyright © 2010 by E. Henry Schoenberger.

ISBN 978-0-9266606-1-8

Library of Congress Control Number: 2011918953

DEDICATION AND ACKNOWLEDGEMENTS

To Marc Loewenthal, for his help and encouragement in reading and criticizing my first draft. To Dave Satterfield, for his support and insight, and for putting his reputation on line by writing a memorable foreword. To my daughter, Meredith, for her social networking expertise and writing critiques. And to my exceptional, articulate wife, Julie, who liked my first three chapters or I might not have continued with this book. She had my back for the duration of my difficult to live with process of writing, and then proofed and added clarity to the entire manuscript.

TABLE OF CONTENTS

FOREWORD

By: David Satterfield, former Business Editor of the Miami Herald with two Pulitzers for investigative journalism.

The financial meltdown of the early 21st century is one of history's greatest debacles. Herein is an autopsy of the disaster. It chronicles motive, cause and result, and it offers a sensible prescription for prevention.

If history is any guide, it will be ignored.

At the core of the great Wall Street meltdown is mankind's innate tendency to be greedy, taken to unimagined extremes.

Greed is a word that gets overused all the time. I subscribe to the belief that a little bit of greed, after all, isn't necessarily a bad thing. The overwhelming desire to "have more than is actually needed" – as greed is defined -- can have some very positive influences. It can motivate, it can attract investment capital, it can result in real invention and innovation; it can lead to job creation. It can make my kids take out the trash.

Like so many things in the right dosage, greed can, in the words of the fictional Gordon Gekko, be good.

But like everything in life, too much greed – good or bad -- can be devastating. The historical record is not kind to man in accounting for greed. Throughout the ages, greed has gotten the better part of us all. It's one of those attributes that's not unlike water – it can help sustain life, but in excess, is one of earth's most devastating forces.

This book helps explain what happened when a flood of greed gripped this country in the early 21st century. Henry Schoenberger explains why the meltdown occurred, and most importantly, how it happened and how it can be prevented, or at least, mitigated, in the future. At its root is man's innate tendency toward greed, which today manifests itself in our nation as **Financial Darwinism – survival of the richest.**

You won't agree with everything in this book; Henry has strong opinions and he is never shy about expressing them. He is unafraid to flay sacred cows. He exposes the Emperor's lack of clothes, then demonstrates that the Emperor also lacks a heart, a soul and the better part of a brain. Few actors in this tragedy are spared from Henry's wrath, and the perpetrators are deserving.

Henry's victims – many of whom also were caught up in the greed -- are the middle- and upper-middle class families who have seen their housing values soar, then plummet and their tax dollars go to rescue the very people who created such anxiety in the market.

In Henry's detailed account, a relatively small band of people – driven by seemingly insatiable greed – were able to convince an entire nation of consumers that unattainable things were suddenly attainable. They convinced seemingly smart investors that one and one could equal three, and that two sides could bet against each other and yet everyone would still win. Their financial engineering turned a segment of the mortgage industry into conniving thieves, concerned only about the compensation bonus and not the client. And they convinced a huge number of hard-working Americans that they could afford things they could not. In sum, they brewed a variety of new flavors of poisonous Kool-Aid, and convinced everyone from seemingly smart hedge-fund managers to newly arrived immigrants to drink it and enjoy it.

When reality finally intervened, the tsunami of greed nearly brought a nation to its knees.

A cruel irony is this: not only did government fail to prevent it, but government had willingly torn down the levees that had been erected some

60 years earlier to protect a nation from that tsunami. And when the newly "free" market neared collapse, government stepped in and handed over billions of dollars in taxpayer funds to rescue that hardy band of financial engineers and their multimillion-dollar pay packages.

Henry calls this excess of greed Financial Darwinism – aside from the terminology, the trait is nothing new. As he says, the latest debacle "is the progression of man's concern for wealth as well as man's historical inhumanity toward his fellow man." It dates back to the days of Emperors and Kings, coliseums and harems. In more modern times in our country, it has taken shape in the Robber Barons of the 19th and early 20th centuries. And it led to the Great Depression of the 1930s.

Economic theorists promote Financial Darwinism through laissez-faire economics – the market will take care of itself, winners will be sorted from losers. Leave the markets alone and they will function properly. Which all sounds well and good – not unlike Karl Marx's socialism. In theory, it sounds great. Unfortunately, mankind is left to execute. And mankind isn't suited for such theories.

That's where government is supposed to step in – to provide some framework and rules to prevent chaos. That's why we have traffic laws and drug laws and criminal law. Imagine if everyone were allowed to drive as fast as they want, not need to stop for traffic lights or signs, and had no responsibility to stop when they hit someone. That's what our financial markets became in the early 2000s.

Financial damages from the resulting pileup became our responsibility. The pricetag is incalculable.

So you would think that our legislators and regulators would be fixing the traffic rules? Not a chance. And Henry explains why.

The book is replete with examples of the dangers ahead. It's never good for a society to have such a small percentage of people control such huge wealth. We scoff at Latin America, but the trend line looks as though we're headed to the same place. Our of our nation's greatest assets and greatest accomplishments was its ability to create and sustain a large middle and upper-middle class – that is in danger today.

Our ancestors wisely took note of the dangers of too rich, too big and too big to fail. That's why we ended up with the Sherman Anti-Trust Act, Glass Steagall and the Bank Holding Company Act of 1956. They were erected for a reason.

So is all regulation good? Certainly not. But neither is all regulation bad. This is not an argument for socialism; it's an argument that might again be espoused by none other than Thomas Jefferson, who said government's role is to protect the public good – even if it's at the cost of private profits.

This book should be required reading for business and economic students. It helps explain why free markets are rarely, if ever, free and why Adam Smith's invisible hand – because of man's inability to control his urges – will often have something up its sleeve.

David Satterfield

PREFACE:
A ZEN PATH THROUGH THE MINEFIELDS

For the past twenty years I have considered the adverse effects of the undeclared pursuit of Financial Darwinism which, ironically, is a *derivative* of the Social Darwinism practiced by Andrew Carnegie, John D. Rockefeller, and the ultra rich prior to the Great Depression. Social Darwinism was based on the writings of the British philosopher Herbert Spencer. Spencer profoundly influenced Carnegie by providing him with the philosophical justification for his unabashed Greed in pursuit of personal riches in business. And the philosophy of Social Darwinism freed Carnegie from any moral reservations about *the pursuit of unbridled financial acquisition at the expense of the wellbeing of his workers.* This philosophy *also* freed Carnegie from any concern for his avaricious behavior's toxic effect on society; certainly not the high society type.

Spencer applied Darwin's idea of natural selection to those who could acquire the highest pile of gold. It was **Spencer** who **coined the term** *Survival of the Fittest*, which he used to explain the fate of the rich and poor in a laissez-faire capitalist society. Spencer argued there was nothing unnatural, and therefore wrong, with competing and rising to the top in a cut-throat capitalist world. Capitalism is not the problem – it is how it is used, or abused in the name of freedom.

So it is important to begin this book with the knowledge that **Financial Darwinism is simply the metamorphosis of Social Darwinism which never died.** And that the Social Darwinism of Spencer is still fundamentally vital to the so-called free-market capitalism practiced by Wall Street. Therefore **Financial Darwinism is the core belief underlying how we got swindled; which means** – *Survival of the Richest*, as David Satterfield explained in his foreword.

Before beginning keep in mind that the sum of the parts equals the whole. So do not expect a logical progression of causes or events or a plot to follow. Because there are so many seemingly isolated but related issues and culprits that must be individually examined and explained - before it is possible to achieve a true understanding of what happened, and why our economy and society has arrived at this point in time. **Additionally keep in mind** that swindles based on a return to the Laissez-faire economics which caused the Great Depression are not straightforward. **And keep in mind that swindlers do not care about victims.**

In 1988, when I was writing my first book, *Invest for Success, How to Avoid Getting Ripped Off by; Real Estate Partnerships, the Stock Market and Diversification*, I sent an outline about Financial Darwinism to Senator Christopher Dodd, Jonathon Katz Secretary of the SEC and to Senator George Mitchell, (who had asked me to present testimony through him for the Senate Finance Committee hearings for TRA 86.) I have provided these communications in an appendix so you may conclude that - if I knew about the growing proliferation of egregious financial manipulations and the lack of regulatory oversight – some members of Congress had to have been aware of how regulations from the 30's, enacted to protect us from the unbridled greed and self interest which caused the Great Depression, were being unraveled.

I believed in 1990, which is now manifestly apparent, that **deregulating Greed would lead to a devaluation of ethics.** Certainly many members of Congress had to have read Paul Samuelson or Lester Thurow or Robert Heilbroner, as I did in the early 60s when I was in college; and when I reread them to write *Invest for Success*. So the value of regulating greed was known.

In 1989, I furnished readers with my own theory of how to reduce risk and improve investing results which I called The Predictability of Substance Theory (PST). And if investors, including counterparties and Madoff aficionados had followed the simplicity of searching for substance to identify value - much of what has now gone tragically wrong could have been avoided. Predictable results cannot be expected from financially engineered, egregiously leveraged derivatives or worse than junk bond debt. Too much leverage simply equals too much risk!

Congress claimed, by the end of 2008, that *it did not know there was so much risk in the system.* And too many well educated, hubris laden financial CEOs - with tens of millions of fees and bonuses safely stuffed in their pockets - have also claimed to be *surprised by the impact of so much risk*!

Was surprise only an excuse to avoid prosecution? Is lack of knowledge a defense even in tax court? So much surprise in the wake of so much "Financial Engineering" that by the end of 2008 the U.S., along with the "Global Economy" was experiencing a meltdown of Great Depression proportions!

By mid 2009, some of the same economists who refused to recognize the meltdown until the markets blew up, tentatively contended that the "recession" may be nearing the end because they clung to the misnomer, "recession." In 2011 the media and too many idiot economists still reason from past recessions in their attempts to describe why this "recovery" is taking place but with an extended recovery period.

It still has not occurred to so many PhDs who have not rethought the present that the deficit is not the issue yet, because the lesson learned from the Great Depression is that Government spending is the only way to create jobs. The Greedy private sector certainly has not stepped up to the line when demand is down and the private sector is still intent on searching for the lowest global wage level.

The stock market has recovered to a surprisingly large degree, but not the people whose retirement savings were wiped out, not the investors who invested in all the failed banks. There is still about 18 percent real unemployment, which now must be regarded as structural unemployment according to economic theory. Great difficulties exist for graduates entering the job market; flat or vacillating consumption continues; housing foreclosures are still proliferate - and all of these issues result in a mélange of related adverse consequences. Sure, there is a lot of optimism coming from Wall Street's unabated profits; the resurgence of Mega Banks; oil companies still are doing what they do - however small business is not doing well; and big corporations are still reducing costs by eliminating jobs or by attrition. One thing for sure banks are not lending yet to small businesses.

CEO's of banks, and investment banks (which are bank holding companies since September 2008) as well as their financial executives and analysts - self important with their array of righteous, fancy brains, egregious bonuses and important degrees like; masters "of" finance or business as well as Econ Doctors – (from places like MIT, Harvard, Yale, Penn, or the University of Chicago where Milton Friedman created the theories behind Trickle Down Economics) - must have read J. K. Galbreath's book, *The Great Depression* as well as books by the other economists who crafted theories to circumvent nuclear meltdowns. Some might have even heard of John Maynard Keynes whose basic question was: how do rational people behave under conditions of uncertainty?

Early in 2009 a large majority of the massively bonused claimed they "did not realize there was so much risk" under the surface of their financial engineering - which is irrational, and not believable. Is that because they laid off, flipped, the risk on to everyone else gullible enough to believe in ratings and that risk measurement of indefensible leverage could provide a crystal ball view of the future? Or is it because they relied on the rationality of the market, and assumed the market they had taken advantage of would ultimately self-correct? Does self-correct mean implode like the Great Depression?

Economists like Friedman and Alan Greenspan were believers in the efficient-market theory and that the market is rational. Perhaps they were also Christian Scientists relying upon belief in lieu of an appendectomy. **Financial markets are emotional bandwagons.** So the controlling substance underlying and subverting the crazy, ludicrous notion of market rationality has always been greed. It does not require more than a paragraph to deflate this bizarre absurdity. Greenspan talked about how the rationality of the market provided a self-correcting mechanism. Greenspan probably is a genius at math but has retrospectively clearly failed psychology 101. Perhaps he should write an essay, as punishment, arguing for the rationality of human behavior. He could refer to all the wars and the history of man's inhumanity to his fellow man; he could explain the rationality of judging people by skin color and then address the rationality of the Nazis in Germany, and explain the self-correcting nature of slavery beginning with the earliest known records of man. He could refer to the Great Depression or our own great recession – which is (let's face it) a depression. (There is reason to be vehement, as a result of so much greed in the name of rationality and freedom.)

Freddie and Fannie did not know enough about the risk of massive leverage either; or maybe they did but relied on rationality and human nature to control it. Appraisers did not realize that if they lied to banks the result would be massive defaults. Banks like Washington Mutual lied to themselves about borrower suitability and stipulated to employees that they had to lend, lend, lend for fees. Fundamental to Wash Mu's incredibly stupid act of blind greed was their assumption that flipping worse than junk bond, but rated AAA, debt to any takers would remove them from all the massive risk. Swaps, which Congress voted for, provided assurances to investors who bought mortgage backed securities, eagerly sold by Wall Street, without questions - just like we accept the existence of God with unquestioning belief. Do you really believe the American public did not know that if they bought a house with no money, let alone no money down, they might not be able to remain in their "home?"

And as the "great recession" unfolded a plethora of important members of our media reported, as if in a public confessional, that they really did not understand the financial matters they reported on. Of course it is necessary to exclude all the Wall Street shills who are cheerleaders for Greed, because they ought to have understood the toxic effect of deregulation. Did anyone read Thurow, Samuelson or Keynes? Is our economic education that bad or is this nothing but early on-set? Did parents not tell their children not to buy what you cannot afford and that the more debt the more uncertainty – i.e. risk in your life!

In this book I will revisit the little understood fact that cash, or equity, reduces risk – which is easy to grasp and better even than reading L. Tillman Columbia Econ Doctor's 2009 book, *Financial Darwinism: Create Value or Self-Destruct in a World of Risk*. Tillman's book along with a foreword from a Nobel Economist is living proof that the etiology of his form of Financial Darwinism is nothing but a more arcane and heavily credentialed validation of Herbert's justification for Social Darwinism. Nobel Prizes in Economics must be awarded by the ultra rich.

There is a critical need to be aware of any new validation of Social Darwinism which alerts, currently troubled, financial engineers to new ways to fabricate financial investments using better tools and strategies to survive. Because this only promotes unbridled Greed at the expense of investors and our economy – and the fabric of our society! Tillman's book told readers how to better deal with risk management to build risk analysis into strategic decision making. "This is not for how investors or our county can survive, but for Wall Street to be able to navigate the astonishingly complex and rapidly changing world of finance...," which is what the Vice Chairman

Emeritus of J.P. Morgan said about Tillman's book. Tillman's book is blatantly for the *survival of the richest,* and J.P. Morgan was a primary cause of the Great Depression – does the apple fall far from the tree!

Galbraith called my parent's generation's aversion to debt "Depression Psychosis!" To quantitatively measure the risk of debt, which is qualitative hence subjective, with ArVs, deltas, quadrants, graphs and formulas is high tech but now we have seen - just plain stupid. What about the laws of physics as applied to leverage? How many econometric models have worked lately, ever? Financial Engineering is merely double-speak for Financial Darwinism. Why not be honest and just grant a PhD. in the dictum of: "*the ability to camouflage risk and manipulate Greed to culture fees and leave investors and society holding the bag."* (EHS 2010) I would ask Bernie Madoff to chair that department at Columbia, he has the right credentials.

Where have the regulators been, asleep at the switch or worse? I contend much worse because there is a pattern to what the SEC, the NASD, and the New York Stock Exchange - and their own, self described, self regulatory arms, now merged in to something called FINRA, have not done. The FDIC and the OCC also missed the boat. It is impossible to think that any regulator could have heard the phrase "too complex to understand" as applied to any innovative financial product and not have the thought of fraud immediately come to mind! There is enough prima facie (empirical) evidence to conclude that - under the surface of things there has been a drive to promote fees and profits at the expense of a complexity of societal, ethical and moral concerns. And to me, this sounds like Social Darwinism revisited. The **regulatory "Oversight in Absentia Ethic"** (ehs) seems to have only served the infinitely self interested - termed "masters of the universe," by Thomas Wolfe in *The Bonfire of the Vanites.*

This book is a path to illuminate what was and is still wrong in order to find truth.

To search for Truth it is necessary to understand that the sum of the parts equals the whole. It is not logical to reason from a part to the whole – so we must make an existential leap into the world of the macro to avoid only a few snapshots of what or who to blame. **The context of how the U.S. got swindled is a conundrum of complexities as well as a compendium of interrelated greed enabled by regulatory, rating agency and congressional failures,** as well as investor greed and stupidity. There is adequate blame to go around, and we will not achieve a proper understanding unless we follow all the culprits, indentify their motivations and rationalizations, and see who wound up with all the bonuses. You may read individual chapters out of order; however you will not see the true insidious controlling substance of Financial Darwinism until you complete the whole.

Everything that follows may not be fun to read; as it was not fun and was emotionally draining to write. If you care about truth and fairness and responsible government then it is fundamentally depressing (even if you have assets left) to consider that we have not left the world of Social Darwinism – an ideology which saw nothing wrong with calling for the National Guard to break strikes by shooting indiscriminately into crowds of peaceful protesters who only wanted a living wage.

My first book alerted readers to financial problems looming in 1989, when financial investment was replacing real investment. *Invest for Success* warned readers about the danger of not asking enough questions to get reasonable and understandable explanations. This book is more strident and vehement because of all the lies, the absolute breakdown of any protection for investors or people who rely on banks, and because of the lack of recognition of the fact of the total abandonment of prudence snowballing along since 1980. There ought to be outrage because there has not been an outcry by members of the Forth Estate and Congress to stop all the financial engineering and innovation for fees and bonuses at the expense of all of us, and at the expense of Real Investment.

I have written this book to help my fellow Americans, including Congress, understand the essence of what it has really meant to have torn down **firewalls erected against greed – torn down in the name of deregulation to "get the government off your back," when deregulation really got the government off the backs of the greediest.**

"Swindled" is a treatise on the context and substance of the history and the current state of the core issues, the events, nuances and culprits which led our economy to the brink of total collapse in 2009.

This book is an insider's accurate analysis and passionate objective discussion of facts which will arm you with a true understanding of what went so wrong and what must be done to remedy the continuing disruption of our economic world. You have my promise that when you have finished reading you will have far more knowledge and insight than the superficial books before this have offered, and an overview which books that have analyzed only a few culprits do not provide.

The insights to be gained by reading this book will allow you to know why we are still in the clutches of Wall Street and Trojan Mega Banks protected by a political process primarily concerned with payoffs from lobbyists to sustain reelection and power. Special interests come before Public interests!

And you will realize why we will not fix the economy or our society for the middle and upper middle classes to build a more secure and ethical arena for all of us and for the future of our children – until everything under the surface is out in the open. It is time to fully identify and reject the ethic of Financial Darwinism - or more than 50% of all the money in the U.S. will continue to belong to less than 1% of us!

There is an economic war being conducted by the Uber-riche against the middle and upper middle classes, and we are losing. So this is the moment in history to understand why and join together to do something. Just like Social Darwinism was identified as evil in the beginning of the 20th century. And nothing was done until the world collapsed in the 30s.

CHAPTER 1

SOCIAL DARWINISM PRACTICED BY "ROBBER BARONS" AND PYRAMID BUILDERS

TWO THOUSAND YEARS AGO the ultra rich and most powerful people on earth were referred to as Kings and Emperors. Some of these self-anointed rulers even attributed their right to power and to the riches of the kingdom to all kinds of deities. It was their god given right. In the days of the Roman Empire, slaves and gladiators were commonplace and the population served at the bidding of Caesar or whomever he elevated to help him rule. The money and the power of the Empire belonged to him and there was little thought given to the common man's struggles to survive. The kings of Egypt were similarly not involved with the tragic lives of the slaves who died building pyramids. The kings of England were primarily concerned with their own needs; however there were Earls and Dukes who as members of the court were also included, like senior executive vice presidents. Almost everyone has heard of Bloody Mary, who happened to be a queen who was not so nice. And today the Queen still owns much of the land under most of the buildings in London, which is why so many properties are called "leaseholds." When I was in the Roman Coliseum some years ago and walked through the tiny prison cubicles, which were at one time under the Coliseum's floor, the tragedy of the slaves and gladiators was palpable 2000 years later.

This is not a history book; however, it is instructive to begin by remembering the roots of our economic society. Robert Heilbroner's *The Making of an Economic Society* and Adam Smith's *The Wealth of Nations* have given us some foundation to understand how our economy developed. From numerous historians and philosophers there should also be some awareness that the present is the progression of man's concern for wealth as well as Man's historical inhumanity toward his fellow Man. Certainly most of Man's wars provide empirical evidence of this fact. And it is self evident there are certain commonalities Man has shared with each succeeding generation.

Some of these common traits have driven certain types of individuals to achieve great wealth and power far in excess of what is essential or fair to the society they lived in. Among these traits are: greed, lies, self-interest at the expense of society and a thirst for power for the sake of power. Bibles have chronicled stories to guide Man to reject evil traits and behavior, and religions have tried to speak out against these evils while at the same time conducting their own wars for power and money – so hypocrisy must also be a human failing.

On Mayday 1886 workers at the McCormick Harvesting Machine Co. in Chicago began a strike to achieve a shorter workday than 10 to 12 hours a day, six days a week. There were no benefits, no safety, hardly a living wage and no hope to not be worked to death. Police were called upon to protect the workers however a fight broke out; one person was killed and others were injured. The following day, May 4 (my birthday) a riot ensued when a pipe bomb was thrown at police who went into the crowd to break up the protest of police brutality; and so police fired indiscriminately into the crowd killing four; seven policemen were killed and sixty injured. In the aftermath hundreds of workers were detained and beaten, eight were put on trail; seven were convicted for conspiracy to commit murder. Four were hanged in November of 1887, one committed suicide and three were pardoned by the Governor. This signaled the beginning of the labor movement and at the same time set it back for many years.

When Andrew Carnegie, in 1892, called upon the United States National Guard to break a strike at his steel mill in Pittsburgh, 8,000 troops were sent to help Andy. And our National Guard shot and killed 6 people who only wanted a wage that would allow them a higher level of subsistence to overcome their poverty. Carnegie, of course, was merely following his philosophy of "Survival of the Fittest" based on his greed and self-interest and Herbert Spencer's Social Darwinism. So Carnegie's lack of concern for the lives of his workers was justifiable, and not unnatural.

In 1914 the US National Guard was called in to attack striking coal workers living in a tent city as they had been evicted from company housing because they needed a higher wage level to subsist on. The Guard torched the tents which killed 3 workers, and severely burned 11 children and 2 mothers. Once again the US Government had helped advance the great cause of Social Darwinism.

This is not an argument for unions, however what would the minimum wage be and what would the lives of workers, including non union workers, be like without unions. Consider that unions led to the creation of our middleclass and the growth in demand for American products like cars and refrigerators, something we need to reawaken today to revive our economy. Congress for twenty years voted nineteen times against an increase in the minimum wage, not until 2008 was it increased. John McCain, who was adamantly for deregulation until the day after the market and Lehman tanked, voted 19 times with the majority.

Of course there were all kinds of justifications for voting against increasing the minimum wage, but how is this not reflective of an undercurrent of Social Darwinism? Let's remember what created the union movement, the same mindset, in a way, as the Kings of Egypt who built all the pyramids on the lives of their citizen-slaves. Laissez-faire capitalism just left the robber barons alone to bask in the glory of their survival of the fittest profits — profits at the expense of society. **To argue for finding some self-interest in the common good is not socialism, but Jeffersonian. Jefferson said the role of government is to protect the public good.**

There has been a transfer of wealth based on tax laws which have increasingly favored the rich since the end of the 1970s. In the 70's there was a best salary level determined by the IRS to be a multiple of the wage level in an industry, perhaps using a guideline of 30 times. This did not apply to closely-held, private, companies as it did to publicly held companies. The reasoning was, in part, that stockholders could not exercise enough control over a board to be able to influence top executive compensation, especially considering that the board was appointed by the CEO. So to protect shareholders from exorbitant compensation there was a "best salary" level, and furthermore if compensation exceeded the level then the excess above the best salary was considered a dividend – which was not deductible to the corporation and taxable as a dividend to the recipient at a rate of up to 90%. Tax laws were often considered a form of "Social Engineering" and were used in some ways for the public good, or what Congress du Jour deemed to be a public good. Much of the social engineering was, I believe, used to reverse the ravages of Social Darwinism – and the practitioners' were termed Liberals, a word Republicans' have utilized to brand Democrats as being against free-market capitalism.

If you can find the 3rd edition (the one I use) of the American Heritage Dictionary you may be amazed to learn that Liberal only means to be; "… for flexibility of thought, for humanity, and against prejudice." Liberal does not mean that you should throw your money against the wall and if it sticks to the wall it's yours, but if it falls to the ground it's the governments.

Somehow a majority of the ultra rich have circulated a ruse that the government has no business providing any support for the public good, and that individuals are only entitled to the bounty of their own efforts. And this ruse to keep taxes low was bought by Republicans and the T-Party. No one wants taxes to pay for waste, or give a ways, subsidies, to help the richest oil companies. However too many Americans, are either too self centered or have been fooled into thinking that transfer payments to those less fortunate, payments like Social Security (which is not a transfer payment,) or Medicaid, or unemployment insurance or even public education should be based only on individual effort and the government has no business taking our tax dollars to provide any social services. This directly takes us back to Herbert Spencer's *Survival of the Fittest* philosophy as practiced by Andrew Carnegie and all the other Robber Barons' who cared so little for their workers lives. And this selfishness is absolutely a derivative of Social Darwinism – which is unlike all the grotesquely leveraged derivatives packaged and sold by our favorite Wall Street Godfathers, because this kind of derivative is easy to connect to its' source.

There is a need today to understand these social derivatives to understand how they contributed to the underlying fundamentals of our Great Recession, which should more properly be termed depression. Additionally it is important to remember (if history is really studied because it teaches us how to avoid self defeating behavior from the past) that a lack of critical concern for humanity has taken down major civilizations in the past – like Rome and many others, how about Hitler's Germany.

In the late winter of 2010, and building momentum in 2011, the collusion of Republican Governors to eliminate unions rather than negotiate, and defund public education to set up charter schools signaled a return to Social Darwinism. So history continues to repeat itself.

CHAPTER 2

FINANCIAL DARWINISM IS BORN AGAIN SOCIAL DARWINISM

S ocial Darwinism was simply a belief in the creative force of greed and that the survival of the fittest is ethical and the manifest destiny of the best and brightest practitioners.

Charles Darwin's theories were based on his postulate of natural selection, and natural selection, or evolution, did not mean that a shark's role in life was to gobble up everything it was capable of eating. Social Darwinism had nothing to do with Darwin.

Since 1980, there has been a relentless pursuit to return to Laissez-faire, unfettered capitalism. Economists like Milton Friedman and Alan Greenspan (and Phil Graham) joined by other prominent, **well respected economists believed that greed was a driving force to grow a strong economy and that deregulation to return to a state of free enterprise would allow markets the freedom to self-correct.**

Under the surface it should have been concluded that their belief in deregulation was a product of substantial consulting and speaking fees paid to them as well as a number of other prominent economists by Wall Street. Even the Dean of the Columbia School of Business was a highly paid consultant to Wall Street, and he was a trusted Bush advisor. And the infinitely toxic and disingenuous Phil Graham is now the Vice Chairman of the UBS Investment Bank Division. (Follow the money.)

On the surface free made sense as the U.S. was founded to be a Democracy free from the Rule of England which at the time was not a Democracy.

The United States was the only Democracy on the planet in 1776 and the only country or large collectivity of people whose expressed goal was individual freedom.

Individual freedom, of course, did not apply to slavery which was the economic backbone of the United States cotton-based economy. Cotton and slaves were important to the North as well as the South because the North also was heavily involved with growing cotton. So the United States, founded on the ethic that "all men are created equal," and that all men deserve to be free and pursue individual happiness, was hypocritical from the beginning.

The owners of plantations did not care about the welfare or individual rights of their workers. And the U.S. Government, until Abraham Lincoln, did nothing to apply the U.S. Constitution to a large group of their fellow Americans who had taken advantage of the economic benefits of slavery to further their own self interest, which was based on greed and the philosophical justification that slaves were inferior therefore, existed to be taken advantage of like chattel. So prior to Lincoln's "Emancipation Proclamation," slaves were people who could legally be bought and sold – therefore owned like any other property.

Slaves were the first large group of immigrants following the English, so Americans with complexions darker than white were among the founders of our country.

The United States did not have a royalty class so money, and the power that money begets, became the new order. And globally, autocracies failed because man seems to have a drive to obtain individual freedom, as well as money and power. The intensity of this drive made men who were able to get the biggest piles and derive the most poser from their newfound wealth the new rulers of the planet.

In the U.S., the most successful driven by greed and power had philosophies to support their activities which, not unlike the pyramid builders of yore, still depended on taking advantage of their workers.

22

Social Darwinism's economic philosophies' were based on a Laissez-Faire model of Capitalism as supported by J. A. Schumpeter's Theory of the Firm and his Theory that the role of the firm is to Maximize Profits. The Maximization of Profit Theory came from his idea of liberal democracy, meaning a Laissez-faire economy. At the same time Schumpeter believed the most profitable firms should drive the least profitable out of business. Certainly John D, Rockefeller, of Cleveland mastered this concept until he grew the Standard Oil Co. of Ohio to become a world-wide monopoly. So in 1890 John Sherman, a Republican from Ohio, got the Sherman Anti Trust Act passed, the legislation passed with a 51-1 vote in the Senate and a 242-0 vote in the house. Even Congress, in 1890, may have recognized the evils of restraint of trade and the adverse effects on commerce. Sherman was more than likely reacting to a number of Cleveland's Robber Barons who did not like Rockefeller or his tactics because he either drove them out of business or to the brink of going under to buy them on the cheap.

Remember that Herbert Spencer, the English Philosopher, gave us the "Survival of the Fittest" ethic which Rockefeller mastered as well as anyone alive. Laissez-faire was addressed legislatively for the first time by a Republican, maybe the ultra rich Cleveland Industrialists who were damaged by Rockefeller's ruthless tactics curtailed political contributions to Sherman – maybe for the public good, always follow the money. The irony of the Sherman Act at the time of Carnegie is truly bizarre. However incongruous, it is important to know the etiology of Wall Streets' and Banks' current Laissez-faire free market economic theories. It is telling to realize that Milton Friedman bought the Laissez-faire Theory and along with Alan Greenspan, brilliant economist, sold this to the entire country. In 2009 on national television Greenspan said he, might have been or was wrong to rely on free market correction. Brilliant!

The modern heads of Financial Empires did not go public to espouse their philosophy, as Andrew Carnegie did, but wisely cultivated economic theories and mathematical risk measurement models to encourage the masses to think that all of their unfettered, greedy, flimsy financial products were in the name of freedom. Kings did their dastardly deeds in the name of God and now the U.S. did everything in the name of individual freedom and the right to achieve as much financial success as possible. This was called the American Dream. The American Dream for 'who' must now be the question. Let's have Goldman Sachs put a wafer on the tongue of every fleeced investor to share in the belly/body of all the ultra rich CEOs who were instrumental in bringing the U.S. back to where it was prior to the beginning of the crash of 1929 and the ensuing Great Depression. Let's have the same rules that helped create so much wealth in the 20's that 20% of all banks failed and people starved in food lines and lived without heat in tent cities.

There are lots of theories from the late 19th century and into the early 20's which supported making as much money as possible no matter what - what simply was the tragic social cost to the lives of the people being exploited as the devastation to the fabric of society became manifestly apparent in bread lines. And today the exploitation is far more extensive than just to workers who were used up and cast aside by Andrew Carnegie, cast aside because they could no longer work.

It is time to identify the fallacious nature and rancid substance of these theories as they keep popping up. In 2009, *Meltdown: A Free Market Look at Why the Stock Market Collapsed, the Economy Tanked and Government Bailouts Will Make Things Worse* by T. E. Woods with a PhD in history who is a right wing rigid "conservative," and purist Economic liberal in the mold of Schumpeter, contended the blame was not deregulation or unfettered free markets. And this is only a survival of the richest irrational denial of the reality of the disarray caused by the hands off approach! Thirty something Woods further argued that greed can only go so far. But everyone should know that greed is geometrically worse when it is supported by the Government. Woods can't even say it can get out of hand. Woods is either a bizarre example of misplaced trust, or a good example of a born again Social Darwinist. Certainly he is a prime example of how a PhD is not a clear path to lucid, clear thinking!

So Woods did not acknowledge the fact that the Government supported deregulation which is exactly how greed turned into **Galloping Greed**. How can Woods or anyone justify all the financial gluttons gorging themselves on oceans of fees flowing from the huge transactional velocity of all the "too complex to explain" sugar coated financial products. Woods, like so many other **Closet Financial Darwinists**, has chosen to return to pure **Laissez-faire Economic Theory** – which is **an economic doctrine that opposes governmental regulation of or interference in commerce beyond the minimum necessary for a free market system to operate according to its own economic laws.**

It is self evident, in the daylight of our continuing economic devastation that a - leave me alone philosophy to do whatever I want no matter what – in the name of FREEDOM – is against the public good. And this return to the "I don't give a shit about people philosophy," only 120 years after the US National Guard killed striking workers, is obviously only for the good of the greediest.

Maybe we need Laissez-faire drug policies. What if your children adopted the philosophy of a belief in non interference parenting? Some of us know the results of this kind of parenting; we have been in restaurants with their families. Personally I am for deregulated motor vehicle laws – no more tickets, and no financial responsibility. Why not when there has been no financial accountability for the bankers who fabricated vast amounts of highly complex leveraged financial products and then stuffed the financial universe full of a plethora of complex instruments until the entire economy contracted stage 2, 3 and 4 financial melanoma. The free market wonks do not give up because they are Greed Zealots; and those of us who are progressive flexible thinkers must know more to be able to understand reality to search for a better and more secure path to the future. Ideologues' cling to what they think they know because change makes them insecure – and man hates to be insecure.

You know that Financial Darwinism (*survival of the richest*) is alive and well when Republican politicians during 2008 campaigned that Obama was going to "redistribute" the wealth by taxing the ultra rich at a higher rate. Another and more logical way to regard the fallacy of "redistribution" was to acknowledge it was merely a return to the tax bracket before Bush lowered it, and deficits soared. When the ultra rich have gotten so much richer during the past 20 years and the real income of so many Americans has fallen – does redistribution ring true even to Republicans. Can a lie this big make sense to the liars. This is would be like Andrew Carnegie calling the Guard, and our government says you bet, and then today's Republicans justify the carnage by claiming the workers killed were anarchists and spies.

Today with Wisconsin Republicans taking the national lead, unions are again under attack. Unions may not be perfect, but they still have the right to be heard and exist to avoid a complete return to the days of the robber barons. And this attack must be recognized as a war against the middle class.

Born again Social Darwinism is a derivative like a warrant. Consider there is ancient adage in the investment banking business which holds that - "warrants just come back to bite you in the ass." It seems that a Derivate like Financial Darwinism, which for years has been fundamentally concerned with creating transactional financial products offering great fee velocity has now come back to bite our entire country in the ass, and worse – has ripped it off.

CHAPTER 3

PARTY PRINCIPLES VS. HUMAN CONSIDERATIONS – DEMOCRATS VS. REPUBLICANS WHO JUST SAY *NO*

Philosophy is what everyone or almost everyone has. Today there is an entitlement to have and cling to your own "philosophy," which has become your own idea and your opinion, and it is okay whether true or not. Standards for right or wrong, or for an ability to back up your own idea/opinion have been demolished over the course of the past 40 years. Perhaps it is not politically correct to think that an opinion can be stupid or just plain asinine; or wrong to expect any informed logical reasoning in support of an opinion. It is wrong to be judgmental, so to condemn anyone's opinion is to be judgmental? Opinions are often derivatives of ideas or philosophies which make no sense. Try to challenge your 20 year old brilliant daughter's opinion and see where it gets you. Or worse, try to make economic sense to a lobotomized member of the Tea Party.

For years Republicans and Democrats have subscribed to or espoused different philosophies in order to differentiate themselves from each other, which seems necessary in order to have a two party system. However product differentiation often is superficial, and political parties need to sound different to get elected, but in reality the American political system may not really thrive on differences because extreme positions whether right or wrong make people nervous and so it becomes difficult to get elected.

Republicans describe themselves as the party of business and Democrats consider themselves the party of the people. Democrats believe that government ought to be concerned for social good and is necessary to help promote and protect the public good. Republican's seem to believe the government should not interfere and that individuals are solely responsible for their own welfare. Both believe in having the government protect the safety of the country. Now here is where there are differences:

Republicans like to brand Democrats as "tax and spend" as if they are more fiscally responsible; and many Republicans like to lead with conservative social personal value judgments based on religious beliefs, even though this country was supposedly founded on the separation of church and state; and many Republicans believe in free enterprise, Laissez-faire free markets and that a free market is self- correcting, certainly a difficult position to hold today based on all the empirical evidence to the contrary.

Democrats are more concerned with the government making up for what some people cannot do for themselves. They favor a greater role in society for government and are more for transfer payments when necessary. Democrats are for working people and so are more concerned with the middle class, and with taxing those who can **best afford to pay**. Consider a small thought from basic econ 101 - that affordability means the people **with the highest personal disposable incomes**. Hence clearly Democrats should favor regulations to protect the public good, because greed interferes with what is right, so Democrats should not believe in Lasses-faire economics or "trickle down Economics." And if you understand the root cause of the Great Depression and recognize the Laissez-faire philosophy behind our Great Recession you know that anyone who gives one half of a shit about humanity ought to know that trickle down was a total lie!

Concern for the public good is a basic ethic in many economically developed countries today. Political systems are a product of philosophers who have searched for elusive truth and wisdom based on logic and reasoning on a journey to find enlightenment. Freedom is a product of this search and so is economics. However it is impossible to find enlightenment within a rigid posture toward not rethinking ideas from the past in terms of the present. So if you cling to what you have always believed even though reality proves it to be wrong – you are doomed to repeat the same mistakes over and over - like clinging to the philosophy of Laissez-faire unregulated markets.

It is clear from the past thirty years of Republican war against the middle and upper middle class that Republicans have more interest in the self and that Democrats have more self interest in the common good, but that breaks down when considering how we got swindled. Is it conservative or liberal is a big question to debate and in so many ways definitions and labels are worse than inadequate – sometimes they are just name calling when used by Republicans. It is considered bad taste, by some, or politically incorrect to discuss religion or politics but as human beings these are fundamental concerns and universal to achieve an understanding of life in order to evolve to be better as human beings and as a society.

Republicans are "philosophically" on the side of "free" unfettered markets and so it might be understandable how they have been led astray by Greedy Wall Street Godfathers and hubris ridden Bankers (like Pandit of Citi who spent $10MM of taxpayer dollars to redecorate his offices in March of 2009). Republicans believe in the free market myth – **but the Democrats let this bogus belief remain alive as well.**

Democrats with Republicans sucked up Greenspan's testimony about his Laissez-faire free-market self correcting 19th and early 20th century pre Great Depression economics; and encouraged Freddie and Fannie to lower credit rating standards to 580 to qualify unsuitable mortgages. Prudent bankers know a credit rating so low is adverse selection by giving credit to dead beats! Both parties allowed the unraveling of Glass-Steagall, and both parties went along with Phil Gramm's Credit Default Swaps. Whether a politician voted for it or not, it was contributory negligence, if it was not filibustered until there was enough public awareness of the "toxic" impact of what the consequences had to be! Insuring ludicrous geometric debt with nothing has to be dumber than dumb.

How dumb is the T-Party with their creationist slant, religious moralizing about how this is a Christian Nation, apparent lack of any knowledge of economic history or theory, and rigid adherence to a Constitution which fanatic Republicans refuse to acknowledge is brilliantly visionary in its elasticity. It is blind stupidity that the very middle class T Ps support lower taxes because their taxes have been lowered. So they are really only supporting lower taxes for the ultra rich – which is not ultra smart. Eric Cantor, a staunch T Party supporter to retain a base for reelection, wants to lower taxes to create jobs whenever he opens his mouth in public. Hopefully you know that taxes are half of where they were in the late 70s – so where are the jobs? Reduce taxes to create jobs, nutso talk from our Republican/Tea Party core ethic – Financial Darwinism on high! (Should this be added to Handel's Messiah, and sung in tongue by the quitter Governor of Alaska?)

The Tea Party and their rigid adherence to - their ignorant posture toward taxation as inappropriate revenue, and the job creation myth that lowering taxes has or can create jobs has changed the Republican Party in 2011 to a fringe cult which cannot reach decisions based on logic and reason. T-P lack of economic knowledge about the terrible impact of Laissez-faire behavior coupled with abhorrent value judgments regarding religious and private sexual freedoms has inexorably changed the party of Eisenhower, Reagan and even Nixon to a group of fanatic's intent on getting their own way at the expense of the rest of our country.

Relying on T-P ignorance big oil and many other large corporations give the T-Partiers lots of money to get elected so they can vote against raising any revenue from higher taxes levied against incomes above $500,000. Additionally they can vote against the elimination of the carried interest tax for billionaire hedge fund managers; and vote to continue to not tax billions of profits shipped offshore. And the Tea Party and lots of other Republicans will not increase taxes on huge corporations still doing great, and, of course not on Wall Street "Banks." The Tea Party is a barrier to our government's responsibility to protect the public – especially when the Financial Darwinists in the private sector are at war with the middle and upper middle class.

What our elected leaders do uniformly believe in is the money they need to get elected to remain in office to have better pension and health benefits than the citizens who pay for everything. Regrettably most of our politicians are primarily concerned with pandering to the lobbyists' for "special interests" who pander to their election syndrome. So we live in a political system built on self interest supported by panderers, who justify the unjustifiable by espousing a superficial moralistic philosophy supposedly based on individualistic freedom, bereft of any wisdom or enlightenment.

The philosophies of "conservative" and "liberal" ought to be replaced by a new philosophy called the Doctrine of Fairness based on a critically introspective analysis of empirical realities. It is time to stop debating whether free markets self correct and that government regulations inhibit individual freedom. It may sound dated to address this when our collapsed stock markets have recovered for some; and the banks that committed immolation were bailed out and are now living high on huge interest rates charged to credit cards and on hundreds of billions of dollars freely given to them by the FDIC, and even more directly from the Fed.

We have partially gotten over the fact that rating agencies rated for bucks, and that our politicians blame dumb laws on lobbyists. Health "reform" provided a modicum of assistance for the 45 million people without health insurance, but Republicans want to cancel this! And our schools are failing while Republicans cut finding. But our polished sports stadiums remain as glitzy symbols of misplaced priorities and values rising above the shadows of our disintegrating urban schools, and our deteriorating environment.

It is time to join together as fellow Americans and lay aside our "philosophical" differences in the name of sanity. Albert Ellis and Robert Harper in *A New Guide for Rational Living* pointed out, from years of clinical evaluations that too often people reach inappropriate conclusions based on irrational thoughts - which is to not think straight. There is a choice to think rationally. So there is a choice to not get upset; or to choose to spend time thinking about whether the Earth is flat, or that Iraq attacked the twin towers or that there is no global warming – because we really have not damaged the environment. There is a choice to think the Republican "Budget," to counter the Democratic Budget, with more tax cuts for the highest taxpayers and billions of tax brakes (subsidies) for oil companies makes sense, or is it a distortion of reality.

Political parties need to be more Jeffersonian in that there should be some consensus that government is to protect the public good, and the public good should encompass more than the wealthiest who can best afford to lobby for unfettered freedom for unbridled self interest at the expense of the public good. Politicians need to be accountable and Americans must become better educated to stop buying sound bites from liars.

Our government should set the tone for Wall Street, Banks, Regulators, Raters, Appraisers and Americans to behave ethically. Government could start by choosing to make sense and conduct itself with appropriate fiduciary responsibility to protect the economy for everyone – not just for ultra rich. Self righteous verbal behavior flowing from long time members of Senate Banking and Finance Committees sounds pretty empty if you examine the past twenty-five years of hands off guidance. Pandering to lobbyists and telling voters what they want to hear, rather than what they need to know, in order to get elected and remain in office is Business of the election and by the election – instead of Democracy by the people and for the people.

Americans need to demand that politicians make better sense, and should start by individually thinking straight. Politics should not depend on personal religious beliefs, which are value judgments and not necessarily reality. Samuel Johnson the great 18th century English philosopher said, "Religion is the last refuge of all scoundrels and liars." Politics should not depend on fair and balanced reporting, but on objectivity. And individuals have a responsibility to know more than what can be learned from one slanted sound bite.

Over forty years ago, when my father voted for Goldwater and I voted for Johnson, to be a Republican was not to be against everything Democrats were for. Republicans were not obstructionists as they are today. So there are a growing number of independents who are refugees from the party of Lincoln because it has become the party of Palin. Maybe more members of each party will become Independent and when this party is a majority party there will be less rancor and more agreement over what makes sense based on a new political philosophy – The Doctrine of Fairness.

Politics is the most fundamental cause of how Financial Markets have gone back to the Robber Baron mentality. Although our government would no longer call out the guard to kill striking workers it has allowed our investments to be slaughtered for fees for the ultra rich. So our own elected Government has subscribed to Financial Darwinism, just as it bought Social Darwinism when it sent out the Guard in support of survival of the fittest.

Evidence of Financial Darwinism is apparent in the fact that the IRS has not enforced tax law which has enabled CEOs to have incomes of five hundred times, or more, the wage levels of their workers. Forty years ago a multiple of more than forty was unheard of, and would have been considered obscene – not just a way to retain talent. There is a tax doctrine of reasonable compensation. There is still tax law which limits executive compensation, and if you want to really get aggravated go immediately to Chapter 18 and do not pass go. Bonuses in 2009 for AIG and Merrill were a spec of sand compared to what has really taken place!

Is anything about how we got swindled reasonable? Has the conduct of Government or business been acting in "good faith?" Does what we have allowed to happen make any more sense retrospectively than the events leading up to the Great Depression. Does it make sense that nothing fundament has changed with so-called reform? Does it make sense that we are still teaching bogus economics in colleges everywhere? Does it make sense that so many young adults graduating from college can not get appropriate jobs; while talk of recovery has become a buzz word among economists! If you stop to think about it common sense is the least common thing around. And the students coming out of universities now must reject all the Laissez-faire free market toxic economics they may have been taught to understand all the lies which are motivated by the *survival of the richest* ethic.

CHAPTER **4**

HOUSING PRICES IN FREE FALL
OR IN A RETURN TO VALUE,
COMMERCIAL IS ROTTEN TOO

" Housing bubble" meant - Alice in Wonderland bloated housing prices, as mortgage brokers played – Red Rover, Red Rover let everyone come over. It seems as if millions of people abandoned any sense of value and jumped through the looking glass into what everyone now knows was a bottomless pit. Of course they were enabled by all the name players: Congress, Wall Street, Banks, Freddie and Fannie, Appraisers, Rating Agencies, Investors, Home Buyers, and Regulators. Everyone believed in the myth that everything keeps going up.

HGTV had a show revealing the value of buying a "fixer upper" in a hot market, and then adding value to an 800 square foot house for $450,000 so it could be sold for $700,000 or more, sometimes the "target" price was a little lower, but never a loss. Supply and demand curves went out the window in the rush to buy and real estate geniuses were created out of thin ice in the deserts of Las Vegas, Phoenix and the grid lock of LA. New York City the financial Mecca of the World could never go down, my Neuro radiologist son who trained there told me. And this is what a lot of bright successful people believed. I don't know if the name players really believed this when their vision was occluded by so much wealth creation for themselves.

So pricing accelerated well beyond the cost of the materials to build, well beyond the cost of the labor to build, and well beyond the cost of developer

35

land. Developers banked land at high carrying costs knowing that they would be able to continue to build and charge prices for new construction in many areas at crazy multiples of retail price to cost per square foot to build. The cost of new construction pulled the cost of existing homes up based on unrealistic duplication costs – and so too many buyers stretched their incomes taut to the breaking point to be able to participate in what the media and our politicians tell us over and over is the American Dream. The dream of keeping up with the joneses has now clearly been dashed on the rocks of despair and the realities of the madness are simple to see.

The cost to buy 2x4's in Shaker Heights, where I live, is similar to the cost in Phoenix, LA, Vegas, Connecticut or Long Island. Wage levels may even be lower if there are workers from Central or South America. Land cost does depend on how much is available; so for California or areas with infill and gridlock land costs are higher, however there is a lot of desert around Las Vegas and Phoenix and no shortages in a considerable number of other locations where builders created an artificial paucity of supply. The DeBeers people know about this - you can always get by on a cz if you put the brilliant stone into a Tiffany setting, who really can tell. Who could tell that housing prices were in a parallel universe where values vanished like socks in your dryer?

Certainly the banks had an obligation to know this, and so did Freddie and Fannie, but they were making so much money for their executives that their motivation and obligation to be prudent vanished. They had a fiduciary responsibility to depositors and borrowers to not let them self destruct, but money talks and prudence walks.

Piggish builder markups coupled with an ability to obtain financing made a house under water, in many instances, from the date of purchase. When appraisers search for comps and not value as a function of actual replacement cost based on materials and labor, with ever growing market prices – it is easy to get trapped in an upward accelerating pricing spiral to nowhere. In Las Vegas, using accepted building techniques which allowed a house robber to get inside by just swinging a sledge hammer at a paper thin exterior wall, a house constructed at a cost of $40 to $50 per square foot turned into a sales price at $250 per square foot. So a house that sold for five times the cost to build made a 2,000 square house worth $500,000. So when the prices crashed by 50% or more, realistically, this must be considered a return to some semblance of value. Think about falling prices in the Hamptons because not everyone got a grotesque bonus to make certain they would not leave the company they helped destroy.

Obviously the pride of owning a $1MM house, even if it was only 1000 square feet, allowed many buyers to feel important. Pride of ownership and status goes a long way. Think about all the fancy cars on a lease and the houses bought with reverse mortgages – where the interest and the non-existent principle were subtracted from the value of the house – which was under water from day one. People knew, people had to know that someday the lack of value and too much debt would begin to haunt them. It does not take a mathematical genius with a masters' in financial engineering, because there were not enough jobs for physicists or mathematicians, to hear the death rattle of so much leverage and viscerally sense the palpable lack of value. Think about how lots of desert, high arid desert and West Coast locations are running out of water. There is so much denial I'm surprised Wall Street has not securitized it.

The housing bubble was only part of the mortgage problem for banks, borrowers and investors. Commercial mortgages pose large problems today and could get worse in the near future because commercial properties like; office, retail, warehouse and multifamily rely on tenants. And tenants are people or businesses with economic problems like: no customers for clothes, or cars, or legal work, or investments or a multitude of diverse economic resources which drive an economy.

Commercial mortgages customarily have balloon payments and less leverage, less than houses for example which were financed for **zero down** or less. A balloon payment is when after paying interest only for 5 years the mortgage principle is due, or sometimes the entire amount borrowed is not due until the 10th year. Even if the debt is only 50% of the purchase price it is usually necessary to refinance most of the initial mortgage because very little has been paid to reduce the balance. Many commercial mortgages were given to properties which were priced too high, especially as a function of replacement building costs. So what will the valuations be when it is necessary to refinance because the balloon payment is due and there is no cash to pay the mortgage off? It is simple – banks will reappraise at a lower value because market prices are less than when the bank made the mortgage, so either the borrower will have to find more equity or the bank will foreclose.

Commercial real estate prices were bid up by buyers with investors clamoring for properties to satisfy an ability to participate in a 1031 tax free exchange. This was not a loophole because investors merely deferred or postponed paying taxes on the gains from their property sale by investing in a replacement property. And if you can defer taxes it often makes sense to do it.

Many real estate investors opted to defer their taxes, especially in California or in any area that experienced significant accelerated pricing. So real estate companies, referred to in the securities business as issuers or sponsors, purchased Billions and Billions of dollars of real estate to put into Limited Liability Companies for investors clamoring for replacement properties legally structured as tax free exchanges with Tenant in Common ownership to satisfy IRS rules. So billions were raised by real estate companies, sponsors, who needed the equity to buy the properties for all the investors selling their properties.

And the demand for tax free replacement properties became so large that the self-important participants decided to call tenant in common ownership, the tenant in common industry and named it the TIC industry, which sounds more important than the IO (individual ownership) Industry. I guess everyone wants to elevate the importance of what they do. Many of these properties were bought to do the deal for fees rather than based on an economic purchase price. So today too many properties remain trapped in the wake of our Great Recession (*Depression) economic problems and what was not a truly great purchase price will not have an ability to pay the mortgage, and without additional cash a workout is a mirage. (*ehs)

In addition to 1031 TIC investments there was a huge demand for high profile properties and assumptions were done to accommodate all the leverage necessary to fund huge purchases and developments. Assumptions always assumed rents would go up; prices for condos would always go up and be affordable even in Manhattan at $2,000 to $3,000 per foot, for 2,500 square feet overlooking the New York skyline. This same equation played out around the rest of our planet for equally exclusive locations and buildings.

Commercial mortgages were also used in the fabrication of complex financial products. And this had nothing to do with Freddie and Fannie who were partially to blame for the sub prime swindle, or ponzi-like thought that another buyer will always come along to pay more than the last sucker. Commercial properties are supposed to generate returns to fund mortgage payments, so Banks and Wall Street packaged these loans into sub prime colloidal suspensions of crappy loans, based on the fallacious premise, that diversification is deemed to reduce the risk - and we have seen how safe it made all the bad stuff.

In later chapters I will simply explain financial products too complex to explain, but for now think about the marketing scheme to slice and dice various types of leverage into trenches (does tranche really sound better) containing loans of different risks. I will also analyze how the risk was branded AAA to encourage investors or counterparties to gobble up all the trench filled pools of leverage.

Everyone knows someone who lost their job - from executives, to Lehman financial analysts, to auto workers to sales clerks who might have worked at Circuit City. And the implosion of jobs causes tenants who pay rent to have problems. Tenants have walked from leases, down sized space requirements and gone out of business. Huge real estate developers walked from projects that had been underway, considering the paucity of tenants and their ability to borrow to complete vanished.

Many banks have the ability to lend now but they have either lost their nerve to assume any risk or do not trust their ability to make a good decision. But under the surface it is worse than this because big banks can still make big returns by leveraging their capital by issuing complex financial instruments, they can make more than through mortgage lending or commercial. And projections are still being contrived to justify the risk, which is what got us a Great Recession. So the slicing, and dicing backed by swaps continues.

Because of all the financial slicing and dicing, and trenches - when there is a problem paying a mortgage **who do you talk to about restructuring** the debt, either for residential or commercial properties. The servicer might not even have paper work to properly claim rights to foreclose on the property! Who do you deal with if there is a feasible way to achieve a workout to reposition a property to survive? The idiot in the bank who did not understand the word prudent to begin with?

Many commercial properties had totally unrealistic purchase prices or crazy development costs and these properties will go to chapter 11 with fingers crossed. The big question is - are any bankers smart enough to have enough wisdom to recognize that a workout is far better than more black holes in their capital base? Can bankers step up to the line now to become reacquainted with a rational perspective toward borrowers to recognize the crucial symbiotic relationship they have with customers, as well as a responsibility to lend to small businesses which will create jobs Certainly rational recognition was a missing element in the mad scramble to shovel money into complex financial instruments for fees flowing transactions designed to flip.

Somehow, Banks need to return to a realistic understanding of their fiduciary responsibilities' to preserve and maintain the financial stability of banks to protect depositors and shareholders. In the Eighties banks made enormous loans for important buildings and exacerbated the supply so that it was possible in major urban areas and not so major, to drive around at night and clearly notice the lack of lights in so many buildings. When a building has no tenants there is no reason for a cleaning crew to come in at night to clean. These buildings were called "see throughs."

Today the problem does not stem from the insurance companies and Savings and Loans funding of overbuilding which was the problem in the 80s. Today the problem is far more systemic, because of the nuclear impact of so many trillions of contrived complex financial products, based on even more trillions of Swap lies.

Housing foreclosures on the surface seem more heartbreaking than underwater commercial loans; however the problems with commercial properties are derivatives of human problems so the linkage is immutable – disastrous. The American Dream, or illusion, is to always expect the future to be better, to expect a new buyer will pay more, to expect rents to go up along with stocks and the value of your real estate. This expectation is the real bubble and too many of us have lived in it.

CHAPTER 5

GREEDY DEREGULATED BANKS ABANDONED PRUDENCE AND REASON FOR FEES AND BONUSES

Banks are not chartered to be on a Zen path or journey of discovery which may retrospectively provide a destination based on the quality of the trip. Zen holds that the trip is more important than the destination The quality of the trip is important for individuals searching for truths, however if a bank lives only in the moment – "by making hay while the sun shines" the quality of the trip will be temporary. And for too many years the journey of our banks was to search for executive compensation with little or no thought that the quality of a banking path should be to maintain stability.

Banks have lived in the moment of the bonus as the shadow of the Glass-Steagal Act was lifted and unraveled beginning with the Depository Institution's Deregulation and Monetary Control Act of 1980. So the rebirth of free enterprise and bigness for banks began under the reign of Reagan aided and abetted by lots of Democrats. Two critical features of this pivotal act allowed banks to merge as well as charge any interest rate they choose.

In 1982, the Garn-St. Germain Depository Act continued the war against regulations to curb greed. Savings and Loans were freed from any constraints to participate in their inherent Greed and outright stupidity. This legislation was sponsored by Republican Senator Jake Garn of Utah, and co-sponsored be three Democrats including Charles Shumer and Steny Hoyer! This act allowed only one shareholder to own a bank. So one fraudulent uber greedy individual like Keating in Arizona could use his own S&L to culture wealth by any fraudulent means necessary. Keating went to jail. Further Garn allowed commercial lending and adjustable rate mortgages so by the mid 80s commercial real estate was grotesquely overbuilt, oversupplied and S&Ls, originally intended to make loans only for homes, were either dead or on their way to a painful demise. Painful for our economy and society.

Glass-Steagal was enacted in 1933, in the wake of the Great Depression, in order to prevent overly large commercial banks being involved with stock market investment. It was clear that huge banks had taken huge risks with depositors' assets as well as with their own by buying new issues, lending money to companies whose stock they invested in, and encouraging their customers to invest in their investments. The consensus then was that banking activities were the fundamental cause of the depression due to bankers' unbridled, greedy appetite for the vast rewards to be had from egregiously leveraged, highly speculative risky investments. Banks were allocated one year to decide whether they wanted to specialize in commercial banking or investment banking, because Glass-Steagal set up a regulatory fire-wall between the two types of activities. This was primarily designed to preserve banking assets in the event risk underwriting failed. And it seems that risk underwriting then, like today, was done essentially to justify participation in selling anything – no matter how much leverage - to generate fees.

By 1999 all was forgotten and all the lobbying to allow all financial entities to get into each others business (pants) resulted in huge profits for Wall Street and Banks, profits which were not properly added to surplus for stability but paid out as bonuses. All the CEO and executive officers became Bull Market geniuses in the race to pile individual incomes, fees and bonuses higher than Mt Everest.

The Gramm-Leach-Bliley Act of 1999 repealed: the Banking Act of 1933 known as Glass-Steagal; and the Bank Holding Company Act of 1956, which prevented bank holding companies headquartered in one state from acquiring a bank in another state and from engaging in the insurance business – further, the approval of Federal Reserve Board was required under this act to establish a bank holding company. Graham-Leach-Bliley, once again, allowed Mega, Trojan-like Banks to come alive, like dinosaurs rising from the dead to gobble up our economy as they did in 1929.

On December 21, 1999 the Commodity Futures Modernization Act was signed into law by President Bill Clinton as it was attached to an 11,000 page omnibus appropriation bill. This bill was drafted by lobbyists and Wall Street lawyers for Phil Gramm (PhD) Chairman of the Senate Finance Committee, who specifically wanted a deregulated atmosphere for over-the-counter energy trades and trading on electronic energy commodity markets. Further, it willfully and intentionally (two characteristics of fraud) created the Credit Default Swap to get around state regulators who regulate insurance, because this was insurance called a Swap. Which was not regulated – and really a bet that nothing "insured" would ever go down. This bill was introduced in the Senate on December 15, 2000, the last day before Christmas recess by three Republican Senators led by Gramm and joined by two Democrats.

It is probable that only Gramm, and his lawyers who drafted the bill, read the dire terms of the bill which was referenced and buried in a long and complex conference report to the 11,000 page "2000 omnibus budget bill. However after it was passed there was enough time to have read the bill before it led to the surreptitious, unregulated behavior of Enron which caused its collapse, not so long after.

The Democrats did introduce legislation to close the so-called "Enron Loophole" after the fact, which Republicans killed. But the Democrats were not loud enough in their condemnation of the Enron Loophole and not focused on the most alarming consequences of worthless Swaps being used to insure the geometric leverage of pooled sub prime loans banks made as fast as they could flip the paper and sell the "insured" derivatives.

By the end of 1999 everything was in place for Bankers, led by Citi Group and Wall Street Godfathers to become innovative enough to do whatever they could dream up to build personal wealth. The CEOs did not have to call in the National Guard to shoot naysayers - unbridled, unfettered greed was once again unleashed on humanity.

Andrew Carnegie rolled over in his grave in glee knowing he was right to have taken advantage of his workers, because his Social Darwinism was still alive and vibrant in the less obvious format of Financial Darwinism.

If banks had not been allowed to be like insurance companies and insurance companies to be like banks - it is probable the free-for-all world of complex financial products backed by Swaps to insure no one could lose would never have been born. And in 2008 to help investment banks survive - the Federal Reserve Board in its ultimate wisdom, showing no awareness of the reasons why Glass-Steagal had erected a fire wall between banks and investment banks as well as no awareness of why there was a need for the Bank Holding Company Act of 1956 - allowed investment banks (like Goldman) to become bank holding companies.

This seems counterintuitive considering it is self-evident that the **unfettered nature of things greedy has again led the world again to the brink of financial ruin and the resultant human devastation.**

But when you examine Wall Street financial ties to the members of the Fed's board of governors as well as to the leaders of the Fed – especially Alan Greenspan, the Treasury and the Regulators - it is simple to understand. Through a mélange of consulting fees, studies and speaking engagements paid for by investment banks and mega banks like Citi; and Goldman's direct infiltration of the Fed, financial regulators and the treasury; and ex Goldman CEOs spreading out like moles into control positions in mega banks - it is self-evident that the influence of unimagined riches triggered an outpouring of support for deregulation motivated by personal greed.

Think about this when considering how the banks so swiftly abandoned reason carefully cultivated for the decades following the Great Depression. Or was reason and prudence simply a mandate imposed by regulations designed to protect the public?

In 1973 when at the age of 31, I applied for my first mortgage, I had 40% down and wanted a $75,000 loan, which would have required 20% of my income to carry, for a new 4,000 square foot house. I went to a bank where a good friend from high school was the general counsel. My attorney told me it was a mistake and made me apply to two other Savings and Loans.

When the first bank reviewed my detailed application, which included supporting financial information, my friend at the bank scheduled a meeting to tell me that the "loan committee" had carefully reviewed my application and "sometimes found their role to be that of a loan counselor and not a lender." Further my friend said he did not see why I needed such a large house at such a young age and that the bank did not participate in "jumbo" mortgages. The mortgage was for $75,000. The two other lenders were happy to offer me the loan at favorable terms. Perhaps the first bank was concerned about my age, or it was my friend's value judgment to protect me from too much debt. One problem was my lack of credit history. My father taught me to pay with personal checks, based on the cash in my account. So I relied on personal checks until every one wanted a credit card. I have built two other houses and refinanced three times and been with the same bank for 35 years, since I refinanced my first house. Tax returns have always been required, the appraisals have always been low, and my credit score has always been considered. Maybe I have been discriminated against.

So when I first discovered that banks had loaned huge amounts of sub-prime debt as well as a huge amount of additional debt on houses which were valued at accelerated prices based on phony assumptions and fallacious appraisals I was "shell shocked" at the rampant stupidity. **But it was not mere stupidity - it was sociopathic greed.** And now this rapacious greed has eaten alive so many banks, as well as so many who should not have borrowed so much. And our country's taxpayers have funded all the stupidity, while most of the top executives exited with their pockets stuffed full of green parachutes, contracts that had to be paid upon severance. What about contracts breached for fiduciary irresponsibility!

Lenders needed to know more about real estate fundamentals than appraisals, because if appraisals take accelerated pricing into account, rather than lend into a "bubble" then tons of properties would not have been financed at bloated purchase prices which would have caused sale prices to be lowered in order to obtain a loan. Therefore, the bubble would not have been so large for home prices. And the prices of commercial real estate would not have blasted through the ceiling of reality in bidding wars for "signature" properties, signature developments, and all the stuff necessary for all the 1031 Tenant in Common private placements.

MAI, as most savvy real estate people will tell you, stands for appraisals "made as instructed." My bank probably lowered appraisals to protect its depositors and capital base from unknowns – so if it made a loan at 80% to value, there was still a substantial cushion. However, it makes sense now to get off the "comp" approach to life and try to estimate value based on real intrinsic value along with perceived market value.

Banks have a responsibility to say "no" responsibly. But if they just say no then any real recovery in housing will be significantly delayed. Knee-jerk reactions hurt the economy as well as suitable buyers. Freddie and Fannie, as they are now on government life support, must determine new appraisal standards which more accurately reflect market value based on total living space and the quality of the finish as well as the immediate neighborhoods market for the level of the finish, rather than merely checking a box or indicating average or good. The cost to finish a house is what sets an average, or good house, apart from the exceptional. Comps are easy to rig and even the appraisal professional standards make the clear, not that most appraisers want to deviate from the superficial aspect of the report form - unless it is good for their business.

In this market, the exceptional house in certain locations will still command a relatively higher price as house buyers who demand excellence, who can still afford not to settle do not. If appraisers had a qualitatively more profound form than the "Uniform Residential Appraisal Report" signed under penalty of perjury - many of the fraudulent reports would not have taken place. Now there is a problem with knee jerk appraisers, who are knee jerk thinkers, just making it easier on themselves which makes it difficult for qualified buyers and sellers to obtain financing. And this is a problem for first time buyers as well as established buyers.

Of course Banks did not say no when there was an opportunity to just say yes and flip the mortgages (flip the risk) into giant pools of debt called Collateralized Mortgage Obligations for Wall Street to sell to investors around the world as a function of the higher interest rates generated by all the sub prime loans.

In the aftermath of all the carnage motivated by the vast amount of compensation flowing from fraudulently misrepresented "AAA investments" must now be logically regarded as billions of income and net worth fabricated out of thin air. When the shit hit the fan - Paulson's TARP (the ex Goldman CEO who made $500,000,000 in the years before he left Goldman for Treasury) added oxygen, at the same time that bankers clung to the idea that they must "honor" employment contracts.

So TARP shoveled money into the pockets of executives either on the way out or who argued the "need" to be overpaid or they would leave. This is honor among thieves at best. Remember all the excuses that a contract is a contract. Remember this was the reason to honor a commitment to someone whose lack of fiduciary conduct to depositors and shareholders and the banking system which led to failure and collapse deserved to be protected by contract law?

What about legal consequences for executives for making misleading and inaccurate misrepresentations to investors, to Freddie and Fannie and for representing that their bank was solvent up to the end – like National City Bank in Cleveland! I grew up in business as a customer of NCB for 35 years. I had offices in the NCB bank annex building initially and knew many of the top executives including David Daberko when he was a trainee.

When I began in business in 1965 (choke) NCB was a paragon of virtue and astute banking. When Daberko assiduously, like "Chinese Water Torture" his colleague told me, rose to the top - suddenly there was a new order to the way banking had been done in the past. And Daberko creatively figured out how to geometrically increase profits and his compensation at the risk of the entire bank. So Dave jumped head first into subprime debt along with his chief cohorts, among them was Peter Raskind who replaced Daberko as CEO in time for PNC to send him packing with an $8MM reward for some of the responsibility for having lost so many billions that TARP did not trust NCB management enough to award them TARP money. TARP funds went to PNC, in Pittsburg, knowing that it would take NCB in from out in the cold. Daberko supposedly got a $20MM severance bonus for ruining NCB, which cost shareholders billions in worthless stock.

This is a small case study, but relatively accurate. The question is how this can be allowed when there are enough characteristics of fraud to conclude or contend that this type of behavior constitutes fraud. In my opinion, after forty years of experience in two businesses concerned with misleading representations, fiduciary responsibilities, the omission of significant information and disclosure – there is plenty of fraud to go around. The good news is there is no statute of limitations on fraud. So if it takes more time for more people to think, fraud(?), all is not lost – except for the trillions of dollars of personal net worth, more trillions of dollars of bank shareholders' capital, etc. and the lives of so many people who were and remain financially destroyed.

Firewalls are gone. And Bank Holding Companies are the new menace which has swept the US. The Fed has promoted this, formerly taboo (forbidden under the bank Holding Company Act of 1956) practice by having allowed investment banks to become Bank Holding Companies. Why? In order to provide funding only available to banks and not subject to TARP or Congress.

Regrettably, there is so much overlapping of substance which has been deregulated that it makes writing a book about the entire context of what went so wrong seem redundant, at times. However, there is a redundant plethora of financial comingling which is critical to observe in order to fully address and understand the insidious and profound nature of the systemic failure of Banking and Wall Street – which are the same as our "Capital Markets," or our "Financial Markets."

The trick seems to be how we get these markets to stop existing primarily for the needs of the self-interested to work for the societal need to preserve the system for the good of our economy. And the only way appears to be to restore fire-walls. Which were the barriers against greed, coupled with requirements that any bank must lend a large portion of its capital, including almost free capital from the FDIC to small business. Capital formation should be of paramount importance; and real investment strategies must replace all the financial instruments which are primarily devoted to a velocity of fee creation for the Banks!

Paul Volker asked in 2010, "should banks be allowed to trade for their own account?" Trading which allowed (allows) banks to generate enormous profits and bonuses when successful – but when they screwed up to the tune of $300 Billion Dollars the government bailed them out. And the government bailed out their counterparties. Lloyd Blankfein, GoldmanCEO, addressed Goldman counter-parties as, "the most sophisticated investors in the world." Banks, at the time of TARP paid back TARP with FDIC money – which is not well advertised. You must know that "bankers" have not missed a step considering the record profits still being generated by Wall Street - still using the same strategies that created havoc. Think $600 trillion of derivates today - where's the beef?

Banks should have known (had to know) that too much debt to leverage is not good. Certainly for decades banks were extremely concerned with loan to value ratios. But over time, especially with the advent of Swaps (non existent insurance) leveraged on capital went up to 30 or 40 times capital - by the time everyone who could charge fees was done with the original capital (if any.) Insurance companies acquired banking and investment functions, as banks acquired insurance and investment function – and of course Wall Street was the big cheerleader and enabler.

Forgotten in the flurry of fees was the sad lesson of 1929 that Mega Banks are prone to Mega Failure.

And the question remains where all have the firewalls gone? To quote the Kingston Trio, from a time when the system was protected from itself, "a long time passing, a long time passing."

Some banks did remember Money and Banking courses from the 40's, 50's and the 60's and are still doing well expanding the money supply based on real economic theory which worked for four or more decades. Some smaller bankers chose prudence over the unbridled galloping greed that caused too many to mortgage their future (**our future**) to the hilt; so some bankers saved their banks and remain alive without a bailout.

There is a reason no one has confidence in banks. It is simple - after ransacking our economy for their own selfish reasons why would anyone trust Banks who have not cared about whether their customers have a job, or can hang on to a home originally obtained in accordance with legitimate mortgage lending standards. Why would anyone trust Mega banks that invested in and created egregiously leveraged "too complex to explain" financial instruments/products – Mega banks that misrepresented the quality of their loan portfolios and participated in home lending which directly caused so much human tragedy? Confidence no – outrage yes.

Why should anyone have trust in the Bank Holding Companies until Congress takes control to protect the public by putting the firewalls back in place!

CHAPTER 6

WALL STREET: FINANCIAL INVESTMENT VERSUS REAL INVESTMENT, THE ONLY ETHIC IS *SURVIVAL OF THE RICHEST*

The stock market formerly was a place where savings were invested in corporate growth except for times in the past, like the events leading up to the Great Depression - when unbridled speculation and greed ruled. Many corporations, still alive today, were started by Wall Street Financiers. Financiers helped innovators like Thomas Edison and Henry Ford obtain the capital they needed to build their companies and sold stock to raise capital. Shareholders understood why they were investing and knew there were risks that could not be guaranteed. Shareholders accepted risk investing in ideas or men who had ideas – which if successful would result in expanding companies which produced products in demand, and the companies along with their stock price, and dividends would grow in value.

So the Stock Market used to be a market which raised money for and sold shares in new companies or was a market to trade in existing investments called securities - which could be either bonds or stock. And **the process works when investment is real rather than financial.** Real investment produces improved, more productive, and more innovative plant and equipment which lead to increased GNP. Real is different than financial, because financial investment may only be reflected by a larger or lower personal income or net worth which is not translated into economic growth.

We have lived in a forward looking economy, and counted on the free market myth to push everything up. Personal savings for some time have not been invested in the growth of corporate values translated into dividends for shareholders. And corporate profits, for too many years, have not been invested in corporate growth, but have been paid out to CEOs and upper-level executives at an accelerated pace for the past thirty years, while necessary cash was borrowed. This equation works as long as everything goes forward, meaning up. So, as investments became more financial than real our markets turned into casinos where shareholders bet on the direction of stocks, or indexes, or anything that could be securitized to bet on.

A similar misdirection of savings occurred in the late 1920s when the stock market soared and "investors" gobbled up stocks on margin (LEVERAGE) in order to have a larger- than-life position in the market while stock prices soared due to unbridled greed and unfettered speculation. When Wall Street's stock market specializes primarily in complex (too complex to explain therefore too complex to understand) financial instruments, real investment is lost is the frenzy of an infinitely speculative, feverish and dogmatic pursuit to manufacture fees and bonuses. The stock market is now for the benefit of Wall Street Godfathers, who have little concern for what happens to investors' savings except for the conversion which has taken place for many years – the conversion of investor savings into Wall Street Godfather family pockets.

Clearly - capital formation has been replaced by fee formation. And "financial masturbation" reigns supreme. This is a concept I raised in *Invest for Success*...which holds that masturbation is OK as long as you do not want to create anything real, but if you expect to achieve real financial results of substance in the future then it is not the right approach, and as **I observed in 1990**: *"If the stock market becomes an arena of financial masturbation, then our economy suffers, as real investment is lost in the mad scramble to shuffle dollars."*

All the firewalls are gone. Wall Street achieved a great victory at the expense of our economy and the financial lives of millions of Americans.

Banks were the cohorts of Wall Street in the 20s and since 1999, (aided and abetted by Congress) have been joined at the hip once again. The Fed in September 08 approved Goldman to become a Bank Holding Company – so now Goldman can take money from the Fed and can return TARP money, because the FIDC money comes in under the table to prop up banks without Congressional oversight or approval. How can this make sense when we have so much empirical evidence to support the rationality of the wisdom behind the firewalls established in the wake of the Great Depression to protect our financial system from its self destructive tendencies?

Wall Street still argues for not too much regulation, because it needs the freedom to quickly react and maintain its ability to be innovative. That's about what I heard Goldman CEO Lloyd Blankfein state in his remarks at the spring meeting in April of 2009 to the Council of Institutional Investors. The following is a direct quote:

"The events of the last year have put into stark relief the tension between innovation and stability. But if we abandon, as opposed to regulate, market mechanisms created decades ago, like securitization and credit default swaps, we may end up constraining access to capital and the efficient hedging and distribution of risk when we mutually do come through this crises."

This is significant and fundamentally illuminating if you want to know how bad Wall Street really is. So I thank the brilliant uber rich Lloyd for exposing the real greed and fallacious self serving reasoning of a Godfather who is so accustomed to getting his own way that he did not hear what he actually said. So he was defending innovation – does that mean the complex financial products, insured by Swaps, which defy understandable explanations? Certainly he did not argue that innovation is to promote increased real capital formation. Credit Default Swaps were created by Dr. Phil, you know the economist who called us "whiny," and it seems the sole purpose was to mask risk and avoid state insurance regulations.

Therefore Blankfein's essential contention was that we "constrain access to capital" if we cannot issue baseless insurance or phony guarantees. To Wall Street hedging means using a Swap to hedge risk - in other words Swaps lower or mitigate risk because the risk has been insured – or layed off on "counter parties," really? So let's not abandon the instrument, the Swap, which is more to blame for how our financial institutions and markets tanked - than Blankfein's ludicrous explanation of the housing price bubble and why lending standards "simply deteriorated."

Where is the real truth that fees and bonuses flowing from an enormous velocity of transactions backed by the hedging illusion of safety called Swaps motivated the demise of lending standards? And how does Blankfein characterize his involvement with the "counter-parties" and total lack of any due diligence regarding the substance of loans termed sub-prime, loans which should have been regarded as worse than junk bonds. At least it was possible to know the issuer of a junk bond. Did anyone ever ask what the credit rating was for sub-prime debtors or follow up with what is the experience of banks with 580 or below credit scores. Who cared when so much money was being made by the few at the expense of the many and the system itself? If you want to read the entirety of Blankfein's remarks go to www.2goldmansachs.com/ideas/public-policy/lcb-speech - if Goldman left it there, which is not likely.

Consider that Goldman achieved record profits in 2010, and agreed to Obama "reform" because it did not materially limit their activities. This was not reform, but optics. And the media has moved on from a story it really never understood. Because the Godfathers have specialized in propaganda to obscure and lie about the substance of deregulation; deregulation used to free the survival of the richest ethic to prey on our society like a giant vulture.

Read Paul Krugman religiously who seems to be a solitary voice of reason, a flickering candle of light in all the darkness. Apparently he has not become a paid influence peddler of Wall Street propaganda.

It is self-evident that Wall Street has not cared about results for investors. Led by Goldman, the Street specialized in selling - "too complex to explain" innovative financial products comprised of geometrically leveraged, quantitatively measured for safety and reduced risk, diversified trenches of emptiness, based on AAA ratings and Swap insured against failure. And this contrived fabrication for fees was fueled by demand flowing from a huge amount of liquidity in capital markets, both foreign and domestic, which created an unquenchable thirst for products that Wall Street knew it had to flip like hot potatoes to get rid of the egregious risk. This is a long sentence – however, it is easy to follow as compared to any professional explanation of complex financial products. The world of the too complex to explain can also compared with Minimalism, an art form which requires a lengthy explanation to avoid the thought that it is nothing.

Perhaps you probably don't remember when 70s Goldman, in the 70s, unloaded tons of Penn Central Bonds on Chase Manhattan Bank from their overstocked inventory, at a time when Goldman was intimately familiar with the bank and the railroad. So when Penn Central defaulted on the bonds, shortly after Chase bought them based on Goldman's advise, Chase' lawfirm Deckert Price in Philadelphia prevailed upon Goldman to take back the bonds and eat them. Goldman had not offered to make a complete restitution relying on the old theory of *Caveat Emptor*. And clearly neither Goldman nor most Wall Street investment bankers nor Banks have stopped relying on this theory, which for generations has been considered egregious and immoral, as well as typically legally indefensible – illegal!

Congress passed the Securities Exchange Act of 1934 in part, "to substitute a philosophy of full disclosure for the philosophy of *caveat emptor* and thus to achieve a high standard of business ethics in the securities industry." And this goes to disclosure. So if anything that has been securitized has issues which have not been fully disclosed: like you cannot measure risk which is qualitative, therefore subjective, quantitatively; and you cannot issue pools of debt backed by insurance which has no reserves and maintain that Credit Default Swaps have any material value then all of Wall Street and the Banks who participated in this should have, along with their heavily bonused executives, severe legal problems in my opinion and in the opinion of several prominent Cleveland attorneys.

How is Wall Street in the investment business when it has turned from real investments to contrived, easily manipulated financial products? What does Hedging really mean and is it technically or mathematically possible to reduce risk with so-called "hedges?" Are Swaps hedges, certainly they must be from Blankfein's talk, and if they are how are they not a lie. What is the fiduciary responsibility of anyone in the security business to not misrepresent the substance of any transaction?

These crucial questions and many others are rhetorical because Congress, regulators and Wall Street itself cares more about propping up "financial markets" than integrity and acting in good faith toward investors and the country. Let's face it Wall Street Godfathers got paid to use swaps to protect investors (the old protection business) and AIG provided the muscle, along with all the other sub-prime lenders who also sold swaps and got paid to issue the empty promise of Swaps. These Godfather families pretended that no one would get killed as long as all the toxic stuff got flipped to the last person standing – just like the investors left holding their Madoff bags, not Bergdorf which at least has an important logo on it. So Wall Street never thought about the systemic effects all of its innovation would have on "Main Street?" (OK I said Main Street.) Is it believable that so much B-School brilliance never thought they were killing so many 401ks – they knew but did not care when considering their own brilliance and such huge payoffs.

In 2009 I went to Goldman's website and read the posted humanitarian concerns of Lloyd Blankfein from the "conclusion" of his "remarks." His conclusion exemplifies the true meaning of lip service. The following is

Blankfein's direct quote to be certain that you have a complete and profound awareness of Wall Street's premier CEO's societal concerns:

"I want to conclude today with the following thought: **we are fighting for nothing** *less than the immediate health and security of every person.* **We can never forget the products of economic growth – more accessible health care, better education, less crime, tolerance of diversity, social mobility and a commitment to democracy.** *In so many respects, change is the order of the day. We have much to do to repair our financial system and reinvigorate our regulatory structure. At the same time, our financial system, rooted in the belief of putting risk capital to work on behalf of ideas and innovation, has helped produce a long-term record of economic growth and stability that is unparalleled in history. We have to safeguard the value of risk capital, which is at the heart of market capitalism, while enhancing investor confidence through meaningful transparency, effective oversight and strong governance. But, there should be no doubt markets simply cannot thrive without confidence. Though honest disagreements will occur, the best companies don't shy away or selfishly frustrate efforts to compel better industry practices. These companies recognize that they are the first to benefit from better standards, especially if their business requires extensive dealings with partners or counterparties. But, we have to recognize a higher responsibility: to speak up, to draw attention to potentially destabilizing trends and to act like an owner responsible for the integrity of the system. I, for one, know we have not done the best job in the recent past but working with you, as many of the world's most important investors, Goldman Sachs pledges to recommit itself to this fundamental obligation."*

How does this sound: self-serving, self-important, absurd, ludicrous, dangerous - or just like plain, dishonest, hypocritical, pretentious verbal behavior from the CEO of a company bailed out by the taxpayer's who were so badly screwed by the all the financial innovative concoctions. **This is verbal surrealism on high – even evangelical.**

Blankfein is not the only one responsible. He is merely the current CEO in a long line of Goldman CEOs, and so many other Wall Street Godfathers who went out of their way to sound good while engaged in avaricious, rapacious greed at the expense of anyone, even one of their own like Dick Fuld of Lehman. Thank god Paulson retired from Goldman in time to be our Secretary of the Treasury to save Banks and Wall Street by throwing vast amounts of TARP money at them in order to save market liquidity so Goldman could go right on "fighting for the immediate health and security of every person."

Goldman is a microcosm of what is and has been wrong with Wall Street and as the self-admitted most successful firm on the Street it richly deserves to be studied, because Goldman infiltrated our Government decades ago! And the essence of its motivations, government relationships as well as its conduct ought to be exposed and understood. There is a prodigious amount of empirical evidence to examine. Empirical means the evidence is easy to see and to comprehend - like **Blankfein's self-evident morally bankrupt and absurd "remarks."**

It is amazing to consider that Goldman's chutzpa is so vast and that Goldman has such a strong faith in its own BS that it went out of its way to post Blankfein's "remarks" for the world to read on the internet.

Years ago I had a therapist who explained the importance of listening to myself to hear how I sounded to my family as well as friends. I have gotten decent at this in time to have established a close relationship with my children, but not in time to have preserved that particular marriage. I guess if you are a billionaire there is no reason to listen to how you sound to anyone other than your self – because the sun rises and sets on the self.

Blankfein is not necessarily a bad person – he is just carrying on the Goldman tradition without stopping to either hear how he sounds or re-examine the substance of Goldman behavior to conclude the obvious, that it has been toxic. Blankfein has no social conscience, or at least not one larger than the sometimes charitable Andrew Carnegie, the pioneer of Social Darwinism.

It is important to realize that Wall Street will deploy any ruse (lie if you will) available to further its own ends, so when it extols the merits of self correcting markets it really means leave me alone. If Japan had left Hiroshima alone after the horror of the nuclear bomb, perhaps it would have returned to normal, but how long would it have taken? We know that forests after a great fire return to normal over the course of time – so we do know that given time some tragic occurrences do return to normal.

Our economic explosion is not a recession so will not return to normal without extraordinary measures, like our Government investing in our economy when there are no others stepping up to the line.

Maybe our political system can return to normal after we dump the Tea Party into Boston Harbor!

The problem is that for the market to be left alone to return to normal – so many lives will remain lost to the desperation stemming from their lack of financial ability to survive. Too many members of the middle and upper middle class have been displaced with not enough food, or medicine, or education for kids or hope for the future, not enough money to ever retire, just grim bare existence. And suicides are on the rise. Wall Street Godfathers and their families are not likely to notice all the human suffering because their pile of cash pillaged from all the past innovative financial transactions allows them to focus on how to preserve Wall Street's freedom to remain innovative rather than focus on how to remain alive without any money to live on.

Do you remember what these Godfathers actually said in late 2008 and in 2009? They unanimously expressed - *surprise at all the risk in the system* (risk they financially engineered into existence). And at the same time they **defended free markets and the fallacious ruse-myth that *free markets self correct*.** Further they expressed little remorse for the devastating damage caused by their greed to so many of their fellow Americans.

They continue to vigorously lobby Congress to remain relatively unfettered. When reform was proposed they paid lip service to some *"regulation reinvigoration."* Why? Because they wanted to continue to sell all types of leverage backed up by a "more judicious use of swaps." Absolutely ludicrous! Because knowledge of historical and current realities reveal there is no rational reason to justify the murderous abuse of leverage.

"Main Street" may not understand the lack of common sense and lack of concern for the devastation caused by so much leveraged debt financial instruments that Wall Street cannot explain its complexities. But it feels the tragedy. Mainstreet may think that deficits are the real problem because that is what Wall Street Shills (and Republicans intent on getting rid of Obama) repeat over and over and over, aided and abetted by all their Republican Shills, and the T Party. The Tea Party should be called the D Party – D for denial, a common psychological refuge from reality.

I realize I am redundant, but my redundancy seems infinitely more rational and logical, based on all the empirical evidence, than greed-based shills redundantly irrationally arguing for free markets for the last thirty years. Keep in mind there is still an ongoing philosophical argument for the merits of free market, Laissez-faire capitalism even though the results of taking down all the fire-walls designed in the aftermath of the Great Depression to protect all of us from the ravages of greed, are so painfully apparent.

It is easier, as well as more politically correct, to engage in a professional discourse about the substance of what Wall Street really is about when writing a book. However, the lack of passion and the brilliance of technical, no matter how improbable, analysis misses the point - which is simple. As once again, our country and our fellow Americans have been brought to their knees because we forgot that Wall Street is not for us, and not for real investment. Wall Street is for fees spewing forth from speculation which is volatile. **And Wall Street - like any sociopathic Swindler cares only for its**

own wants and needs. Wall Street stopped providing real investment when, long ago, it stopped promoting price to dividend ratios.

Wall Street makes money by innovatively **contriving** financial products, which result in a geometric velocity of transactions generating huge amounts of fees. Wall Street is for immediate gratification for its own Godfathers and their families. And if nothing real is created for anyone other than them – well they can live with this thought. Because the executives of all the failed companies (like Merrill and Lehman) still have millions and millions to fall back on. And the CEO of Goldman still has a mandate to maximize Goldman's profits going forward, no matter what - that's his job description!

Blankfein was firmly on this path when the Fed, surreptitiously, allowed Goldman to become a bank holding company in time to receive billions and billions, of almost zero interest capital from the FDIC. (No votes from Congress like TARP.) The Fed is not governed by Congress and has little or no meaningful transparency. Our Secretary of the Treasury was the Vice Chairman of the Fed when it made its decision to turn investment banks into bank holding companies!

One thing for sure - neither Goldman nor any bank holding company wants to rebuild the firewalls that worked for 50 years in the aftermath of the Great Depression. Possibly now there could be a modicum of agreement that we should "reinvigorate regulation," but not enough to interfere with innovative complexities which defy an understandable explanation for anyone who comprehends English, French or German. Possibly if you can speak Chinese or Finnish you could understand the mystical nature of nothing.

My suggestion for Wall Street to inspire confidence would be to embrace, possibly for the first time, a sincere posture of real concern for results to "Main Street" investors. This must involve relinquishing some of their self-interest to acquire a modicum of self- interest in the common good. And this could be evidenced by a return to value investing vs. *too complex to explain* speculation. At the same, time Wall Street would have to rededicate itself to rediscovering functional ethics and look in their mirrors of self deceit to determine a clearer view of the truth. Truth is not to be found in posturing in amazement over all the risk that no one realized existed. Wall Street created the risk and then did not recognize it, and to accept this BIG LIE would be like Dr. Frankenstein not recognizing the monster he created. Where is Lava soap when you really need it? (Mothers, in the 50s washed out kids mouths for lying or swearing (me) with this terrible stuff – now you would use Neutrogena.)

Innovative financial products hedged with financial tools for safety just do not inspire my confidence today. Financial engineers have riddled Wall Street with math rather than real investments and that is not a confidence builder for anyone who does not remember the purpose of Algebra, but may remember it used to be important to invest in value as measured by a price to dividend ratio. Financial products do not produce growth in GNP, or any meaningful measure of capital formation - and have not produced anything of lasting value for anyone except the Godfathers and their families who assiduously saved all the booty. Goldman's brilliance was to flip the risk faster and better than the rest and then retreat from the scene of the accident - as if the financial death of so many Americans can be thought of as accidental. To me it looks like murder one.

Blankfein and his Wall Street (banker) colleagues, along with Congress, want us to have confidence our in financial markets to maintain our financial might. **Confidence comes from trust.** There is no reason to trust Wall Street if you truly understand how little it has cared about you. And our government allows Born-Again Social Darwinism to have its way with our economy as well as sabotage providing critical needs in our society like: health insurance and public education and the rebuilding of crumbling infrastructures.

Can you really trust CEOs and the firms who hired financial engineers to camouflage all the risk? Trust the CEOs and their brilliant heavily degreed executives who completely understood the risk of fires while they spent decades working on tearing down all the firewalls! Why - because they feed on fire like vampires feed on blood!

Wall Street is only in business for itself and does not give a small shit about you and me. Or else how could so many emails within each firm express amazement at how investors could buy the "shit" they sold so aggressively around the world? Why did the Congressional hearings where these emails were made public not result in the personal prosecutions of all the participants? Where was the integrity to stop selling "shit" to investors - and at the same time short the "shit knowing (inside knowledge) the "shit" eventually become obvious and gap down in value or just be worthless.

CHAPTER 7

APPRAISERS AND RATERS DROVE THE GETAWAY CARS

Raters became involved with Banks and Wall Street's innovative "too complex to explain" debt, which was securitized, packaged and sold as bonds. And they were paid significant fees to rate the risk which was deemed to have been mitigated by the fallacious assurances provided by Credit Default Swaps. So raters enabled Wall Street and Banks by providing ratings too good to be true.

A rating is like the depth meter on a sailboat in that you always think you know where you are until you hit rocks. I know I have hit rocks, which is always possible when you are dragging 6 ½ feet of lead around under your waterline. And for most of summer of 1986, I was shippedwrecked in Bayfield on Lake Ontario in Canada, just months after Congress passed the Tax Reform Act 1986 (TRA 86.)

There is a difference, however, because sailors know better than to have too much faith in their depth meter because any large body of water has charts which chronicle or attempt to gage the depth and also indicate the unevenness of the bottom. Raters, based on a preponderance of past nonperformance, seem unaware of the degree to which the future depends on variables, like substance, chance, and even integrity. And this is where appraisers and raters are so alike – integrity is essentially absent, again based on performance and the empirical evidence surrounding the highly specious results of so many appraisals.

Investors depend on, hopelessly conflicted, third party judgments to be able to make decisions without having either the expertise or experience to know what something is worth - like a bond or real estate. Banks loan money or issue debt, referred to as a mortgage, to people who want to buy property, whether residential or commercial. Wall Street uses credit rating agencies to measure the quality of debt which it securitizes and sells as bonds. Appraisers rate the value of real estate; credit rating agencies appraise the risk as well as the value or strength of the bond after analyzing the issuer; so both are deemed to be analyzing substance in order to provide risk evaluation to all concerned parties.

Banks have the fundamental responsibility to evaluate and do due diligence, regarding the substance of who they lend money to in addition to evaluating the real estate behind the loan. Wall Street, like Banks, has the primary responsibility for doing due diligence to understand the substance of **any** investment securitized and sold. Neither is supposed to primarily rely on third-party judgments. Yet, it seems that is what they both relied on to market and flip so much never underwritten debt, innovatively fabricated into financial products. The ratings were their excuse to sell shit.

Simply put, Banks churned out the debt for Wall Street to securitize into bonds to sell. So approval by the raters and the appraisers was fundamental to the process of creating a huge velocity of transactions and was of paramount importance in helping the ultra rich grow their pile of fees by enabling the swindlers to financially rape the economy and the society we live in and depend on for survival.

Credit Rating Agencies, like S&P, are accustomed to analyzing the risk of corporate, municipal, state or government bond issuers. Because so many bonds were blind pools of various levels of mortgage risk, raters got in over their heads and jumped into a murky pool of unfathomable debt based on the quality and market value of real estate - as appraised by real estate appraisers. Companies that rate bonds and their issuers are generally unfamiliar - not experienced - with analyzing real estate fundamentals, which mortgages depend on.

Investments with phony ratings catered to the Investor Risk Avoidance Syndrome – (which has a well documented history.) Raters, who must have known better, relied on financial engineered, risk measurement tools. And these esteemed "professional" tools were intentionally designed to mask risk in order to sell blind pools of unmitigated, fallaciously appraised real-estate sub-prime, over leveraged, mortgage debt. It is obvious that raters were paid to bless all the lousy lack of substance with alphabetical grades like AAA or AAb. The reliance on these tools and the ability to hide behind the use of the word projection is absolutely form versus substance for raters to avoid prosecution. The IRS has used form vs. substance as a well documented reason to overturn tax avoidance schemes. And if the form is willfully and intentionally contrived to cheat the IRS then prosecution is the conclusion.

Fictitious, phony triple A ratings were a pretty neat trick and an impressively innovative marketing tool considering how instrumental ratings were in helping Wall Street sell trillions and trillions of crappy debt. And Wall Street led the way to the Promised Land of riches beyond belief by creating the market demand for the banks (themselves) to flip as much debt as they could place.

Real estate appraisers were given the high sign by banks to appraise high enough to do the deal. Mortgage brokers were also encouraged, even pressured, to generate lots of loans. To be certain there were enough loans to flip to Freddie and Fannie and ultimately to Wall Street to securitize into huge pools of tranches (trenches) filled with different qualities of debt and debtors (from residential to commercial.) The more loans the more money for compensation for banking leaders and the more money for everyone, except the borrowers who stupidly were in over their heads from day one. Something for everyone, how great!

The quality of subprime debt was admittedly worse than rotten. However, raters approved putting the crappy debt into diversified pools containing some higher quality debt, which allowed raters (their bogus justification) to award the AAA to the vast trillions of dollars of Swap "insured" debt.

When you eat at a 3-star restaurant in Paris and the tablecloths are grimy, and you commence to vomit midway into dessert you know immediately the revered French Michelin Guide screwed up. However, when you gobble up AAA mortgaged backed, swapped backed, sub-prime, but laundered into diversified trenches, debt securitized into bonds - it takes a few years or more to know that everything has been a lie. And this lie from Wall Street and Banks was enabled by all the phony appraisals and phony ratings. So now we are stuck with massive chronic dry-heaves for the foreseeable future.

It is overkill to explore all the causal factors of the conflicts of interest fueled by the greed and **blatant idiocy of appraisers** and raters as this is self-evident. Anyone who wanted to peer beneath the surface of all the sham transactions while raters and appraisers were helping grease the wheels of LAISSEZ-FAIRE free-market capitalism could have smelled the stench leaking out from the growing piles of money based on financial products that could not then or now be explained to any rational person.

After forty years of experience, retrospectively, I have had zero confidence in most of the appraisals of the commercial real estate that have been included in all the real estate private placements that I have analyzed, and I have reviewed too many to count.

My only experience with residential appraisals is when I have bought or refinanced my own homes; and each time my opinion of residential appraisers was that they were equally rotten, because they were so comp dependent and rigidly pedestrian. Comps are often not comparable, and cannot be unless the quality of interior finish and exterior construction is truly similar. This is true for commercial buildings as well. However, commercial buildings are classified as A and B or lower – so commercial appraisals are done to make a B look like an A.

Several years ago, I refinanced my house in a neighborhood which supports the quality of a top of the line renovation. In some locations there are buyers who prefer to find an older house totally finished to high standards, which moved the house forward in time. At certain market levels there are buyers who prefer quality in the right location and can still afford it, although it is possible some houses at the highest end of the price spectrum are so expensive and the market is so thin that buyers are not there. The market for a house is also stronger in certain markets where prices never accelerated beyond reasonable duplication costs, and never became part of the bubble. Again, my bank's appraiser looked at comps which did not require any personal or judgmental validation and simply appraised my house below market value, which did not disaffect what I needed from the bank. But this approach today will materially affect sellers who want or need to sell or refinance, as well as all the home buyers who may not be able to get loan due to faulty, lowball appraisals. And this scenario will not help turn housing around.

I vividly remember an appraisal for a private placement offering for a large apartment complex. It concluded the property was well located and in good condition, although the property looked like a dying whale in color photos. The appraisal specifically stated the roofs would need to be replaced within the next few years – which really meant the roofs were shot and there were no replacement reserves. I have an elephant memory for the absurd.

One of the largest national sponsors specializing in institutional quality properties for 1031 exchanges and blind pool investments for individuals and pension funds actually put out a 40 page appraisal (from one of the largest real estate brokers in the US) for a 1031 TIC property comparing the per square foot purchase price of $280 to five other office properties. The others were in downtown Denver, and actually cost $170 to $190 which included adequate parking. The $280 psf property was not located downtown, and without available surface parking. Therefore this property required its own "structured" parking garage. The downtown purchase prices were increased to reflect what the five properties would have cost with structured parking – which they did not need. So the appraisal for the more expensive property made the downtown purchase prices equivalent to an office building not as well located that had a purchase price of almost 50% more per foot than downtown. The huge national broker in this transaction was also the appraiser. Can appraisers have a conflict of interest?

Conflicts of interest govern how S&P has furnished ratings for years. The more in-depth the rating the more the cost to be rated. And when you are paying so much to be rated and have lots of other stuff to rate think of the business that can be generated by being generous to your client. Nothing like a willingness to issue favorable ratings to generate fees!

Years ago, I was a General Agent for one of the top mutual companies in North America. Duff & Phelps, S&P along with Bests gave this company top ratings shortly before its unannounced fraud took a 125 year old company down in 1994 due to a glut of see-through real estate loans. See-through means, no tenants and no lights for cleaning at night.

How the raters and the Department of Insurance in Michigan could not have noticed the Canadian Trust Company, set up to provide worthless trust certificates in exchange for all the trusteed cash held in the states to protect US policyholders as required by US law for foreign domiciled insurance companies, I don't know. The bank in Connecticut holding the trusteed assets just silently watched the account dwindle from $750,000,000 in cash to nothing; while E&W was called upon to consult with their client, the insurance company, about a "liquidity crisis" furnished an unqualified audit statement only a few months before Confederation Life was liquidated in Canada in accordance with the Winding Down Act. At that time (it might be different today) there was not a Chapter 11 filing available, so there was no ability to reorganize for the benefit of anyone. Should the raters have been able to understand that a trust company, created to launder US policyholder assets into a sham Canadian Trust Company, merits alarm? Obviously not a AA, or an A+ from Best's.

So why do we trust appraisers and rating agencies given the conflicts and terrible breaches of integrity, along with all the failed judgments? Why should S&P be allowed to rate the credit of The United States of America? In my opinion, uncharged felons should not be in the rating business. Or is fraud not a felony?

Real Estate Appraisers are not as large or as influential as the major credit rating agencies like Moody's or S&P. They do not generate similarly huge profits – so are more susceptible to financial conflicts to survive, which is not much of an excuse to furnish fraudulent appraisals. If individual appraisers' commanded higher fees based on an improved, more thorough residential appraisal format for Freddie and Fannie which included all residential lenders it might be better. If all residential lenders were required to retain 50% of the loan (commercial loans too); and if residential appraisers were subject to integrity checks which reviewed their track record for a percentage of the failure rate of their past appraisals - maybe matters as they stand today could improve.

Certainly appraisers, who participated in any bogus appraisals of sub-prime house loans, or any real estate loans, should be run out of town. Appraisers who have committed fraudulent appraisals should be prosecuted, along with the banking executives who encouraged them and the Wall Streeters who securitized the debt into bonds, now termed ***too complex to explain*** – again to generate a velocity of deals for fees and bonuses.

After so many years in the securities business and having preached to my investors, like a zealot missionary - *do not invest unless you completely understand and the investment makes sense.* I cannot get the absurdity of the *too complex to ...* out of my head/craw. How does anyone with an ounce of sense and experience invest in interest rates well above market rates and think a debt instrument - termed an innovative financial product -can or should be AAA?

The concept of "too complex to understand" sounds to me like **"go directly to jail, do not pass go, do not collect $200,000,000."** I realize, I sound like a broken record, I return again to this absurd explanation of the bizarre nature of what took our economy down. Perhaps *too complex to explain* should be on the next Wall Street "tomb stone" bragging about how much money it raised, essentially for fees for their firms, definitely not for results for investors or their equally greedy counterparties. Our current type of Depression ought to be termed the Great Depression of the too complex to explain era.

Why did Freddie and Fanny along with Banks not require better appraisal standards with better forms to illuminate reality? Maybe Congress was partially to blame. But Congress did not tell them to totally abandon prudent underwriting. Perhaps better appraisal standards might have protected the two Fs from their rampant greed and stupidity; certainly the advanced degrees of their officers did not.

Rating companies like S&P certainly deserve to be investigated infinitely more than Martha Stewart. The executives of these institutional raters helped cause the destruction of so many financial lives and their response was merely an expressed a desire to do better. Is that fair? Especially when considering how their bogus ratings helped cause the downfall of our economy and so many financial deaths. How do we trust raters and appraisers in the future, because it would be crazy to trust them now! Confidence in ratings and appraisals would be an irrational oxymoron, which would also be moronic.

And now in August of 2011 the raters have lowered the rating of The United States of America.

Regrettably, this toxic mess is inexorably and symbiotically connected; hence it is impossible to avoid the overlapping nature of the context of this book without leaving some of the truth out. So once again it is necessary to stop and think about how the media and our government, along with Wall Street and Banks, always talk about the importance of the need for confidence in our markets. What about integrity. What about the rational market lie?

How many times do you lie to someone before trust is demolished? How can there be a return to confidence in ratings or in appraisals when there have been no consequences for all the malfeasance and misrepresentations? Kids without consequences grow up to be unruly adults who either are involved in the self-destructive behavior of too many inner-city kids who no one, including our society, has cared about enough. Or they grow up to be sociopathic, self-interested and self-indulged Financial Darwinists taking advantage of the public good. This does not include all the creative entrepreneurs who have made money by ethically creating real businesses which add value to our economy and society.

Appraisers have not cared enough about standards and integrity, and have been used by banks and others to sell real estate as well as flip it to the Freddie and Fannies of the world. Congress should take notice and work with real estate specialists who understand the failings of the appraisal process as well as the appraisers.

The executives of the major rating companies who helped - aided and abetted - their clients flip giant pools of debt to counter-parties (still lurking in closets), hedge funds, individuals and pension funds - should be held accountable. There should be immense fines for the companies, with the recapture of bonuses and jail. There also ought to be prosecutions for not doing appropriate due diligence as well as misrepresenting the quality of all the spurious debt securitized in blind pools of toxic waste. There should be huge liability and punishment for not pointing out that the Credit Default Swaps (CDS) were a sham contrived to sell securities rather than provide any semblance of a back up or insurance. CDSs were explained to be insurance!

The major **credit rating agencies** have exhaustive, in depth experience and expertise with rating insurance companies for risk and stability. Therefore they certainly **knew how to analyze for reserves behind insurance products as well as analyze the competence of insurance company management** – AND THEY DID NOT DO THIS. These executives are guilty, in my opinion, of driving the getaway cars which SIGNIFICANTLY CONTRIBUTED to the greatest financial pile up since the Great Depression. How do you build confidence when it is now self-evidently irrational to trust ratings and appraisals – and the Investment Banks and the most prominent Banks, which today are all Bank Holding Companies engaged in Wall Street activities? Now they are blurred into Wall Street. But the Goldman family has ruled the Street – it seems, along with our government.

Today we are still ship wrecked on financial rocks of deceit and despair – and we have been asked to have confidence in many of the people, and entities who caused this. Let's let S&P put our country into default – along with the T Party. In January of 2011 many of the culprits proudly announced they will have record incomes. Wall Street's return to explosive profitability (as far back as 2009 when the market crashed) came on the heels on of TARP and FDIC funding, and the Fed's injection of an extra trillion – as well as the continuing huge amounts of contrived leverage. Does this restore our confidence in Wall Street's business acumen and engender faith and trust in their integrity? Or does this create the opposite? Why is there still a discussion of trust? Gee wiz, where is it?

CHAPTER **8**

SELF-SERVING REGULATORS SERVE THE SELF-INTERESTED ULTRA RICH

W̲e know it is wrong to lie. And we know what the SEC did to Martha Stewart for lying to their investigators; they put her in jail, although no individual was injured and the financial markets did not implode. Why? Because you and I cannot lie to SEC investigators. Congress also habitually prosecutes us if we lie to them. But what happens when they lie to us, or allow Wall Street and Banks to lie to investors (us again)? I guess lawyers would argue that to be a lie the false statement must be given under oath. Let's put them under oath and ask them if they have tried to identify manipulative, contrived financial products. And follow up by asking if they think these products are or were deceptive. Let's ask if they ever smelled the odor of Ponzi – or if all the flips were, in fact, an innovative chip off the old Ponzi.

What happens when Wall Street Banks promote investing in large, **securitized**, blind pools of sub-prime debt termed bonds – and then add diversification and Swaps to assure investors the "bonds" are safe? And even better the bonds are rated AAA by Credit Rating Agencies to provide further validation of the prudence and safety of the Bonds! After all these safety procedures to further affirm the safety and prudence to be obtained by investing in the Bonds, Wall Street then advertises how the risk has been quantitatively measured using the latest financial engineering tools available to reduce risk. We know what happens.

First, focus on the SEC (the Securities and Exchange Commission) which is easier to understand than the complicated economic responsibilities of the Federal Reserve System (informally referred to as the Fed) whose Board of Governors is in charge of the supervision of banking, and primarily comprised of bankers and investment bankers. It gets complicated, but to follow all the conflicts is to follow the money, which is the source of motivation for all the betrayals of public trust.

Section 10(b) of the 1934 Securities Exchange Act makes it "unlawful for any person...to use or employ, in connection with the purchase of sale of any security.., any manipulative or deceptive device or contrivance in contravention of such rules and regulations as the SEC may prescribe." 15 U.S. C. sec.78j. Rule 10b-5, which implements this provision, forbids the use, "in connection with the purchase or sale of any security, "of any device, scheme, or artifice to defraud" or any other "act, practice, or course of business" that "operates...as a fraud or deceit." 17 CFR sec. 240. 10b-5 (2000) One of Congress' primary objectives in passing the act was "to insure honest securities markets and thereby promote investor confidence" after the market crash of 1929. *United States v. O'Hagan*, 521 U.S. C. 642, 658 (1997) Further Congress wanted " 'to substitute a philosophy of full disclosure for the philosophy of *caveat emptor* and thus achieve a high standard of business ethics in the securities industry.' "

So far the SEC has not applied the concept of "deceptive device or contrivance" to the lack of substance of Swaps or Mortgage Backed Subprime Bonds – but it is very clear that these bonds and many Swaps were definitely securitized. It is self-evident that innovative financial products embody many of the basic elements that rule 10b-5 was designed to address, and this chapter will argue that the SEC has been more derelict in its responsibilities than anyone has imagined. The controlling issue behind financial products is that they have been manipulated to camouflage and misrepresent risk and the lack of explainable real substance.

The SEC was not the only regulator, until recently. Several years ago, there was the National Association of Security Dealers which was created by the 1938 Maloney Act to be a self-regulatory organization of the securities industry responsible for the regulation of the Nasdaq Stock Market and regulate broker-dealers. In regulating broker-dealers, it oversees all the business activities of registered representatives and by 2001 the activities of 5,400 securities firms (like Lehman Bros. and many smaller firms), 58,000 branch offices and more than 505,000 registered security professionals. I was among the 5,400 in the 90s.

In 2001, the NASD was carrying out a substantial portion of the functions of the SEC, its parent organization's responsibilities of being the securities industry's primary self- regulator. This information was directly from my July 2001 NASD manual, page 151. Further the manual stipulated that the NASD was responsible for testing, on-site examinations of securities firms for compliance with federal securities laws (I still remember my audit when I was a broker-dealer). And the NASD reviewed advertising and sales literature as well as underwriting arrangements proposed by securities firms in connection with new securities offerings. Although you may have little interest in understanding the arcane, or obscure structure of security regulations it is necessary to know just how badly the SEC has failed to protect Main Street, and to more profoundly understand that our SEC has provided refuge for their ex, chiefly Goldman, ultra rich partners to swindle us.

Stick with this for a little more background. In July 2007 the NASD was merged into something called the Financial Industry Regulatory Authority (FINRA.) At the same time the "self-regulatory arm" of the New York Stock Exchange was also merged into FINRA. Consider that the SEC approved the NASD to pay each member firm $35,000 (out of the very large surplus the NASD had accumulated from all the fees charged member firms) to, in my opinion, induce or bribe them to approve the merger. A number of broker dealers that I have known for years endorse this opinion. Mary Schapiro who was the president of the NASD engineered this event and her salary went up to $3MM it is reported.

FINRA oversees 5,000 brokerage firms, about 173,000 branch offices and approximately 656,000 registered representatives (like stock brokers.) Its web page contends that: *"FINRA is dedicated to investor protection and market integrity through effective and efficient regulation and complementary compliance and technology-based services."* It goes on to say that it is "dedicated to keeping markets fair..." Mary Schapiro is now the head of the SEC at a much smaller salary, but she was in charge of investor protection leading up to where we find ourselves today.

Investor protection is an interesting concept; to me it means not allowing the proliferation of all the contrived financial products. And it ought to mean not allowing the fallacious practice of mathematical risk measurement, which is to quantify the subjective, hence qualitative, nature of risk. Even without firewalls Securities Regulators have a clear legal basis as well as an obligation to protect the markets. Regulators are obligated to look past form to the substance of anything securitized that creates hazardous waste. (So does the Fed.) Have regulators stopped to hear that innovative financial products are **"too complex to explain." That remark from anyone who sold that type of security should be more than enough for any regulator to prosecute based on the plethora** of existing rules - pick one!

The Fed Bank Holding Company Supervisory Manual of about 1,500 pages stipulates: **IM-2210-1. *Communications with the Public About Collateralized Mortgage Obligations (CMOs) – (a) General Considerations, ... (3) Safety Claims - A communication should not overstate the relative safety ... (5) Simplicity Claims - CMOs are complex securities and require full, fair and clear disclosure in order to be understood by the investor.*** So if something is too complex to explain it seems that it would be illegal to sell it. Credit raters must be able to understand a complex transaction to rate the security, and credit ratings should reflect the amount of risk – as well as disclose it – right? So there ought to be an explanation from the rating agency that is understandable as well as from the issuer – or how can the investor understand? Comprehensible explanations seem to be few and far between (trite but true). Another looming question is: **why should banks be allowed to invest in complex securities based on excessive leverage, which is apparently allowed by the Fed's Bank Holding Company Supervision Manual. What kind of protection from the risk of insolvency is this?** We ought to know better now. Does it make sense to trust the Fed with additional responsibilities when it failed so miserably in the past? A regulation has the full force of the law behind it so if the regulation is violated the law is broken.

Again consider the conflicts inherent in the Credit Rating Agencies relationship to their Wall Street and Banking clients who profit from good ratings as do the credit raters. So when the enormous amount of fees stemming from the huge velocity of transactions became obvious the SEC should have looked for conflicts. The SEC has rules against stock churning, which is illegal when stock brokers do it. Churning takes place when stock brokers generate large numbers of trades by rolling money from one stock to another to create commissions rather than performance for their customers. SEC regulators and firm supervisors vigilantly guard against an unusual amount of transactions within a short time frame - so the SEC could have reasoned from all the announcements of huge profits for Wall Street and Bankers that something was amiss. **The SEC could have applied the concept of stock churning to derivative churning.** Further, executive compensation must be revealed in annual reports for public companies to shareholders so the SEC could have stopped to think about why all this egregiously leveraged, now "toxic" stuff, was so easy to sell. Don't forget that without the Swaps the market was not interested, so the investment bankers and banks had to slice and dice to add a pinch of diversification, as well as back up the crazy, crummy debt to provide assurances.

83

The SEC and FINRA are very concerned for compliance and conflicts regarding individual securities salespeople (registered representatives) and apparently the small broker dealers. There is a litany of censures which support the fact that any little conflict, or breach of compliance issue, whether material or not, will cause the wrath of the regulators. As the entire Godfather system is so full of self-interested conflicts (beginning with so many ex Secretaries of the SEC) the rating conflict is at the highest level; so if investigated and the fallacious essence of the ratings had been exposed this would have adversely affected ultra rich bonuses, so rating agency material conflicts were not disclosed by the issuers, or the rating agencies. And our regulators did not (do not) want to be deal killers, especially for Goldman Sachs, or Lehman, or Bear Stearns, or Morgan Stanley, or Merrill, or AIG, or Citigroup.

Disclosure is an important issue. Often this has been a way for security regulators to **go after** an individual registered rep, or the issuer of a private placement, or the law firm that drafted a Private Placement Memorandum the legal document furnished to any investor if disclosure was inadequate. Therefore it is now important to consider the following questions for Wall Street Godfathers to answer: Were the conflicts disclosed between the raters and their clients (like Goldman or Morgan) who needed to give worse than junk debt good ratings to help their clients sell, sell and sell, and flip, flip and flip? Did the issuers' disclose they had to use an assumption that everything always went up in their complex, infinitely obscure and arcane risk measurement models. They had to intentionally do this to elicit paid for assurances of low risk from raters to sell their financial instruments. So was DUE **DILIGENCE** done or used (using is better) to justify that it is logical or possible to measure qualitative risk mathematically?

Was any Due Diligence done to discern if credit default swaps had appropriate reserves to back up the implicit guarantees? (Where were the state insurance regulators in seeing through the implausible nomenclature of credit default swaps?) Was there any regulatory concern for advertising to ascertain that it did not offer the implicit promise of something that could not be promised - like reduced risk through diversification and numerical risk management and swaps? Did the NASD or FINRA ask itself how swap bets provide "market integrity?" If an individual rep used a word that implied guarantee, or worse stated that something highly leveraged was not risky; or implied or held out that future returns would follow the results achieved in the past (although circumstances in the present were not parallel) there would be hell to pay. And the ads would not be approved by the firm, let alone regulators.

As a matter of fact FINRA/ NASD want to see all registered rep ads to approve before an ad can be used. Compliance with superficial rules to control behavior and reporting is infinitely more important to our regulators than the profound scrutiny and material analysis of worse than malignant, innovative financial products and contrivances to bet on.

Because the SEC has been so concerned with advertising, especially with language that holds out the implication of riskless or greatly reduced risk for an investment, it seems implausible that the use of Credit Default Swaps could have avoided their radar. So regulators turned their radar off to accommodate the culprits. Just like the SEC did when it audited Madoff and his colleague – Frank Avellino. The SEC searches for people who lie to their investigators. When it ought to search for logical justification for claims of lowered risk. Evidence of any search for valid risk reduction stemming from Swaps is simply missing (in action) from assurances of lowered risk behind all the innovative financial products. And Goldman was willing to "reinvigorate regulations" as long as it "does not interfere with innovation." Innovation means only this – financial contrivances for fees! It is illegal to contrive, that's what SEC regulations state.

Fee splitting is another no-no for individuals; however, it must by OK if there are billions for Wall Street to share as fees paid to Credit Rating Agencies. Therefore, the more AAA ratings the larger the volume of the fees. Fees which accelerated like a space shuttle leaving the Earth's gravitational field. Fee splitting is considered a conflict even when disclosed. Even when the substance of an individual's business relationship with an outside consultant results in a reasonable consulting fee. This behavior raises some concern – even from state regulators. But it did not raise any concerns about the Wall Street Godfathers, or the Mega Banks before everything became a Bank Holding Company.

Where is the substance? It is a matter of how high up the food chain the money goes. Did any firm disclose that the enormous fees paid to the raters could possibly constitute a conflict? The fact of the matter is that if credit rating agencies did not give geometrically leveraged derivative debt good ratings, then the fallaciously mathematically risk measured debt could not have been sold. Hence, the issuer, the one who bundled and stuffed the debt into all the trenches would not have had all the huge fees – and the heavily bonused issuers could not afford to care how much the credit rating agencies charged. This is an unforgiveable conflict, even if you read this upside down – isn't it?

The tear down of the fire-walls – barriers against greed - allowed Wall Street and Banks to get the bit in their teeth, and if you have ever been on a horse heading for the barn you know what happens. Still there are and were rules which were selectively enforced like compliance rules which govern new customer forms. The NASD and then FINRA always carefully monitored this. It is so important to give these regulators recognition for always being concerned with having proper forms as well as the completion of continuing education courses. Let's not forget suitability standards like the reg. D requirements regarding $1MM of net worth or an income in excess of $200,000 to be able to invest in a private placement. Reg D is protective because the government deemed this level of net worth made the investor, "sophisticated." However, important substance may be our regulators are more concerned with superficial form!

Too bad our security regulators were not "sophisticated enough" to understand the misrepresentations and the omission of significant information inherent in financial products *too complex to understand*. It's too bad securities regulators, even at the state level, were not aware of the fact that Credit Default Swaps were explained, (like a Shakespearean aside to the audience – which constitutes insider-like information) as "insurance." Too bad it was not disclosed that Credit Default Swaps were (and still remain) nothing but bets that everything would continue to go up. And there were and are bets on the direction of swaps - in the "unlikely event that there might be defaults. Too bad the Fed did not notice the egregious crazy risk of Credit Default Swaps (CDS) which were sold by every bank that had any amount of sub-prime debt. CDSs did not just emanate from AIG. And the Fed is supposed to watch the Banks. Too bad the Fed watches banks trade and bet on swaps, while they indulge overt speculative, highly volatile derivative leverage of 35-1 - which is functionally nuts! **Too bad the Fed in its role as the central bank of the United States enables greed!**

The Federal Reserve System (**the Fed**) was created by an act of congress on December 23, 1913, and serves as **our country's central bank**. There are twelve Reserve Banks (12 districts each has its own board) and seven members of the Fed board, with the Chairman (T. Geithner) being the member known to the public. Further, there is a twelve member Federal Open Market Committee (FOMC), which makes the key decisions affecting the cost and availability of money and credit in the economy (called Monetary Policy). The seven Fed Board Members along with five Reserve Bank presidents, one of whom is president of the Federal Reserve Bank of New York, comprise the FOMC.

Typically, the President of the Bank of New York is the Vice Chairman. In addition to setting Monetary Policy (which I promise not to explain here as this is not an Economic textbook and I do not have a "Piled higher and Deaper"), the Fed is responsible to regulate and supervise member banks, bank holding companies, international banking facilities in the US and other entities it is responsible for. The Fed also sets margin requirements, which limit the use of credit for purchasing or carrying securities.

Apparently, no one has set limits for the amount of leverage used in the fabrication of financial products – products Bank Holding Companies create, invest in, and even maintain markets for. Why? Because limits are against the ethic of the survival of the richest crowd.

The Fed's mandate is "to promote sustainable growth, high levels of employment, stability of prices to help preserve the purchasing power of the dollar and moderate long-term interest rates." In other words, this is the function of Monetary Policy. As the Fed is in charge of supervising banks, it has a fundamental responsibility for examining banks to make certain they practice sound banking standards – which should mean monitoring leverage, risks and debt levels to be certain banks remain solvent with an appropriate amount of liquidity. As banks have become super huge and incredibly complex, the job of supervising enormous Bank Holding Companies (BHCs,) like Citi, has evidently gotten out of control.

The Fed has been an enabler of the danger stemming from Mega Banks – a grave systemic danger it must be aware of if members of the board had studied the Great Depression and derived any valuable lessons from J P Morgan's abuse of its size and power in the events leading up to the moment of truth. Morgan was the forerunner of the true Mega Trojan Bank – bigger than life on the outside, but inside a seething boiling caldron of diverse nuclear fermentation of speculative risk! For many years large wannabe bigger banks argued that they needed to be huge to compete globally. And when they got their way they did compete (conspire) with all the other Global giants (or were they counterparties) – however the competition, in the final analysis, became a contest about which bank could lose the most billions and billions, to the point where every major government has had to bail out all the giant greedy idiots.

In practice, the Fed is an arcane and quasi secretive (non-transparent) US Treasury funded concern that: should monitor banks for liquidity, i.e. adequate reserves; that manages money supply - M1; **that _intervenes only at_** *times of systemic risk.* **But the Fed has a long history of not intervening until well after it should – it does not anticipate when it should intervene because the Fed Bank Board members are among the leading culprits who require the intervention.** Again, the Financial Darwinists are in charge.

Numerous Economic textbooks explain the Fed in great and arcane detail, which is confusing if you are not intent on understanding the whole thing and are not good or interested in quantitative thinking. However, it is helpful to summarily know something about the Fed to truly appreciate how incredible and fundamental the supervision failures were to have not prevented what happened. Certainly there was no timely intervention.

For the past thirty years, the Fed has been far more concerned with galloping inflation and letting markets self-correct which is a function of Laissez-faire economic theory, than intervention or knowing that leaving markets alone lead to the Great Depression. And it is now self-evident that the Fed has had a severe case of macular degeneration regarding its inability to see the all the galloping greed as well as even consider the danger of mega banks, which it helped create.

Keep in mind a bank to become a Bank Holding Company needs Fed approval – which Goldman Sachs got in September. Since many of the Fed leaders are economists, some should remember why Woodrow Wilson spoke out against bigness.

In 1914, the Clayton Antitrust Act prohibited certain kinds of price discrimination and the acquisition of stock in competing corporations, and this led to the establishment of the Federal Trade Commission. Less than 20 years after the Great Depression in 1956 The Bank Holding Company Act was enacted to further prevent banks from becoming too large and too powerful, which was a logical progression from other legislation to deal with the "toxic" effects of unfettered banks becoming, again, too large and too powerful. Too big to fail really means too big to control.

Sandy Weil, at Citi (where Robert Rubin, ex Goldman leader, went in 1999 after his stint at Treasury) spent over $200MM lobbying Congress, for more than a decade, to repeal the Bank Holding Company Act so he could grow Citi Bank to be large enough to compete globally. Citigroup, as everyone knows, is now a conduit into our Treasury sucking out billions and billions of dollars which immediately become part of our national debt. So it is obvious, again, why oversized banks were considered dangerous in the lasting wake of the Great Depression.

The President of the Federal Reserve Bank of New York William Dudley, a former Goldman partner and managing director, promoted and approved that Goldman should become a BHC. And Steve Friedman, who resigned in May 09 as Chairman of the New York Federal Bank's Board, a retired chairman of Goldman, was a part of the board that approved Goldman's ability to become a BHC in September 08, which enabled Goldman to be in the first group to receive TARP money. **Friedman bought 37,300 shares of Goldman stock on December 17, 2008 - which by May had increased in value by $1.7MM.** He purchased the stock while waiting for a waiver from the Fed for approval to have been able to purchase the stock. Without the waiver, on January 22, 2009, Friedman bought an additional 15,300 shares when he was still the Chairman. He made more than $3MM in profit in total based on his knowledge as the President.

In January of 2009, the Fed issued the "SR" letter authorizing the Temporary Liquidity Guarantee Program (TLGQ) which allowed the FDIC to loan an additional $100 billion to needy banks (which was closer to $500 billion). It seems probable this allowed Goldman to quickly announce it wanted to repay the TARP money. Of course Goldman didn't announce it knew it would get, a reported, $28 billion from the FDIC. To have bought the stock, while Chairman of the New York Federal banks board, which was a violation of Fed policy. However it is worse to consider that advance knowledge of how the proposed Fed TLGP FDIC money would benefit

Goldman, in my opinion, this has to constitute insider information. This should be investigated. Of course Thomas Baxter, the New York bank's general counsel issued a statement at the time: "It is my view that these purchases did not violate any Federal Reserve statute, rule or policy." Sounds like all the Bush lawyers who furnished opinions that water boarding was legal.

How awful is this? Of course, it is not an untenable conflict to buy stock in a business you are regulating – it's worse! Let's remember what the SEC did to Martha. In my opinion, all the revolving doors and paving the way for Goldman and Morgan Stanley to become BHCs constitutes more than conflicts - it constitutes collusion, or at the very least a wink.

Holding Companies are a way to limit competition. New Jersey, in 1888, passed a law to permit one corporation to buy stock in another, and shortly thereafter, it permitted a New Jersey Corporation to do business anywhere. By 1911, Standard Oil of New Jersey had direct control of 70 companies and indirect control of another 30. A number of other individual corporations in different industries acquired enormous economic power through the use of holding companies in the same way as Standard Oil. By 1913, Morgan banking interests held 341 directorships in 112 corporations and the total value of this was more than 3 times the value of all the real and personal property of New England. Woodrow Wilson said: "If monopoly persists, monopoly will always sit at the helm of government..." (The Making of an Economic Society, Heilbroner.)

The Sherman Anti-Trust Act was the result of all kinds of problems with bigness. And although Standard Oil was dissolved, broken up into a number of large companies, the Anti-trust Division of the Department of Justice did not have even $1MM of funding until Franklin Roosevelt. And there were few prosecutions for the first fifty years. So size has been considered dangerous to our society for a long time and it is instructional to remember this in the new era of Bank Holding Companies.

The Fed has been anything but transparent! So how well known is the existence of a document of 1,578 pages called the Bank Holding Company Supervision Manual - which details and specificies internal audit functions in the regulation of bank holding companies. It deals with significant non-banking activities as well as significant off balance sheet activities which include securitization and asset management. **Section 2124.01 "Risk Focused Supervision Framework for Large Banking organizations…" reaffirms the definition of the Responsible Reserve Bank (RRB) and specifies RRB responsibilities for conducting inter-district inspection and supervision inspection activities for a banking organization.**

If you read some of this stuff, it's online, you will have some awareness of how appallingly complex it is to monitor such complexities. You will also learn that banks are involved with financing customers Commodity Purchase and Forward Sales (CPFS in the manual) and commodity derivative activities. **There are numerous examples of BHC's speculating in highly leveraged, risky activities; activities which flourished and developed a life of their own after the deregulation and financial consolidation which led to the development of financial holding companies (BHCs.)** Further, this deregulation allowed commercial banking, insurance, investment banking and a plethora of other financial activities to be conducted under the same umbrella. The Fed has been named supervisor of the consolidated enterprise.

Who is smart enough to digest 1,578 pages of arcane, esoteric rules to be able to discern and understand just what the hell is going on in the bowels of these overgrown, apparent Mega Monsters who got out of control when their managers gorged themselves on all the transactions they could contrive for fees?!

And nothing better exemplifies how Social Darwinism has metasta-sized into Financial Darwinism than this.

A friend in Dallas who at 31 had recently received his MBA, had worked for a large bank (if that's what you call a bank) and was personally familiar with bank regulations. One of his finance professors was formerly a VP with a Federal Reserve Bank; and a member of his class asked the ex-Veep – how could the Fed have failed so badly at forestalling the banking crises? His professor responded, "I guess they just missed it." Bullshit!

Will our fellow citizens who are the taxpayers who fund this miss the trillions it is costing to not go down the drain? Will all the people who lost jobs miss not being able to send their kids to college, remain in their homes or miss being able to retire? Where were all the brilliant economists who work for the Fed?! Were they all given consulting jobs by Wall Street?

The Fed in its ultimate wisdom, in September 2008, allowed the investment banks to become BHCs. And in January 09, after this bailout decision for Goldman Sachs and the other investment banks (keep in mind this decision came from an ex Goldman partner and managing director), the Fed issued a letter concerning: "Debt Guaranteed under the Federal Deposit Insurance Corporation's (FDIC) Temporary Liquidity Guarantee Program." This "SR" letter was distributed to all bank holding companies, including financial holding companies, which was incredibly inclusive. So Citi, Wells Fargo and Goldman, and a number of others could repay TARP because the Fed channeled fresh cash from the mint to the FDIC to the BHCs to pass the "stress test." And this made it look like BHCs were in the black? Although the Fed is independent of Congress it has a direct pipeline into the US Treasury, so when the Fed calls for the green the Mint goes into action. Clearly its important governors have not been independent from Wall Street payments for services rendered for outrageous fees; and their brilliance does not extend to any ability to recognize or understand conflicts of interest. Ethics?

It is self-evident that the Fed has failed big time, just as it did prior to the Great Depression when there were no firewalls. Do banks really need to be so large and involved in the same activities as investment banks? Why do investment banks need to be banks, and is all the complex financial innovation positive for anyone other than the executives at the top of the pyramid? We need to demand fire walls and financial entities that can be understood well enough to monitor. How many Einstein's are available to be bank examiners? Does this sound as nuts to you as it does to me? When I took Money and Banking in the early 60's I understood the course and the need for firewalls, but I have lost my ability to understand the rationale for all the complexities and how our Fed has enabled our economy to self-destruct in an ocean of avaricious greed.

It seems from an understanding of the Fed's own mandate to supervise risk that it has aided and abetted the creation of systemic risk and is still on its very own strange Zen path to existentially accept the chaos and disorder. I mean - I have not heard the Fed cry out for the return of the essential firewalls. It really seems as if the Fed has no sense of history and solutions which worked. Although Milton Friedman and Alan Greenspan disagreed with the self-evident nature of the positive impact of firewalls, it should now be clear that fire is inherent in all the risk. And excessive risk still seems to be an integral part of how the old-line Mega Banks and new Bank Holding Companies planed to resume and did resume their innovative lives - propped up by our money.

The working of how our two primary financial regulators operate sounds pretty sketchy, doesn't it? In reality, it is a patchwork of enormous power and influence that engaged in fundamental failures by allowing Wall Street - Bank Holding Companies - some insurance companies and just sort-of-plain-banks get to the brink of a chasm of total collapse. And this brinkmanship has cost millions of Americans a chance to continue to have a decent life. It is time to restructure the Regulators who have not protected us from systemic risk. The SEC and the Fed did not intervene as they should have well before everything got way out of hand. And now we are stuck with the horrendous results of their inexcusable dishonorable breakdown - and massive dereliction of duty.

In addition to the Fed there is the Federal Deposit Insurance Corporation (FDIC) and the Office of the Controller of the Currency (OCC). Both of these entities have significant regulation responsibilities – and both failed to do what was necessary to fulfill their obligations to protect the banking system. The FDIC insures deposits, has the authority to establish minimum capital requirements, conduct investigations and shut down any FDIC insured bank. It is supposed to monitor the ratio of total capital to risk weighted assets as calculated in accordance with the FDIC's "Statement of Policy on Risk Based Capital," and has established a "minimum leverage requirement." It has been reported that Sheila Bair, head of the FDIC, said the FDIC just blew it – no shit! This is only an overview of the context of our regulators and how they all were so derelict in their duties, and their fiduciary responsibilities to have protected Americans from imprudent, reckless and greedy institutional financial behavior.

"The OCC was established as a bureau of the U.S. Department of the Treasury in 1863; and headed by the Comptroller, who is appointed by the President, and approved by Congress for a five year term. The Comptroller also serves as a director of the FDIC. The OCC's nationwide staff of examiners conducts on-site interviews of national banks and provides sustained supervision of bank operations. This agency issues rules, legal interpretations, and corporate decisions concerning banking, banking investments, bank community development activities and other aspects of bank operations. National bank examiners supervise domestic and international activities of national banks...Examiners analyze a bank's loan and investment portfolios, funds, management, capital, earnings, liquidity, sensitivity to market risk and compliance with consumer banking laws...They also evaluate bank management's ability to identify and control risk." This is directly from the OCC website. There is no reason to discuss just how badly the OCC has failed now that you have read this.

There are 50 State Divisions of Securities and 50 State Divisions of Insurance, all regulators. There are thousands of lawyers in these divisions who specialize in writing thousands and thousands of rules to comply with. However, none of the states have been either proactive or insightful enough have seen through all the subterfuge surrounding innovative financial products or insurance called swaps to have penetrated the rancid nature of the lack of material substance or just notice all the contrived misrepresentations inherent in the greed and power of the too big to fail participants in the swindle.

Insurance regulators have typically been better at protecting than securities' regulators – but they blew it when they did not see through contrived form to question Credit Default Swaps. CDSs were nuanced by design, and somehow were kept in the closet until 2007 when the closet could no longer contain the stink. Because it was bulging at the seams with trillions upon trillions of swaps getting ready to explode. (On a personal level the holding tank in my first sailboat almost exploded because it had not been pumped out and could only hold so much methane generating stuff. Suddenly I decided to acknowledge the god awful fumes which I had avoided because I was in denial that anything wrong with my new boat. And I learned the importance of pumping out the holding tank, as well as the sailors theory of the Y Valve, which directs bio-sewage directly overboard – to mix with all the biodegradable fish droppings. Droppings the EPA cannot control.) **Too bad we can't just Y Valve 600 trillion Swaps overboard, before our economy suffers from a new mushroom shaped cloud, and the ensuing toxic fallout.**

Regulators have a duty to open closet doors to know what to throw out. Denial does not work, and the swap odor was not recognized in time; not by any regulators or by Congress who passed the law creating CDSs; and is still not recognized! Individual state insurance regulators are obligated to look past form to substance. Insurance companies, like AIG, certainly know about the need for reserves behind any insurance contracts. So any insurance company that did not reserve along with the executives in charge should be remanded into some formalized custody hearing, if not criminal then for mental competency. There is a legal procedure for mental competence which is called "intake."

Retrospectively, the bottom line clearly is that our self-righteous, non-performing regulators accepted the lies of the Financial Darwinists, because many of the individuals came from Financial Darwinist backgrounds. (Goldman has been the farm team for the SEC, the Fed and too often the Treasury. Or is it the reverse?) Their excuses were and have been accepted due to their past history of mechanically operative mindsets.

But there is no excuse for putting the good of the ulta rich ahead of the public good. And the public good is the casualty in the War Against The American.

There are so many stories about SEC failures now that it would be massively redundant to name them and it is horribly obvious how the Fed has led us astray. Never forget that Greenspan, former Chairman of the Fed, at the end of 2008 begrudgingly admitted that he may have been wrong.

Greenspan's tiny admission, several years ago, of a "possible mistake" is akin to Hitler saying he might have been responsible for a bad war - certainly Bush would never say that about Iraq. Nixon, at least told David Frost and 50MM Americans watching TV that he did things a President should not do. Robert Rubin, Secretary of Treasury under Clinton, was all for tearing down the firewalls, Rubin, of course, was a former Goldman CEO, like Paulson.

It is painfully self-evident that our regulators betrayed us, and Congress let it happen. **There is a desperate need to rethink and redo how we regulate – new firewalls may not be enough to curb all the complex financial innovations,** we may just need to say no to innovation and return to real investments. But this is not happening because Wall Street is making so much money again. And the survival of the richest ethic continues unnoticed in the war against most of us. The war to keep their sun shinning and make as much hay as possible!

On June 17, 2009, President Obama said in his speech to unveil his Financial Regulatory Reform Plan that: "A regulatory regime basically crafted in the wake of a 20th century economic crises – the Great Depression – was overwhelmed by the speed, scope, and sophistication of our 21st century global economy." NOT TRUE – the regulatory regime (the barriers against greed) had been removed by the drive for deregulation. Removed by Graham-Leach-Bliley, and our President's lack of awareness of this fact is alarming.

Therefore, this is not what happened!! I am not a constitutional lawyer or scholar, and I am also not a Financial Darwinist as many of our president's leading economic advisors were. I was not the Vice Chairman of the Fed who egregiously failed to anticipate when to intervene. When to curb the brew masters production of systemic poison emanating from the plethora of contrived financial products. And when to stop the untenable risk to the system from Mega Bank Holding Cos trading in geometrically risky "proprietary" unexplainable stuff for their own accounts! I was not in charge of the SEC as it sat on the sidelines while Goldman former partner colleagues (who had infiltrated Washington) allowed contrived *too complex to explain* financial products generate a huge velocity of transactions from which to generate fees to engorge on.

Twenty years ago, in Invest for Success, I wrote how investing had turned from real investments to financial investments. So **today, there is an urgent need to recognize that the absence of barriers to greed, coupled with all the contrived financial products, and a political process against the common good controlled by Financial Darwinists is the crux of our Great Recession** (depression). This is emblematic of a lack of concern for the public good. And we have returned to the same unchecked greed, the bigness of banks, the lack of regulation of securities markets and no concern for the public good to a social environment not dissimilar to the roots of the Great Depression. One essential difference is that even without barriers there are rules the SEC and the Fed could have used to intervene before the meltdown – but did not.

Regulators require the help of barriers and a common sense definition of what constitutes too much risk - not more rules to further complicate attempts to administer the regulations. Regulators could have applied the brakes to all the churning of derivatives by just saying no based on the fact that existing regulations clearly stipulate that it is wrong to contrive. And there are enough regulations that clearly make it wrong to stipulate that an investment has been collateralized when it has not. It is not OK – it is a lie - to state that egregious leverage has been backed up for safety when the backing was illusory at best. So could more nit picking regulations with more power to the regulators who abdicated their responsibility to protect markets and investors (as a function of being too intimate with current colleagues or former colleagues) be the answer? Regulators well know that **if the rules become too complex enforcement is inversely related to complexity. We need barriers not more regs.**

Congress and the President must look back at the toxic history of "bigness" and realize that the excuses given to not be able to unravel the bigness are hollow excuses promulgated by the free marketers who are hard-core Financial Darwinists. Certainly Government can remedy the lack of firewalls, and get rid of derivatives that are too complex or have zero value if it has the will to correct matters for another sixty year run of rationality. The Global excuse and rationale for bigness was and is a lie.

In mid 2011, Congressional Republicans clearly revealed themselves to be a reactionary group of zealot ideologues clinging to a dysfunctional "philosophy" of less government (or was/is it merely racism to get rid of Obama) no matter what. The hell with the public good. And it is not politically correct to admit to racism.

So, Congress was held hostage by Republicans clearly intent on dismantling Obama and the American Dream in the process! And the evidence to support this fact is proven by so many House Republicans willing to not vote to extend the budget ceiling - even if the US defaulted on its guarantees and obligations. Clearly, both parties indulge in huge waste and overspending. However, it is implausible to believe the pawns of the uber riche will wake up to their own ignorance about being rigidly for deficit reduction and against revenue increases, no matter how fair! Tax revenue from the ultra rich decreases deficits.

It is obvious that Obama financial reform was good for Mega Bank Holding Companies because they accepted the outcome. Mega Bank Holding Companies recovered because of TARP and billions of extra funding from the FDIC and avoided the public spotlight without need for Congressional approval. And Banks continue to exist in their unregulated state - free to charge usurious rates for credit card debt; free to not lend to small business; and free to not restructure home loans. Congress on both sides has been a wildlife preserve for banks, a refuge for decades and there is no meaningful path toward change. Therefore, **our financial world remains a Petri dish to culture riches for the uber riche** - run by the uber riche who are backed up the by Fed and the party that just says "no." A party without concern for the public good that was/is willing to allow our country to default. Regulations are supposed to protect the public.

Samuel Johnson, the great 18th English philosopher said: "Religion is the last refuge of all scoundrels and liars." Johnson applied the same logic to Politics and Patriotism. Perhaps if he were alive today he would have said: **regulators are the last refuge of the ultra rich**. The uber riche have the additional refuge of mega net worth, which is their firewall to not have to care about their fellow Americans suffering in the wake of their financial rape of our country. The survival of the richest ethic has no social conscience, just like the survival of the fittest Robber Barons. **The Fed silently watched the 20s explode.**

In the final analysis, rigor mortis is customarily a condition found among the dead. Unfortunately, our regulators have sought refuge from mental rigor mortis as an excuse for having sat silently on the sidelines watching as well as having supported the tear down of the firewalls that had worked.

Regulators are still silent! Silent about the barriers we all need to protect us from rampant greed. Are they still paid consultants to Wall Street; are they still writing papers in support of greed - are they still suffering from conflict of interest confusion?

Recently, a member of the Fed board of governors called off the Attorney General of New York because he was going after banks that had no valid documentation of mortgage loans which could cost Banks billions and billions – but that would eat into the additional 1.2 trillion dollars the Fed (from Bloomberg) gave them since 2007 to shore up profits. The bottom line is apparent. Our regulators are chiefly concerned for the "markets" which means Wall Street's ability to remain unscathed no matter what!

CHAPTER 9

FINANCIAL ENGINEERING –
THE QUANTIFICATION OF RISK MYTH

S ubstance is the essence of what something is, and in a world devoted to numbers, and the drive to explain everything, including human nature and how man arrived on this planet, numbers are easier to consider than the subjective nature of value judgments. And I logically contend, as would any rational, objective person not depending on a numerical assignment of risk to sell extremely risky financial products to generate mega fees, that the nature of the substance of risk is a subjective value judgment. Therefore, **it is not logical to analyze the subjective by quantifying it.**

Clearly, this contrived method is to camouflage risk with high tech "risk measurement tools" and has not resulted in anything positive except for fees for all the practitioners. If you paint clothing, like army fatigues, with green and black amoebas, and then tell the world that the articles of clothing are really jungle leaves – I think eventually almost everyone will see what you did, perhaps not the people who prefer to see jungle leaves. Is this an example of not seeing the forest for the trees?

Financial engineering is to paint jungle leaves on all the risk and then measure the size of the leaves rather than the size of the fatigues, and then conclude this somehow reduces the size of... this gets too complex to explain further. But you know what I mean.

This is what the International Association of Financial Engineers says: *"Financial engineering is the application of mathematical methods to the solution of problems in finance."* ... *"Financial engineering draws on tools from applied mathematics, computer science, statistics, and economic theory. Investment banks, commercial banks, hedge funds, insurance companies, corporate treasuries, and regulatory agencies employ financial engineers. These businesses apply the methods of financial engineering to such problems a new product development, derivative securities, and scenario simulation.* (my personal favorite) *Quantitative analysis has brought innovation, efficiency and rigor to financial markets and to the investment process."*

MIT Sloan Management's "Laboratory for Financial Engineering (LFE) is an MIT research center created as a partnership between academia and industry, designed to support and promote quantitative research in financial engineering and computational finance. The principal focus of the LFE is the quantitative analysis of financial markets using mathematical, statistical, and computational models. ... Current research projects include the empirical validation and implementation of financial asset pricing models, the pricing and hedging of options and other derivative securities, risk management and control, trading technology and market microstructure, non linear models of financial time series, neural-network and other non parametric estimation techniques, high-performance computing, and public policy implications."

... *"Risk Management focuses on the entire spectrum of issues surrounding the process of rational decision making under risk."* (I give up.) But this is important to read as well before reaching your own conclusion. MIT goes on to discuss "Delta Hedging Strategies and how they play a central role in the theory of derivatives and in our understanding of dynamic notions of spanning market completeness." MIT does reference cognitive sciences and neurosciences and consider that emotions are an integral part of decision making process but concludes with the silly thought that: "Our subjects are finance professionals that are highly trained individuals and who are very well motivated thus allowing us to avoid many of the studies in traditional economics." (And if this is not self important hubris as uttered by outright genius – what is?) Samuel Johnson said this about such ludicrous self inflation: **"A man of genius has seldom been ruined but by himself."**

What is the motivation of financial engineers but to have a job and provide innovative financial products for the ultra rich Godfathers who prefer the immediacy of fees flowing from the huge velocity of bets in lieu of raising capital for real investments - which take time to mature. Try to understand what MIT stated on its own website and then apply this "Croation-baffle-gab" to your own conclusion regarding why financial products are too complex to explain and therefore be understood??

To fully understand the depth of fallacious, fictitious and spurious reasoning behind the creation of financial engineering it is instructive to go back to Saint Thomas Aquinas' theistic medieval proof (QED) of the existence of God; which the First Vatican Council taught can be proven by reason alone. (I learned about this at John Carroll University from my logic professor.)

Saint Thomas raised five primary *a posteriori* arguments, (an MIT sounding statement at a time when the world was flat!) The five basic arguments were: motion..., efficient causes..., contingent beings exist..., graduated perfections understood by comparison with an absolute standard (like a delta) ..., and of course the right wing favorite ... intelligent design. Saint Thomas was instrumental in binding science to religion which slowed its progress for over 100 years and put Galileo under house arrest for the balance of his life after discovering that the earth revolved around the sun – which was blasphemy in the days of wizards.

The controlling issue is that if you do not first believe in God, the arguments do not make sense – so if the first assumption is fallacious, (or cannot be proven with empirical evidence) what follows logically is not logical. The same is true for all the financial engineering – if numbers are logical but the initial premise is not – that risk can be measured quantitatively – then what follows is a logical absurdity. And this is a leading culprit in getting swindled.

Wizards of yore were charged with the responsibility of turning lead into gold for the king du jour. Financial engineers, the wizards of today, are charged with the responsibility of turning nothing (complex financial creations) into fees for the leaders of Wall Street and the Banks. Unlike the wizards of yore who consistently failed, the financial wizards did turn nothing into vast riches for the few but turned gold into lead for the rest of us.

There is a lot of legal precedent, and a law called the Prudent Investor Act (Rule), usually referred to as the Prudent Man Rule, which govern fiduciary responsibilities regarding money management. The fundamental principle for money management was stated by Judge Samuel Putman in 1830: "Those with responsibility to invest money for others should act with prudence, discretion, intelligence and regard for the safety of capital as well as income." And this is the basis for the Prudent Man Rule used by ERISA to establish standards for fiduciaries who manage tax qualified funds like pension and profit sharing as well as 401(k)s. Further, this concept and rule is also intended to protect investors from advisors who recommend shady, too risky or otherwise poor investments, like penny stocks. Should innovative, too complex to explain financial wizardry – based on unmitigated leverage and manipulated into existence by financial engineers who understand e=mc2, but not the Prudent Man Rule not be included in the definition of shady, too risky or poor investments?

Financial Engineering relies on acceptance of implausible math used to measure risk and model investment performance, as applied to "solutions of problems in finance." So Financial Engineering overlooks the real problem which is that nothing real is created.

Finance as utilized by financial officers and individual entrepreneurs running any business activity, is used to establish and manage financial controls within a business to understand and have complete knowledge of current expenses, revenue and overall cash requirements. Further, traditional finance methodology is used to project an ability to go forward based on needs for equity and debt to survive as well as to be profitable and grow.

Personal finance relies on cash management also, because individuals cannot spend more than they make for too long, or they will be consumed by their own consumption. A great majority of us learn from birth that it is dangerous to have much debt. My parents had what Galbreath called "depression psychosis" so I was taught to not have a large mortgage and to pay cash for cars. My father, when his business was not good drove cars into the ground, and when his business was good considered cars a waste of money and drove them for many years. But GM's "planned obsolescence" eventually provided my father an excuse to buy a new car. Of course, "planned obsolescence" was the idea of a financial genius.

I suspect that many financial engineers (as well as the rest of us) learned growing up that debt is not necessarily positive; although projections flowing from huge debt are terrific as long whatever it is goes up in value. Consider a projected return from 30-1 leverage: with 3 cents in the investment, and 93 cents borrowed - if $1 goes up 1 cent in value, there is a 33% return on the investment. Sounds neat, but 30-1 leverage is risky. so financial engineers step in to measure the risk with formulas, instead of common sense. Risk management is the game – not debt management. Risk management for gamblers using other people's money only creates something real for the gamblers. However, when the gamblers can't manage to flip the risk or when all the flipped risk comes back to hit all the risk managers in the face our government has to step in to prevent everything from going down the **toilet.**

Although the risk of too much debt is well-known, unmitigated leverage has geometrically become the favored approach to creating immediate wealth for the ultra rich. So - the more leverage utilized the more Wall Street and Banks turned to financial engineers for high-tech "risk management." And the results of all the mumbo-jumbo quantification of the subjective are simple to observe.

Finance has been concerned with formulas and math for decades, and Chief Financial Officers in charge of money supply within a business are responsible for helping provide management with financial information used to operate in the present and in the future. Any endeavor which relies on cash and debt must also rely on forecasting cash flow – cash coming in and going out. This is simply what finance formerly was used for, but for the past seven years it has been used to justify and either implicitly or explicitly mitigate perceptions of risk. I have restated this to emphasize how far we have traveled from the world of real financial information to the make believe. It is possible to think that our financial world has jumped down through a hole in the looking glass and left the rest of us holding a bag of s— t (poop) or an economy full of it.

This bag did not fill up as fast as it might seem. The US car business is a prime example of what happens when a clear view of reality is not the goal (as it is not for financial engineers). Car manufacturers did not properly reinvest in plant and equipment in time to improve quality and better engineered cars, not in time to compete with foreign companies that beat us at our own game.

David Halberstam's *The Reckoning*, published in 1986, chronicled the rise of Nissan contrasted with the decline of Ford, which foreshadowed what has come to pass. (Ironically Ford may have learned its lesson in time.) It took Ford 20 years to learn what Halberstam learned during the 5 years it took him to write his book. *The Reckoning* used Ford as a microcosm of the advancing decline of American post WW2 industrial supremacy, and tells the story of how America got too wealthy for its own good.

By the mid 80's - Wall Street was embarked on a personal self-interested mission to keep its own wealth growing, no matter what. So the Street turned to mergers and acquisitions (M&A) and leveraged buyouts (LBOs), with a touch of "greenmail" – which was blackmail but regulators did not notice. Wall Street must have read *The Reckoning* because early on it embraced its most important early financial tool (prior to in your face financial engineering) diversification. Diversification was a product of the Modern Portfolio Theory (MPT) developed by finance Phd Harry Markowitz. And this theory allowed Wall Street to always have something to sell. Because, when there is nothing of substance to recommend, diversification becomes something to recommend as it fulfills the mathematical promise of investing in variety to reduce risk. At least that is how it is usually explained.

In 1990, Chapter 8 in *Invest for Success* explained why diversification is fallacious. So this chapter "The Modern Portfolio Theory of Investing: A Posture Toward Ignorance" has been included in the appendix because it logically argues why diversification does not work as advertised, and I can't improve what I wrote almost twenty years ago.

Wall Street, however, has improved on the Modern Portfolio Theory by going to a level of dizzying quantification which has allowed financial engineering to layer our financial world with innovative financial products with so much leverage that these products are too mathematically sophisticated (rigged) too explain – and that is what financial engineering really means. It is too sophisticated to explain because it creates nothing real but financial products based on calculus? I used calculus as an example because my son got an A in the subject and told me it is fundamental to physics. He is a Neuro-radiologist so may not know what a true mathematician would say. But the analogy works because there is no way to explain what financial engineering's real purpose is except to observe that it is fallaciously used to measure and manage huge leverage. And the leverage being measured is too huge to manage, let alone rationally explain. How can you measure leverage that is empirically exponentially risky, and subjective?

Again, I am compelled to point out that the subjective cannot be logically defined quantitatively. And I do not know any reasonable person with a liberal arts degree who does not know this. Leverage, or a lever, is something a physicist would know something about - like how much leverage, force, can be applied before the lever breaks! And all the levers applied by financial engineers have now caused our economy to break. Financial engineering has failed everyone except for the Wall Street

Godfathers and the Mega Bankers who have relied on its spiritual, numerical essence to manufacture vast wealth for themselves.

The following is a list of prominent universities offering a master's degree in "Financial Engineering:"

Cornell

Columbia

Baruch

Berkeley, the Haas School

U of Michigan

U of Pennsylvania, Wharton

Northwestern

NYU

Harvard

Rutgers

UCLA

Princeton

Stanford

MIT has a laboratory for financial engineering which "seeks to spur advances." Just what we all need.

Did you know about the cult of financial engineering? I did not before I started thinking about writing this book. It's kind of a dirty little secret because who in their right mind would have thought we would use calculus to manipulate, or to manufacture innovative financial "products." I guess it is still not possible to use calculus to manufacture real investments.

All of the listed bastions of higher learning have important departments dealing with the Humanities deans of Arts and Sciences. **So there must be many prominent members of their faculties who, if they are aware of financial engineering (the haute cuisine of financial masturbation), must condemn the foolish notion that it is possible to measure the subjective nature of risk with math by quantifying the qualitative. So there may be** some form of embarrassment attached to offering any advanced degree - in the supposed ability of math to measure risk. Especially now that the results are in! Stochastic calculus is actually a small piece of what a well trained financial engineer studies and some of the schools have financial engineering programs to be found in their mathematics departments.

The real question to ask universities who jumped on the financial engineering bandwagon and the economic lies behind the deregulated free market rational myth is - was this done to improve education or was it for Wall Street sociopathic profits and to increase the personal net worth of all the educators who became proponents of all the self-evident lies? Do business school Profs and Deans disclose fees or any compensation from Wall Street as docs and medical school profs and deans must do?

I read an interesting article from 2006 which noted that Linda Kreitzman Executive Director of Berkeley's Haas School had trouble placing graduates in 2001 when Berkeley's financial engineering program started. But, (strangely enough just after Graham, Leach, Bliley) by 2006 banks and hedge funds, "...have come to realize they really need students with strong skills in financial economics, math and computer modeling for more complex products like mortgage-and-asset-backed securities and credit and equity derivatives." She went on to say that in the fall of 2006 all 58 financial engineering students seeking internships found spots at such companies as Citigroup, Lehman Brothers and Merrill Lynch. And their project was to include credit portfolio valuation, artificial intelligence trading models, and structured fixed-income products. I rest my case.

An interesting book to read, only if you are a physicist, on financial engineering, is *Monte Carlo Methods in Financial Engineering*. This is especially interesting to me because my finger was crushed checking into the Loews Hotel and Casino in Monte Carlo years ago. After having lived there for six day I know that Monte Carlo's economy is entirely a function of their casinos! What I didn't know was how to have utilized better risk management tools to not have spent my first afternoon, after flying all night, in Princess Grace Hospital! Personally, I believe you have far better long-term odds playing blackjack in Monte Carlo than you do with 30-1, or 40-1 risk managed leverage. Does anyone really need chance factored into grotesque leverage to justify a professional sounding scam? At least when you are in Monte Carlo you know where you are.

Maybe I just don't get it because I can't remember why I took algebra or what do with it, even though I got a B. Probably, I would relate better to financial engineering if I took Columbia's course in their master's program – "Applied Time Series Analysis which explores the methods used in the analysis of numerical time series. The course will be both theoretical and applied." Although now we know, from all the empirical financial damage, based on the vast number of trillions of Dollars and Euros and Pounds down the drain - that the application of this theory (along with so many other mathematical financial engineered methods) has failed.

The subject of financial engineering makes my eyes glaze over with thanks that the Empire State Building, where I once visited the observation deck, was not built innovatively by financial engineers, or I might have needed a golden parachute to have escaped if I was unlucky enough to have been there when it collapsed. It is unfortunate that all the Godfathers in New York did not use that building as an example of what can be accomplished if you care enough to build something real.

Think about how financial engineers measure risk and fabricate innovative products. To accomplish this you need to have a firm command of the following: standard deviations, value at risk (VAR), betas, alphas and correlation, sharpe ratios, shewness, coefficient of variation (CV), dispersion, expected return, mean, non-sampling error, variance, t distribution, volatility; and my favorites – cokurtos, kurtosis, mesokurtic, platykurtic, tail risk, and let's not forget leptokurtic. I am sure I have missed a lot of other arcane and esoteric areas of consideration. If you eat something with a label like the ingredients just listed you will die a horrible death. Actually some of the nomenclature just sounds like a bad case of bad breath. And if you care to practice speaking in tongue, if you repeat all of these words at high speed you are ready for the life of a devout Creationist.

Here is my only explanation to grapple with – "When a distributions kurtoses coefficient is greater than 3, the distribution is leptokurtic, and when it's less than 3, it's platykurtic. (Try to find this shit in your spell check, whateverrr!) No wonder financial innovation is too complex. Not making sense is hard to understand, but thankfully we have fabricated the wonderful world of financial engineering which understands how to not make sense and has enabled our financial world to dump trillions of the stuff onto the world. Financial engineering is in the final analysis a sham transaction designed to culture fees for the "New Guilded Age" and "new titians," as the New York Times observed on July 15, 2007. This article featured Sandy Weill who led Citigroup to the point of needing $50 plus billions of bailout, and reported how Sandy contended that he and his peer group earned their immense wealth by contributing to society.

Financial engineering has been a costly grave mistake and should be given proper recognition and credit for building a foundation to bring about our tragic financial holocaust. Financial engineering is a form of racketeering and in my opinion the engineers should be required to walk the plank. Formerly a punishment reserved for pirates and mutineers - in the distant past when there still existed a code of honor. If you remember nothing else from this chapter remember this:

roses are red

violets are blue

cokurtos and kurtosis

are only poo poo *   *(poet-philosopher e h schoenberger)

CHAPTER 10

"Too Complex to Explain" Financial Instruments: Derivatives, CDOs, CMOs, Swaps, and Rancid Tranches – Pools of Worse than Junk Bond Debt

" *B y far the most significant event in finance during the past decade had been the extraordinary development and expansion of financial derivatives. These instruments enhance the ability to differentiate risk and allocate it to those investors most able and willing to take it – a process that has undoubtedly improved national productivity growth and standards of living."* Alan Greenspan, Chairman, Board of Governors of the US Federal Reserve System, April 2005, and Genius. Who was the recipient of lots of outside income as a consultant to Investment Banks and Mega Banks, and leader in the fight against regulations!

Greenspan's 2005 inscription in granite, like a commandment from God to Moses, came back into focus, for those of us who remember when all the financial markets fell apart only three years later. Did Greenspan, or any econ Nobel Prize winner from the Chicago School, or anyone else explain how betting on derivative options to buy or sell an underlying asset at a given time in the future at a stipulated, prearranged price, improved anything the brilliant Greenspan contended would be improved. Actually the opposite occurred.

Then **Greenspan in an interview for the CNBC show House of Cards,** toward the end of June 2009, **when asked about CDOs replied modestly, that he had a lot of knowledge about mathematics but,** *"honestly did not* *understand CDOs*." (That's really great.) The entire two hour show was, essentially, a superficial discussion of how Wall Street sold so much of the stuff internationally (stuff that was explained as "safe") and that banks had to go into overdrive to create enough mortgages and refinancing to fuel Wall Street's voracious appetite to package all the debt into securities to load the planet up to its neck in risk. These mortgage loans were made with no origination standards; no questions asked, no brakes - no concern for all the leverage. And these innovative financial products were called CDOs, and CMOs, even structured financial products – but were derivatives essentially of unmitigated leverage.

Of course, anything can be a derivative – which is merely something that is a function of something else.

So it seems that CDOS are, or may be (?) derivatives (which are called contracts) and are a function of the value of something else. Possibly, the amount of equity in a home loan that was under water the day it was approved by Citigroup or some strange, even newly created bank to serve Wall Street's bidding. Possibly the CDOs had 2nd and 3rd mortgages in their diversified tranches or pools. Retrospectively, although it was known at the time of conception, these pools were black holes of debt which consisted of 80% or more lousy loans, "subprime." And when pooled, diversified and properly tranched as derivatives (to nowhere} were then given AAA ratings - so Wall Street and Bank Holding Companies created a shit load of demand to sell counterparties and everyone else as much of the, internal email described, shit as possible.

Mary Schapiro, the Chairman (person) of the Securities and Exchange Commission said in Congressional Testimony the week of June 26th 2009 derivatives; "allow parties to hedge and manage risk, which in itself can promote capital formation." Did anyone ask how this promotes capital formation? How about asking her to explain how this helps manage risk, or questions regarding any supporting realities for our Chairman's reasons for derivatives. And how do Swaps, without real substance, offer any back up for egregious leverage when egregious leverage is the substance of a swap. This is Nuts! By June of 2009, banks appeared to be winning the fight for the existence of derivatives. And $600 trillion derivatives did win, because **the War Against the American Dream has been waged by Financial Darwinists, without any unified defense against the protagonists.**

In September of 2011 Schapiro's self-expressed mission on the SEC website is – "to reinvigorate regulations." (Where in the hell has she been – sorry, but what a load! I have been licensed since 1968 and have heard a lot of BS, but **Schapiro has only reinvigorated the meaning of hypocrite.**)

Richard Bookstaber, one of the pioneers of financial engineering on Wall Street told Congress, "Derivatives are the weapon of choice for gaming the system." Richard went on to testify that, "derivatives provide a means for obtaining a leveraged position without explicit financing or capital outlay for taking risk off balance sheet, where it is not readily observed and not monitored." So derivatives enable institutions to avoid taxes and accounting rules.

A leading **Scottish economist, John Kay, pointed out that –** *derivatives allow risks to be transferred to be shifted from those who understand it a little to those who do not understand it at all.*

Whatever the composition of derivatives - it seems obvious, transparent - they exist so that side bets can be laid off on the presumed future movement of the market's ability to price the derivatives. And because the market is thought of as rational - regulation is not necessary because the market will serve to establish appropriate values. We know this kind of innovation was for Wall Street and the Banks to create a complex casino for the house to profit from.

So how does betting or speculating on a future price movement add value to anything but the speculator's pockets if the bet is successful? How does this promote capital formation for anyone but those who skim off house profits? Maybe Mary Schapiro should have to explain this complexity. When financial innovators introduced the concept of trading derivatives on an unregulated and off the record (meaning not transparent) market unknown amounts of leverage were released like a pandemic into the world economy.

Derivatives have been considered "powerful risk management tools," a contention which defies any attempts to rationally explain or understand, and I am unaware of any well reasoned or cogent explanation. Even Greenspan has confessed to befuddlement. Therefore, **derivatives used to manage risk are too complex to explain.** Further, it was stated that derivatives were contracts that were devised (contrived) based on the need to minimize risk. It is possible to conclude - based on the abundance of empirical evidence of financial tragedy - that the complex derivatives were/are powerfully risky, because **complex derivatives are huge amounts of leverage. Arcane leverage, or too complex to explain dice which ultra rich Godfather Families roll in obscure darkness on proprietary crap tables.**

Plain vanilla derivatives were not the fundamental problem; the customized financially engineered derivatives which created the accelerated profits for AIG, as well as National City in Cleveland, and so many others were. And in June the Obama Plan allowed complex derivatives to remain intact so Wall Street – which could now be called Mega Bank Holding Company Street (BHCS) – can continue to gorge out on financial innovation, which is primarily for its own gormandizing appetite. Just like horses will eat until they are dead, engorged BHCS will eat our money until the government steps in to prevent our economy from death - by saving their collective asses.

Derivatives are like inverted pyramids – with everything, piles and piles of debt "instruments," carefully structured, mathematically arranged to precariously balance on the tip of some tiny substance – which underlies all the leverage. As long as assumptions come true (like fairytales) that the underlying tiny substance goes up – then expectations (confidence) keep the pyramid upright. When there is a hiccup, or a downward trend in economic factors underlining the tiny substance - or just everything heads south – the pyramid crashes on the rocks of despair. Most lost huge amounts of net worth, savings and pension assets, and the economy crashed because of all the financial leveraged products created by financial engineers for Wall Street and Banks to flip for fees. The resultant loss of jobs was a derivative of the financial carnage and led to a spiraling loss of jobs which added up to decreased consumer demand. The few who bet that a constant upward trend could not be maintained made a killing betting against the improbability of inverted pyramid stability.

Two theories or assumptions fundamental to the reasoning behind all the risk measurement quantification are: that the Market is Efficient, and that the Market is Rational. The first results in the notion that the Market is self-correcting, which has now been demolished by reality. The second is ludicrous as well as absolutely preposterous, because the Market depends on human behavior which is governed by emotions and reactions to external and internal personal events – and human behavior is far closer to irrational, or borderline chaos than rational.

At best emotions are erratic and not objective, unbiased or unslanted. ONLY Fox Views is fair and balanced – and it is self-evident that it is not objective, so is this rational? Are Glenn Beck and Rush Windbag rational; are they proof of market rationality? Palin speaks in tongue! And Bachman's entrepreneurial experience and family business is an unlicensed clinic to turn gay men heterosexual, heavily dependant on government funding. Think of the untold riches for her clinic to focus on turning all the heterosexuals gay! What about all the Republican creationists running for president in 2012, who are surreptitiously running against science. And they are all running against Obama because their base cannot sleep at night because of Obama's complexion. And that's a fact unless you are in denial and avoidance. Although a great percentage of Americans below 35 do not care about superficial differences – which is hopeful. Of course, the Middle East is rational and the way we back dictators seems rational, just like we bombed Iraq to seek revenge against the terrorists who were in Afghanistan. Rational – like the rational markets.

Was it rational for over twenty percent of Americans to believe that Obama was not born in the US, or to not accept that Hawaii is a state – or racist? Isn't prejudice a leading form of ignorance? Is it rational for so many Americans to be so ignorant? And Republicans are promoting the free-market rational market lies again now that they have gained control of the House of Representatives. How rational is it to quantify the subjective!

Philosophers have spent thousands of years attempting to explain and understand mankind. Psychiatry, which is a derivative of Philosophy, originated not that long ago with Sigmund Freud and his theory of personality. Most psychiatrists no longer practice talk therapy unless deeply involved with Freudian psycho-analytic theory, so psychologists and LISW psychiatric-social workers have taken up the cudgel of front line talkers. Although most therapists have their own unresolved issues, I would bet there would be a consensus among therapists that rationality is a hard to find human trait. Look at all the prejudice and fear of the different – is this rational?

Most mathematicians who crafted all the innovation have probably never heard of "Rational Emotive Therapy," which Ellis and Harper wrote before most of them were conceived, hatched? And their work has formed the basis for much of the therapy practiced today – even if your therapist will not acknowledge this. It is important to examine why markets are not rational and consider how it makes sense to structure market theory on such silly ideas – could it be Financial Darwinism – which has no concern for any sense of critical introspection, because it could lead to bad feelings about one's self – probably not because of so much denial and avoidance.

None of the dictums attempting to help mankind become more rational and less self-destructive would attempt to argue the rationality of group human behavior, which is more subject to irrationality than one individual. But the Market Theory and the assumption that the Market is rational are akin to saying that these two ideas are like an elegant telescope peering into the center of a universe of investment decisions in perfect order like a constellation – forgetting that constellations have stars that blow up.

Now our presumed rational and effective market has been **outed** as the Black Hole it really is. Because, fundamentally, Wall Street and Banks have turned from the reality of value investing to the infinitely surreal nature of crazy contrived 40-1 leveraged (is the substance at the tip of the inversion) innovative financial products so admired by Alan Greenspan and probably still Goldman, et al. But, Financial Darwinists never give up. So the free market crap has been born again, less than three years after the meltdown, because Wall Street has recovered. But not the American Dream – which three years ago was referred to as "Main Street."

Who can explain clearly irrational and poisonous leverage? Maybe a shrink or maybe a simple discussion of unbridled greed coupled with the volatility of massive speculation based on fees for the creators of the surreal financial products. It is simple to observe that all the financial products combined to create the inverted pyramid. Without the innovation there would have been no way for Freddie and Fannie to have helped create the housing bloat. And the financial engineers cleverly used the sub-prime debt to enlarge their diversified pools of collateralized triple A stuff, which was easy to sell because it was backed up. This is the opposite of real investing, and financial reform did not take this into account.

If you make some doggie caca a little transparent, it will still smell and kill your grass.

Financial products are rigged to produce a huge velocity of transactions. At each transaction there is a fee charged just like buying and selling shares of stock on the NYSEX. The fees and bonuses are not related to results so it is not performance based. When all the financial products contained in the moon sized pyramid started to teeter, because the tiny substance was coming unglued, the pyramid of too complex to explain financial innovation imploded.

It does not make sense to list all the innovation and then attempt to explain the implausible. But it does make sense to consider the broad areas and observe all the products were essentially Derivatives, Secured or Collateralized Debt Obligations (including mortgaged backed whatever,) Swaps and Options. Even Federal Reserve Chairman, Ben Bernanke said, "some innovations in financial products may be so complex that no amount of disclosure can make them transparent to consumers – so that the only option is to restrict or even prohibit them." (Brilliant!)

It is probable that **Bernanke (the Great Depression expert) knows innovative *complex* financial products are the problem; however, it seems that no one in the government wants to erode any shred of confidence left by just saying we need firewalls and that bigness cannot be managed.**

Still, it is dishonest to not advance the logical conclusion that the last ten or twenty years of financial product innovation was instrumental in our financial mess and should cease and desist. Larry Summers, Obama's first chief economic advisor, was a cheerleader for tearing down fire walls and for financial innovation. The disingenuous Summers played an integral role in the Obama Plan leading to the financial reform, and he has a reported net worth of $6MM to $12MM ... from doing what?

Because reform has not relegated the complex financial stuff to the same dumpster of many 401ks; it is clear that we are not on a true path to provide stable markets. Without barriers, meaning no specific laws against complex BS - how have we learned from history? By July of 2011, the requirements of financial reform were yet to be determined.

Trading options is not new. Contracts for commodities have been traded on the Chicago Board of Trade (CBOT) for over 150 years. In college one of my friends and I "invested" in potato contracts. We controlled a whole boxcar load of potatoes for $25 apiece. We knew this was powerful leverage. This was riskier than we thought because if you held the contract too long you had to take delivery and pay for the whole load. So after a short time, I convinced my friend to sell our contract at a "small loss." In today's terms, however, $100 lost in 1963 was not good, especially considering that my only means of support was winning at gin. My friend went back into potatoes, big time, assuming prices would go up and lost $5,000, which was about the cost of one year's tuition then. He stopped eating potatoes for years. And his father, who bailed him out as the legend goes, never ate potatoes again.

The options markets formerly consisted of the commodities futures market and buying and selling puts and calls. At least commodities are real and the stocks involved with puts and calls are bets on the direction of corporate stocks. Although this type of investing or betting is based on the positive value of leverage this activity can be explained and understood. Today *too complex to explain* **options on complex derivatives, or on who knows what, are by current financial nomenclature standards of definition – unexplainable.**

In the 60s, and for decades following the Great Depression, stock market investing was based on dividends and price to dividends ratios. (There was some charting, dollar cost averaging and numerology.) Value investing was the rule. It was possible for an investor to think investing in stock was an ownership position and an opportunity to participate in growing corporate values because companies were motivated to increase dividends so the price of their stock would grow.

Companies formerly used retained earnings to improve an ability to grow (regrettably car companies and steel companies did not reinvest in plant and equipment so could not remain competitive with foreign competition). Investors relied on holding worthwhile company stocks for the long term to participate in growing corporate values.

123

But holding stock did not generate enough commissions for Wall Street. Firewalls were still in place and at the end of the 60s when there was a severe decline in stock prices. Prices then remained relatively flat through the 70s – so Wall Street had to be creative and get more small investors involved. Additionally, in the late 70s, the lowered cost to trade, with the advent of discounted commissions, was eroding Wall Street revenues – so something had to be done. Real investments, unless dot com arrived, typically only grew at a snail's pace. Of course, there were always mergers and acquisitions. But betting on options was a fertile ground of derivatives to culture fees. And strategies were devised to create the illusion that risk was mitigated - but leverage is a double edged sword.

Because so many of the innovative products are called bonds it is necessary to remember bonds are pure debt - which formerly had issuers that could be analyzed. Bonds contained a maturity date - which was a stipulated future date when the face amount of the bond became cash. For some years, too many investments have been called bonds. Too many real estate deals have been compared to bonds. Deals which were represented to have safe returns. Real estate safety is a function of the real estate fundamentals making sense. And most Real Estate deals in this decade definitely did not. Further, there were no maturity dates for highly leveraged real estate– only mortgage balloons.

This short prelude or primer would not be complete without some understanding of the meaning of collateral – because so much of the innovation is said to be collaterized, or backed, like a mortgage backed bond. Collateralized debt ought to mean that there is a recognizable asset behind the debt and the supporting asset was supposed to be able to be made liquid at a moment's notice. So it was necessary to have a ready market to sell the asset.

A home mortgage has the value of the house backing up the loan. A personal guarantee given to a bank to obtain a term loan must have personal relatively liquid net worth to back up the signature. A letter of credit is similar to a personal signature, however, a bank giving the LC will usually require the assets backing up the LC to be placed in the hands of the bank - so the bank is in control.

Collateral is something that can readily be turned into cash. In the case of US Government Bonds, the "full faith and credit of the treasury" backs up US Treasuries and these are considered the safest forms of bonds. So when a complex financial product (instrument of doom?) claims to have been backed up or collateralized, collateral is thought of in terms of the past rather than in terms of the empty promises of swaps. It is necessary to understand that the collateral of yore was totally dissimilar to the collateral of CDOs, which is one reason why they were too complex to explain!

To examine the meaning of collateral should be far easier than to examine the meaning of love, or the meaning of life. So when something is collateralized according to the American Heritage Dictionary it is defined as, "to pledge property as collateral...to secure a loan." Collateral is defined as: "serving to support or corroborate; ... guaranteed by a security pledged against the performance of an obligation: *a collateral loan.*" That's simple enough. The free on line dictionary states: "Assets pledged as security for a loan. In the event that a borrower defaults on the terms of a loan, the collateral may be sold, with the proceeds used to satisfy any remaining obligations. High quality collateral reduces risk to the lender...." Not much different than the American Heritage. Forbes Financial Glossary starts out with: "asset that can be repossessed if a borrower defaults," but then transcends the understandable into the surrealistic world of the too complex to explain: "Collateralized mortgage obligation (CMO) – A security backed by a pool of pass-through rates, structured so that there are several classes of bondholders with varying maturities, called tranches. The principal payments from the underlying pool of pass-through securities are used to retire the bonds on a priority bases as specified in the prospectus. Related: mortgage pass-through security." (??)

So with Forbes we reach the obscurity of surreal language that Louis Rukeyser, in *How to Make Money on Wall Street* termed - "Croatian-baffle-gab." And that is a return to the world of the too complex to explain. Maybe we could use "skewness to measure the asymmetry of "Croatian-baffle-gab" definitions and analyze the metrics to lower the risk of not understanding the definition. And you thought skewness was just for financial engineers. Maybe I sound silly, but how can I be expected to make sense in the face of such a terrible lack of sense – when I **cannot understand how a pool – or sea - of huge worse-than-junk bond debt can be offered up as collateral.** Can you?

I bet the kind of prospectus that the Forbes dictionary referred to has committed some form of securities fraud. My opinion cannot be backed up because I do not have one of these PPMs. However, after 40 years of going beyond disclosure to provide my investors with clarity of understanding that transcends mere disclosure I would like to be Andrew Cuomo, or Spitzer when they were on the front line of protecting us from Wall Street.

It seems to me that **to call CMOs (Collateralized Mortgage Obligations) or Collateralized Debt Obligations (CDOs) collateralized is to misrepresent the substance of what is customarily thought of as collateral.** It is a mystery why regulators allowed BHCs and Wall Street to term the stuff backing up so much leverage as collateral. Because collateral has the clear connotation of a guarantee and implicit in this thought is the idea that risk has been reduced by an ability to immediately turn the collateral into cash.

Swaps certainly are the cruelest joke against investors who believed in the acumen of our financial engineers, and an even bigger lie than oceans of crappy, but diversified, debt. Swaps had no reserves, or if there were reserves they were too tiny to matter. Therefore, to call swaps collateral was a severe misrepresentation of the concept - to back up debt with collateral. It was projected that swaps would not come into play because the essential assumptions behind financial innovation showed the tiny substance constantly going up. So why not issue lots of swaps – trillions and trillions – because they would never be called upon to back up defaults. So the banks sub-prime and not, along with Wall Street Godfathers issued a never ending torrent of swaps and raked in fees (not premiums like insurance) for issuing swaps. And the fees went directly into bonuses – with almost nothing into reserves.

Of course this is hard to explain – because it does not make any sense! And this was not explained because it did not make sense.

Swaps were a trading mechanism to facilitate trading without regard for the empty promises to investors. Clearly, reality proves that swaps were primarily used to generate a velocity of trade for fees. How complex is this? This is pure greed without any concern for the risk to the economy of so much leverage without any security behind its contrived creation. No one can argue rationally that swaps have created anything but havoc.

Certainly, in the genre of Alan Greenspan they have not – "improved national productivity, growth and standards of living..." Remember the prophetic words of Lloyd Blankfein who said; "... we are fighting for nothing less than the immediate health and security of every person. We can never forget the products of economic growth – more accessible health care, better education, less crime, tolerance of diversity, social mobility and a commit-ment to democracy... innovation, has helped produce a long-term record of economic growth and stability that is unparalleled in history." (See chapter 6)

Swaps were and are a scam, and a sham transaction – nothing but a *crap* **table where "investors" stand around and bet on the dice, and bet on the bets on the dice and even the players; and investors were told these empty pieces of paper backed up the risk of defaults.** If Swaps are derivatives, and it is instructive to recognize this as fact, it follows that it is important to disclose that swaps are derivatives of nothing – zero.

Without the lie of backed-up, collateralized debt instruments; the quantified measurement of the risk; and the misrepresentations of the rating agencies - even Wall Street and the Mega Banks could not have unloaded all the specious debt. **No wonder no one wants to explain.** Traders and their august firms who fabricated and sold all the innovation had a clear obligation to clearly explain in all the private placement memorandums how these products worked.

There was a crystal clear legal obligation to explain how the tiny substance functioned to support all the leverage, and a clear obligation to explain the collateral. This is called disclosure. It is not OK to use the expression "too complex to explain," or to contend that it is necessary to pay exorbitant bonuses to retain all the traders who sold the products which caused our economic disaster – because only they could understand how to unravel the crazy products. And the traders, who were licensed in the securities business, had to understand that they had to be able to explain exactly what they were selling – selling what Greenspan admitted he did not understand!

To write about all the details of innovative financial products is to fall into the trap set by all the mega banks and investment banks (the issuers) that contrived the world of the *too complex to explain*. To attempt to explain the rancid nature of the *too complex to explain* is to legitimatize it, plus it does not make sense! As issuers it was their clear duty and legal obligation, as well as the only way to honorably behave toward investors, to have explained everything before it was contrived and flipped. And it is only possible to conclude, in the final analysis, that these financially engineered products (which are not referred to as investments) were and are essentially Bull Shit. If my language seems coarse, because the use of coarse nomenclature disturbs the language police – consider the lack of ethics and total lack of concern for protecting the best interests of investors and the country. At least Bull Shit is an easily understood concept.

There is a new movement for "transparency," which was formerly called disclosure. Appropriate disclosure would have been to have pointed out that all the financial products were designed to furnish the traders and their firms with transactional velocity motivated by fees. Further, it was necessary to have disclosed that the financial products were perched on a precarious amount of leverage and that any down tick in the presumed value of the tiny tip of substance would – not could – cause the pyramid to topple. The contrivers should have warned investors, like a pack of cigarettes tells smokers that smoking causes cancer, that investing in *too complex to explain* innovative financial products is to invest in Bull Shit which may cause financial death.

Transparent markets would be to go back to regulating any securities sold and disclosing transactions, like the futures market which was deregulated and made non-transparent - and off the record, even secrete. This lack of transparency allowed Enron to do its thing along with all kinds of other toxic transactions. How does being off the record, and therefore, not regulated parallel any concern for truth? How did the futures market drive up oil prices to $150 a barrel without any fear of daylight?

If you care about Truth then consider this - there is more substance in a fart which is methane gas, CH4, than in all the innovation Wall Street and Mega Banks have released into the economy. And unlike all the innovation which broke our economy, breaking wind does not cause any damage to anyone; in fact it may even cause relief, which can be positive as everyone knows. **Wall Street's innovation broke the banks.**

CHAPTER 11

RISK REDUCTION, A FINANCIAL ENGINEERING FAITH-BASED HOAX

Since the beginning, of time man has searched for assurances to feel better about the risky nature of life itself. Possibly man's aversion to risk began from the struggle to survive as caveman. Cavemen were probably more dangerous to each other than the other mammals they hunted in groups for food. As early man developed and different cultures grew more complex and life remained consistently insecure because of the finite nature of death, as well as the daily struggle to exist. So the insecure nature of life - based on the inescapable fact that life is fleeting and that death cannot be controlled (although lifetimes have been extended by modern medical knowledge) is an underlying factor in human behavior. And this need to feel better about risk may have become an innate drive in humanity in order to emotionally survive in the face of past life threatening risks.

Religion has been the accepted way to deal with the insecure nature or meaning of life. Fear of the unknown adds a crippling barrier to coping so man turned to various gods from the beginning of recorded time to deal with this. Most of us studied Greek and Egyptian mythology in high school, and learned how good versus evil has historically been set in opposition. (Creationism and Animism were the rage thousands of years ago.) We also have learned if we took one religion course in high school or college that man has an affinity for creating gods to either protect or control mankind.

Historically, man has exhibited faith in all sorts of deities; beginning with the worship of rocks and animals, as well as the sun, water, thunder, daylight and darkness. Almost anything which was not understood and, therefore, threatening was likely to be worshipped. As knowledge advanced, all the gods eventually were merged into the concept of one (**the first big merger**). On the path to advanced knowledge it even took an extra century after Galileo's breakthrough discovery for the world, or the Church, to accept that the sun did not revolve around the earth; and this fact caused the subversive Galileo to be held under house arrest for the balance of his life. The unknown has always been feared and when a new way of looking at life appears, like the orbit of the planets, faith in what was previously accepted before any new discovery made it difficult to accept change. . It was probably difficult to give up leaching.

All of the deities and the big merger, one god, were based on the existence of faith, which is acceptance with unquestioning belief. And Faith has been the operating system of our planet from the earliest beginnings of man. For example, we have faith that we will wake up when we go to sleep; faith that all the money spent on a lavish wedding will result in a lifetime of happiness; faith in the devil; and faith in the deemed objectivity of numbers.

The idea that investment risk can be reduced by financial tools is based on man's aversion to risk and man's inherent insecurities considering the insecure nature of life. So there is a predisposition or propensity to value faith. And this unquestioning belief system seems to be related a human need to find comfort and reassurance in having faith. All humans do not share this need, as some need empirical evidence, so this need is not universal.

Strangely enough, in the aftermath of September 2008, there still exists the idea that risk can be reduced by diversification; and managed better with the newest, super high-tech mathematical tools designed by nuclear physicists. Putnam Investments ran a full page ad in the New York Times on March 3, 2009 which stated, "My advisor recommended Putnam Absolute Return 700 Fund because it takes advantage of a wide range of investment tools that seek to reduce risk." What is the essential fallacy in their ad, as well was in the contentions of so many other mutual funds and Wall Street ads? Is it the idea of investment tools? Is it that the fund only seeks to provide a 3.2% return which would be two times more than a 3-year T-Bill did on March 3, 2009? Or is it that risk can be reduced by taking advantage of (high tech) tools – ranging from screw-drivers to a miter box? At least it is possible to have faith in screw-drivers, unless you try too hard and it, not you, gores your finger.

There is a religion Wall Street has built around the human drive to reduce risk. For example, the concept of God reduces the risk that the nature of life is insecure and finite.

Religions offer the promise of becoming part of an everlasting two-tier existence; first from birth until after death, and then joining God in heaven forever. In the case of Christianity, it is getting in on the "Good News" that Christ rose to the right hand of God. Islam offers heaven with a number of virgins waiting for the lucky martyr. Certainly, an attractive thought compared with any personal thought that this is it, so I better be as nice as possible because I am not going anywhere else. And Wall Street uses the religion called math to reduce risk, while offering returns too good to be true from leverage too high to make anything real. How is your faith holding up?

The drive for reducing risk can also be seen in the United States' quest for guns and the right to carry concealed weapons to fend off dangers lurking around every corner. Consider the possibility of having to shoot a robber who grabbed your bag of perfectly straight green beans that you just finished carefully selecting at your favorite super market; or the driver of the car which just rudely cut in front of your car; or the neighbor who came to your door through your backyard unannounced late at night who had locked himself out of his house next door. Remember, the NRA tells us that guns do not kill people, people do. So guns reduce risk, simple!

There are hoards of risks that can be reduced like: divorce – do not get married; birth defects – do not have children, automobile accidents – do not get into a car; and the best is to declare war against terrorists. I could go on and on. But it may just be that life is tenuous, and so is investing. Especially when you are not investing in the **predictability of the substance of knowledge (PST appendix).** Some risk comes with certain territories and there is no realistic way to provide protection. What if pilgrims had waited for trip insurance or NASA had avoided the first landing on the Moon until there were moon shot swaps to hedge the risk! (MSSs)

The moron Chris Columbus sailed right off the edge of a flat planet. And now we declare war against terrorists, but they are hard to find until they blow themselves up with lots of bystanders at the same time. It seems that our financial tools are based on the same science that produced the flat earth theory. And Wall Street terrorists only blow us up, although reform has declared them to be transparent, but has not inoculated us against Wall Street Flu. Remember the Asian variety? The Wall Street flu has cause far greater world-wide devastation.

Listening for what you want to hear is also risky, because then you may not know what you need to know. So by examining the often repeated mantra of Wall Street - that risk can be reduced, are we not involved with the human failing of seeking reassurance provided by avoidance and denial, as well as the implausible?

If one Street myth should be obvious now it is that diversification does not work to reduce risk and most, if not all, methods of quantifying risk have failed! This is self-evident. **Early in 2009 the leading economist for the New York Stock Exchange was quoted by the New York Times as wistfully noting that, "diversification has been a failure."** Crazy - an economist suddenly recognized and announced that diversification was a "failure." Diversification has been a cruel joke from the Theater of the Absurd, and a prominent economist became alienated at last.

It is clear that diversification has not worked and will not work based on all the available empirical evidence. I guess if you slice and dice pieces of highly leveraged pools of mortgages and dump them into diversified "trenches" (you already know I do not have faith in tranches – too fancy for me, but tranche is the operative term) and then assign these pools a triple A rating, because they are properly diversified, and then they all implode – it should now be self-evident that diversification does not work. If anyone remembers **Peter Lynch, the legendary investment manager of the Magellan Fund, called diversification – "deworseification!"**

In 1990, I explained why diversification does not reduce risk and this chapter from *Invest for Success* has also been included in the appendix of this book. Clearly, in 2009, for investment firms to have continued to advertise it is possible to reduce risk with diversification and high-tech mathematical tools, our regulators should have intervened. They should have required a logical, specific analytical explanation of how this works for their own edification as well as for investors, and required to appropriate disclosure that diversification has not actually reduced risk, and further required a track record of success to support any allegation of risk reduction.

Justice should demand that regulators and Congress provide proof that the utilization of investment tools to measure and reduce risk has worked. Only then will it be fundamentally understood why this approach to reassure investors is nothing but a marketing scheme - a hoax – a hoax which should be recognized and acknowledged as fallacious.

Any contentions of risk reduction or risk management should require: **an explicit and understandable explanation** of the "tools" to be employed as well as provide understandable justifications based on logic, reason and track records. If this information is not provided to support - either stated or implied assurances given to investors that Wall Street recommendations are structured to reduce and manage risk, then it should not be legal to issue or sell such a security. False advertising and false claims advertising are illegal under current regulations. False claims regarding risk reduction should be added to financial reform to make it clear that Wall Street must stop its practice of merely securitizing (meaning sell) anything that it can sell motivated only to produce fees and bonuses for its own benefit rather than results for investors.

The two most fundamental and widely held investor myths are: the belief that risk can be reduced by mathematically measuring it; and the belief it is possible to provide insurance to back up risky investments. And investors have been deluged with this myth. Noam Chomsky, one of the world's leading and most honored intellectuals and linguists, has written about how the more repetition given to false statements or absurd premises the more acceptable the lies become. George Orwell wrote about this in his classic book *1984* – where "love is hate" and "war is peace." Orwell called this doublespeak. Now we have "risk is not risky." Is this honest? What about the death panel lies, and the lies about where President Obama was born? We are awash in a sea of lies.

Suddenly, ethics are now back on the table for discussion. There is an honor code pledge at Columbia Business School, which all students must take a vow to support: '"As a lifelong member of the Columbia Business School community, I adhere to the principles of truth, integrity, and respect. I will not lie, cheat or steal, or tolerate those who do." Strangely enough this code has been in effect for the past three years – while Columbia's school of financial engineering has been turning out mathematicians who have been measuring the subjective substance of risk with calculus and at the same time have been fabricating *too complex to explain* financial products – backed up by the assurances offered by Swaps. How this conforms to their code of ethics I am not smart enough to understand. Perhaps I should hire a financial engineer to provide me with the "metrics" to analyze this. It looks like ethics are only on a table.

It is not functional to have a code of ethics without the ability to understand and put ethics into action. If Columbia took its own code to heart it would have to ditch its financial engineering master's degree and apologize.

Other Ivy League and so-called top tier schools have jumped on this new bandwagon. But they too have not recognized the immoral and fallacious nature of granting financial engineering advanced degrees (advanced degrees in bull shit or toxic innovation with toxic realities). Harvard students are among the leaders of the charge to establish a professional code of conduct for MBA's, like the "oaths taken by lawyers and doctors."

Legal ethics, of course, allow lawyers to defend either side of any issue no matter how self-evidently wrong – so this does not inspire me. Legal ethics make me gag, how about you? (Some of my closest friends, neighbors and relatives are lawyers so I would exclude them.) I know physicians would not be pleased to have their oath to keep people alive compared with the financial engineering MBA's who have participated in culturing fees based on unmitigated greed and have, incidentally, been among the leading proponents for tools to reduce and measure risk. Certainly doctors do not want to have their Hippocratic Oath compared to the legal oath. Ask a doc friend how the medical community regards lawyers. Philip K. Howard's book, "*The Collapse of the Common Good – How America's Lawsuit Culture Undermines Our Freedom,*" should be required reading for those who would align any oath with legal ethics. Howard is an attorney who also wrote "The Death of Common Sense," which should additionally be required reading for financial engineers, Congress, the risk reduction soothsayers and everyone else.

There other tools to assuage man's aversion to risk and one of my favorites is hedging. How often have you either read or heard that "we are going to hedge the risk!" Does anyone ever explain this? This is not an investment guide but a treatise to understand how bad the verbal behavior and actual financial behavior has been. So it is necessary to include some short definitions of hedging from various dictionaries: "to counterbalance one transaction against another; to take equal and opposite positions in an investment so that regardless of the outcome the risk bearer is left in a no win/no lose position; a means of protection; a line of closely spaced shrubs and bushes; hedged – evasively worded in order to avoid an unqualified statement; the practice of offsetting the price risk inherent in any market position by taking an equal but opposite position in the futures market."

These definitions are dialectic at best which beg the question by a circuitous form of reasoning commonly known as Bull Shit. A pure hedge can only provide a cancelation both sides of a position or a zero result – except for transactional fees. Many definitions hold out the thought that hedging is used to reduce or cancel out the risk in another investment. Most investors have heard that "to minimize loss or risk you should diversify your financial portfolio to hedge risk," "hedge your bets." My good friend, Frank Butler, who once ran a very successful and ethical Fortune 500 Manufacturing Company, said: **"Hedging is what you do when what you are going to do probably won't work."**

Thirty Years ago, everything was an arbitrage, not as catchy as *hedging*, or just plain *hedged*. My explanation is that true hedging is to bet (invest) on both sides of the direction an investment can take – sort of like betting on a vector, which is a straight line in one direction. So if you bet that a vector will go up and at the same time bet an equal amount of money that the vector will be downward then if it goes up you win and if it goes down you lose, and the two positions negate each other. So a true hedge produces nothing.

Business Directory.com calls hedging: "Risk management strategy used in limiting or offsetting probability of loss from fluctuations in the process of commodities, currencies, or securities. In effect, hedging is a transfer of risk without buying insurance policies. It employs various techniques but basically, involves taking equal and opposite positions in two different markets (such as cash and futures markets.) Hedging is used also in protecting one's capital against effects of inflation through investing in high-yield financial instruments (bonds, notes, shares,) real estate, or precious metals."

Where is the proof that any of this has reduced risk or the probability of loss? Maybe the proof has been provided by the failure of so many strategies and contentions of risk reduction. Perhaps a good hedging strategy to manage the risk of marriage failure would be to marry more than one person at a time – **a technically perfect marriage hedge would be to get married and divorced at the same time.** But that would be illegal. For hedging to be appropriately used as a tool to reduce risk, the fundamental reasoning must be properly disclosed under the risks disclosed in any Private Placement Memorandum. And this does not happen.

We are told that Swaps are a great way to mitigate, as well as insure against risk. There is even a market to bet on whether swaps will fail in the event of a default or not fail. This certainly is nuts! I have talked enough about the lack of substance behind the empty promise of swaps – or about how swaps are merely lies to provide assurances that risk is backed by guarantees that some amorphous contrivance will pay off should vast pools of sliced and diced coo-coo leverage fail. And the verdict is in: swaps have been a leading risk reducing "financial tool," and were a leading culprit in the "Great Recession." But financial reform has overlooked this empirical fact!

Ratings may not be considered a financial tool to reduce risk – HOWEVER, ratings certainly have been at the forefront of providing assurances to faith-based investors that there is no need to fear – because the raters have assured us that triple A (AAA) means low risk. Faith in rating agencies should certainly be relegated to the same dumpster where all the worthless swapped backed mortgages have been placed to foolishly attempt to get a modicum of the toxic smell out of bank lobbies and investment bank lobbies. Now the worst lobbies are all in financial institutions called Bank Holding Companies.

The most basic and popular risk reduction tool used by Wall Street Godfathers is flipping. Flipping to get rid of all the toxic potatoes as fast as their traders can unload the stuff seems to work best. Because if you get caught holding the last few trillions or just hundreds of billions of hopelessly rotten potatoes, the Government will bail you out and let you keep all the billions and billions of profit generated by all the lousy debt backed up by all the fallacious promises. I guess Wall Street, with so many well placed ex CEOs and partners, has faith in the government. It should, it is full of self-interested Wall Streeters.

God-backed religions, whether you believe in God or not, have produced ethics, values and principles which are essential for mankind to survive as frail individuals in order to build cultures, or societies to live in with some form of order. Faith in risk management and risk reduction tools has produced our massive depression-like recession. No one likes the word depression; however with real unemployment holding steady at 17% in the US, and higher in Europe and Asia, as well as in other developed nations. What should such a tragic and huge economic displacement of humanity be called?

Paul Krugman has called our massive societal displacement, a kind of depression – not a recession. **So don't hold your breath when Republicans are content to let the tragedy continue until they get rid of Obama. And these "faith based" Republicans claim to be religious with "family values."**

There is a need to recognize and acknowledge that misplaced faith is like misplaced anger – it is self-destructive. And now is a time to make a leap of faith into common sense by turning away from all the contrived assurances about financial investment to the world of real investments, and real mortgage lending based on the discernable substance of value. If you invest in the predictability of substance then you will not need false assurances. The Predictability of Substance Theory (PST, refer to the appendix) will protect all of us infinitely better than backing egregious debt with virtual guarantees. I guarantee this (just kidding) Innovative financial products rely on risk reduction tools based on the faith that these tools are meaningful; however there is no substance, because the substance got lost in all the leverage!

It is time to consider the performance of alphas and betas, and whether deviations have ever been standard. Does VAR really work when, clearly, the metric approach to risk measurement has been a disaster based on numerology?

It is time to get rid of all the spurious financial tools and go back to basics. So faith in tools and ratings can be replaced by knowledge of the substance of real investments. Knowledge of substance is geometrically better than "Croatian-baffle-gab" innovations which must be quantitatively measured, because they are too complex to understand! And If you cannot understand something you should never invest no matter how intricate the metrics used to reduce and manage the risk, no matter how many assurances you receive to not worry. Risk reduction is a form of plastic surgery using stuff that blows up after a while. And when it happens at the financial magnitude we are in the midst of - it is like dumping an island sized glacier in a small pond.

CHAPTER **12**

RISK MEASUREMENT SIMPLIFIED

Leverage = risk.   **Less debt = less risk.**

Therefore:

More cash is the best way to reduce risk.

(You do not need to be a mathematician to get this simple equation, because this equation is self-evident!)

Marriner S. Eccles, U. S. Federal Reserve Chairman from November, 1934 to February, 1948 said that:

Too high a level of debt was one of the primary causes of the 1920s-30s Great Depression.

2ⁿᵈ best way to reduce risk:

Eliminate all innovative financial products and invest in real investments.

Plus: the Predictability of Substance Theory*

(*see the appendix)

CHAPTER **13**

HAUTE DEGREES AND SOCIAL STANDING DO NOT EQUAL JUDGMENT OR ETHICS

Too often there is a fundamental mismatch between advanced degrees, measured by the ability to perform on Ivy League and upper-tier university tests, with judgment and wisdom. Further, Ivy League degrees have no correlation with integrity or social conscience. And the self-overvaluation of one's own brains and abilities without any correlation to the results for investors and our society is the essential mismatch. Of course there are lots of other examples, but correlation should be a controlling factor.

Perhaps greed coupled with hubris, or just plain arrogance, is the cause of the mismatch. But the mismatch is self-evident. Plato said, "It is not the role of the one who points out the self-evident to prove it, but it is the obligation of the one who denies the self-evident to absolutely negate it." I think the reason is simply that a lot of heavily credentialed people just do not have judgment or the ability to think about whether what they think or were taught or had to learn to get good grades really makes sense. Lots of these individuals know a lot about what they know – but do not know much about what they don't know, and that is not good, it is the kiss of death.

Let's consider why Larry Sumers PhD, ex Secretary of the Treasury, and Obama's chief economic advisor is an example of a fundamental mismatch. It seems fair to assume that he is brilliant on the surface of things, and he would agree. However, until Obama and our flirtation with a Great Depression he (along with Alan Greenspan, Laffler and, of course Milton

Friedman) was among the leading prominent leading cheerleaders for Deregulation based on a zealot belief, as Financial Darwinists, in the free market theory, which is another way of saying Laissez-faire! Or were these genius' paid consultants to Wall Street?

These cheerleaders, some armed with Nobel prizes, had a zealot belief that the Markets are self-correcting and that the Market is efficient, because it is rational. How does this correlate with judgment and wisdom? Bad judgment and a lack of wisdom often cripple the future which is just around the corner. How do you trust or depend on the judgment of someone who was so wrong in the past? If Summers is an economist he must have read Samuelson, Thurow, Heilbronner and Keynes. He must have been aware that mega banks and unbridled greed led to unmitigated speculative volatility which crashed into the reality of bread lines. He, along with lots of other "important" economists, had to know that certain fire-walls were the only effective barriers against galloping greed. He had to know the trickle down theory pushed by Laffler and the great *Closet Republican* R.Reagan (by own admission) was for the benefit of the ultra rich and had terrible consequences for the rest of us – including the rest of the industrialized world.

So how could Summers have believed in all the phony baloney? Beliefs which influenced the Obama Plan announced on June 15, 2009. His belief in Financial Darwinism which provided the basis for the illusory reform passed in 2010; so called reform which only confirmed Summers' past belief in deregulation - because there was no reregulation!

The Obama Reform band-aids will not, do not correct the fundamental underlying problems – problems his Chief Economic Advisor did not acknowledge because he supported a bogus financial reform bill. The barriers against greed developed by Roosevelt administrations lasted for almost six decades – so we do know what has worked to curb reckless gorging out on fees.

Ben Bernanke, chairman of the Federal Reserve, a self-confessed "expert on the Great Depression," must know the MBHCs (mega bank holding companies) have lobbied and killed attempts to put more regulators on their case. The MBHCs are too complex to regulate and are still trading for their own accounts. To have pushed to give the Fed a new role as a risk regulator was clearly infinitely inferior to have downsized and split the banks from the investment banks once again. From any understanding of economic history we know this worked.

So where has the wisdom and judgment gone? Was it simply a lack of balls to stick up for pragmatic functional solutions which have been time tested; solutions applied to similar fundamental reckless and geometrically greedy behavior. Bernanke is supposed to be brilliant and well-intentioned, and an expert in the Great Depression. Yet his wisdom and good judgment are difficult to see. How brilliant is it to have advanced a plan to increase regulation responsibilities for the Fed. As the Fed absolutely abdicated its clear responsibilities to have enforced regulations against investments too complex to explain. How could such brilliance as well as the fact of his expertise in the Great Depression not have produced an approach that did not focus on bigness and the critical need to rebuild barriers against greed? How could any approach (not based on the survival of the richest) not prohibit banks from being in the complex instrument business; and not make banks to return to provide loans for capital formation? **The answer is the ethic of survival of the richest must be the core belief of the Fed.**

Timothy Geithner, Secretary of the Treasury and former Republican, seems unarguably brilliant as well. The New York Times article on the Obama Plan from June 16, 2009, reported that Geithner said, "We have to make a choice. I do not believe there is a plausible alternative that provides accountability, credibility and gets to the core of the problem." This was in reference to the plan as proposed to give the Fed more oversight and authority. Considering how badly the Fed blew its authority in the past – how more Fed oversight in terms of more regs will prevent the propensity of greed to engorge on unexplainable innovation I cannot imagine.

Although Geithner had many ties to Wall Street, in the form of personal relationships when he was Vice Chairman of the Federal Reserve as President of the Federal Reserve Bank of New York, I do not understand how having studied the approaches of other countries, and with his first-hand inside profound experience from having been in charge of the home of Wall Street he could have participated in assisting President Obama in arriving at such a myopic approach. Where is the judgment inherent in a decision to ignore the history of pragmatic functional solutions which worked for sixty years?

Congress did not get reform right – but it was made more difficult when our leading economic advisors chose to ignore the fact that the *too complex to explain* financially engineered innovation directly led to a vast chasm of despair for so many Americans and so many others world-wide. So Congress (the Democrats) chose the reality of lobbyists, and caved in to the Republicans against everything to protect and help their fellow Americans.

To date, Congress has not done anything functionally effective. Congress, with our taxpayer dollars, bailed out the culprits, but has not provided enough funding to have created more jobs, while most extremely profitable companies and the billionaires who Republicans will not require to pay more in taxes stand by the sideline hoarding their gold. And the Attorney General of the US has not investigated the substance of what really happened and how it has not changed. I guess it was more important to investigate Barry Bonds for lying about steroids; but they did jail Martha – for what, compared with causing a depression.

Milton Friedman, posthumously, has now been as discredited as Trotsky was by Stalin after he died. So, did it make sense to depend on the "brilliance" of a man (Summers) who foolishly could not - **did not reason from the tear-down of fire-walls to the opening of Pandora's Box? He was a Financial Darwinist who believed in the creative power of unbridled greed. He overlooked the destructive essence of too much greed because of his own greed.**

All the Wall Street Godfathers, their families of traders and financial engineers, and the leaders of the Mega Banks as well as their counterparties (the sophisticated investors in their complex financial instruments), must have had equally important degrees and backgrounds of financial success. Probably they had high SATs and high IQs (whateverrr) high enough to impress everyone around them so they could claw and float like cream to the top of the inverted pyramid they innovatively created on a microscopic golden crumb.

These are the leaders of our financial markets; these are the men who hire the financial engineers who contrived all the complex grotesquely leveraged products. These are the leaders who hired the rating agencies, and lobbied Congress to be able to indulge in Laissez-faire Financial Darwinism. And these are the men who skimmed off the fees from all the complex transactions and figured out how to rise above great wealth to the rarified atmosphere of outrageous riches – these are the Uber Riche, the new robber barrons!

Goldman was/is simply the best practitioner of the survival of the richest ethic, the best flipper of the plethora of empty potato skins, and the only one to have assiduously infiltrated our US government. Goldman infiltrators can be found, as well, in many states that have or had governors who at one point in their lives made tons of money at Goldman and moved on. Summers made millions with Goldman during his short stint.

Of course outrageous riches confer immediate social status, notwithstanding the source of the wealth. Society pages of leading newspapers and magazines like Town and Country add to the mystique of money. Bernie Madoff was extremely charitable and the most important leaders of Wall Street and Banks are charitable too. Andrew Carnegie gave to be socially acceptable. But how does what happened to our economy relate to their undying interest in societal concerns and needs? The best way to characterize this is to compare the Hippocratic Oath physicians take to keep people alive with what I call **the *Hypocritic Oath;* which is to give charitably while** *robbing Peter to pay Paul,* **by engorging on the spoils of the innovative and unexplainable.**

I plead guilty to using too complex to be true like Chinese water torture – but I have never heard anyone attack a sincere user of this phrase, so forgive my redundancy, because it should have happened by now. Certainly, the brilliant economic gurus adjacent to the oval office could have expressed more outrage than just adding more regulators to those who have already failed us. What about rebuilding barriers which would be practically brilliant? As paid consultants to Wall Street they pivotally helped demolish barriers.

The brilliant men of Mega Bank Wall Street understood how to make money, but not how to preserve the present or the future for the public good. **Sociopaths do not care about the public good.**

Is it brilliant, or just piggish, to jump headfirst into a bandwagon of reckless, infinitely greedy speculation? Of course, the Public Good of Jefferson is not on their agenda. Maybe they could learn something from Ted Turner, Bill Gates or Warren Buffet – they have lots of money but have exhibited real concern for the public good. Of course the government went after Gates, who has survived in a very competitive environment, while costs to consumers have gone down; and oil companies have become monopolistic again – and raised prices while receiving huge subsidies and generating enormous profits.

Brains have nothing to do with any concern for future economic stability when greed becomes the primary motivation. And brains have nothing to do with lobbyists who are motivated by fees in lieu of what is right. Brains can become addled easily by a thirst for political power at any level, which is simply why it is still OK to have automatic weapons, and not OK to tell Mega BHCs to shove it.

I think my fellow Americans are quietly "mad as hell," and if they do not want to take it any more they will need to vociferously make Congress aware of the fact that a collectivity of voters still has more power than lobbyists. I worked to elect Obama for almost 18 months and do not believe his Financial Reform is anywhere near what must be done. It does not make sense that so many (deemed brilliant) economic advisors in positions of enormous responsibility have chosen to not vigorously speak out, but have overlooked the poison which remains in our financial system. The historical lessons are clear and so is the irrefutable empirical evidence from 2008 as it continues in 2011.

Maybe the problem is simple. Intelligence does not correlate with any self-interest in the public good, and is not necessarily related to integrity or ethics. As politicians and talking heads on TV love to proclaim to circumvent an acrimonious debate or discussion when they are on the wrong side of the truth by noting – *the fact of the matter is...* **The fact of the matter is: Too much greed and self-interest interferes with logic and reason.**

The problem is that Financial Darwinism is the problem. Wrongly held core beliefs interfere with any ability to use brains with objectivity. We have an obligation to rethink what we think based on available realities. And unless we are open to critically questioning what is in front of us that just does not make sense – like too much leverage, both personal and in complex investments without understandable explanations - then we will not survive in a world controlled by Financial Darwinism. Think about it, does it make sense to invest with people who would tell us that free markets are the answer because markets self correct because they are rational? We need to stop buying lies.

CHAPTER 14

ARCANE PROFESSIONAL NOMENCLATURE UTILIZED TO OBFUSCATE AND SELL EMPTY PROMISES

Collateralized, swaps backed up by derivatives of sub-prime (way below decent) debt with pass through securities and innovative CDOs and CMOs that are self-correcting based on the Efficient Market Theory as long as their deviations are standard and diversified with appropriate Alphas and Betas based on metrics that have been engineered by physicists. This sentence (which makes no sense) is a prime example of the arcane nature of professional financial nomenclature – as arcane means, "knowledge known by few," or may even be – "secret knowledge." (Am. Heritage)

Too complex to explain *phinancial** (*ehs) instruments have been created - massaged by verbal behaviorists who can't spell or is it smell empty rotten promises – like backed up, i.e. collateralized. When a toilet is backed up – well we know what that means. Is a plunger a professional tool which is utilized to provide back up? Plungers have been far more dependable than swaps, or standard deviations.

The real question is - are your metrics in place – not, do your metrics make sense. How could anyone have the nerve to question metrics anyway, when it might make you sound ignorant. Certainly, proper metrics include underwriting fees – not commissions which are crass. **Is integrity a metrix?** Spelling mistakes are easy to correct, but not metrics.

Risk measurement strategies are so important when Wall Street sold enough leverage to kill a number of leading world economies. Everything depends on dealing with leading everything and whether you can afford a penthouse for $2,000 or $3,000 per square foot. The more something costs, the more important and the closer to professional nirvana, a peculiar nirvana not to be found on a Zen path to professionalism.

Looking-glass language with equally obscure explanations supervised by regulators, loaded with professional behavior and professional degrees has turned our investment world into a prurient sewer of greed-backed securities. And few have vehemently questioned the arcane nexus of the meaningless verbal behavior. Try to make sense out of the first four paragraphs without achieving an epiphany. Regrettably, some of the most important investors in the world did not question the sense (or lack of sense) behind the words, the nomenclature. The genius mathematicians enveloped in their professional cloaks of "secret" arcane knowledge did not stop to question either - perhaps because their concepts made sense in some dictums, like physics – just not in investing. **So risk measurement is empty fallacious rhetoric.**

Everything in the professional and emotionless world of flim-flam, contrived innovative investments must always sound even and monotone-like, to not jar the listener or reader with reality. Financial Darwinists go out of their way to sound and act professional as they advance against their investors like crusaders hiding behind shield-like credentials. Sounding professional is to use nomenclature at the highest level of attained degrees; being professional is to care about the substance of what you do, to care about results for your investors (or patients) as a perceived specialist or "expert."

Perception means everything when you are marketing the "too complex to be true" or to be explained. When something is not true it is hard to explain, often impossible. So, **when Demeanor becomes a larger than life issue** (and no one's demeanor is perfect) **no one seems to notice all sorts of**

crazy nomenclature. Demeanor matters, but being professional is to care about results. Good bedside manners coupled with a high mortality rate for a thoracic surgeon is less than professional.

Professional sounding "professionals," heavily-laden with important degrees in senior positions with Mega Bank Holding Companies (which included the investment bankers of yore) does not necessarily constitute professional behavior. According to the online financial dictionary acting professional encompasses: **"meticulous adherence to undeviating courtesy, honesty and responsibility in one's dealings with customers and associates, plus a level of excellence that goes over and above commercial considerations and legal requirements." Whata joke! Is this Wall Street or Congress, or Lobbyists or Lawyers? Is honesty an operative word? Are Republicans professional?**

Is it courteous to unload killer debt on unwary investors in the name of financial innovation backed by collateral, which is composed of more complex empty implicit promises designed to generate fees rather than results? Is it honest to apply the word *collateralized* to crazily leverage rotten mortgages loans? Have rating agencies been professional by endorsing all the "collateralized" complexity with so many triple A ratings? And how professional have our regulators been when there was no intervention before everything hit the crapper? **Where were the questions – and where are they now?**

To act professional has become the mantra for perfect business and financial behavior, In fact, for practically everything, because everyone wants to be considered professional. And to be considered professional - demeanor has replaced substance. So much depends on adherence to façade creation to avoid detection that behind the façade there may only be a little man with a bullhorn - like the Wizard of Oz.

(For example the tone of this book is not professional because of my passion and intensity to get the objective truth into your hands. So Swindled may be considered a rant – which is defined by the American

Heritage usage panel as, "to speak or declaim in a violent, loud, or vehement manner." And I admit to being vehement which is defined by the same panel as, "Characterized by forcefulness of expression or intensity of emotion or conviction.")

Professional behavior ought to be termed the – Wizard of Oz Syndrome. And this syndrome has become so pervasive that if you become intense about idea-backed- principles and the realities of empirical evidence, you will regarded as a *ranter*. Often, if you become vehement, you will be accused of yelling by listeners hoping to avoid a clearer view of reality than they chose to embrace or accept. To either act or react with passion for principles in a search for truth is considered abrasive by the throngs of humanity who may feel bad about not joining the search or who are just unwilling to acknowledge that they have not cared enough about truth.

The insidious dissemination of professional demeanor-based standards, which includes verbal behavior, has replaced standards to be forthright and candid, as well as to be functional and make sense. (Iran's president is always pleasant no matter how outrageous his behavior or what comes out of his mouth.) This demeanor also encompasses political correctness. So let's never let on what we really think or that we don't…really think.

Therefore, we now live in a world which admires how we seem to be ahead of who we are. We decide to trust or hire based on initials after a name rather than listen for whether something makes sense. From more than 40 years of personal experience dealing with investors, I know most prefer to hear what they want to hear rather than what they ought to know. Therefore the smoother and simpler the financial pitch the more acceptable the nonsense. And the less you challenge someone to think critically and listen, the more acceptable you become.

It is not professional, notwithstanding a perfectly polished Ivy League demeanor, to have allowed financial innovation to hide in the obfuscated shadows of complexity.

Transparency has suddenly become the new code word of our Government. Regulators and the Obama administration's economic experts (with too many ties to conflicts from the past) put transparency out there as their goal in their mid June 09 financial proposal. And the reform that ensued was transparently nothing much.

Barriers to greed must be rebuilt. And this along with an explicit understanding communicated to investors - with accurate disclosure that can be understood about the substance of anything securitized to be sold as a security, should be a priority, well before mere transparency. Transparent would be to place a warning on a pack of cigarettes that smoking kills and has killed lots of people. Smoking killed my father at 64 thirty seven years ago. Cigarette packages did not have warnings then, but they did have lethal addictive additives.

A financial warning could be: Warning – this is too complex to fully explain so that it may be understood, so proceed at your own risk because investing in this could destroy your ability to retire. Or could be like a warning for a bridge – **the bridge is out** – so if you can take the risk, go for it, drive at high speed hoping to fly over the missing part of the road. Disclosure provides limited warnings, but no barriers.

Few know or understand the wonderful world of arcane financial nomenclature, after all my research and 40 years of experience, I admit I don't. However, if someone sounds like a *shit-talker* (a sports expression) no matter how elevated the professional verbal behavior the substance is probably **feces**. (Now you know that I can sound professional.)

No matter how elevated the wealth and credentials of those who contrived the toxic innovation, individuals who are regarded to be at the top of their profession I really can't understand a lot of what they talk about – like having *liquidity in the markets*. Liquidity for what or for whom?

Liquidity for what? Not to lend, because banks don't really lend that much. Certainly it does not mean more lending to people or to small business, or to restructure existing home or commercial real estate loans based on any sense of fairness or concern to not further implode real estate. It appears to mean (I am guessing) more money for Mega Bank Holding Companies to create proprietary financial innovation to either trade for their own accounts or to flip to counterparties?

I also do not understand how to measure risk with math or how to back up worse than crappy debt with contrived derivatives, like swaps that have no substance. And I do not understand what meticulous (a Wall Street word) means when so many financial professionals utilized no underwriting standards to make all kinds of loans and issue worthless swaps to back all kinds of securities. I do understand meticulous as applied to clothing, because I grew up with a meticulous father who was not tall and special ordered suits from Saks.

This chapter is about what I don't get, and I wanted to share my confusion in case we suffer from similar confusion. It is OK to admit that you just don't understand when confronted by arcane explanations as a function of arcane nomenclature, or just a lack of any sense. Just because someone is devoted to sounding professional do not assume they are not shit-talkers. We respect the word professional and we respect professionals; but to be professional, respect must be earned.

To be a financial professional there must be a concern for positive results to investors, and not at the expense of the many for the benefit of the few. There must be a concern for a truthful and explicit explanation of the substance of the investment.

Financially contrived nomenclature is vocabulary used to convey the impression that risk has been managed and therefore reduced. And words which do not properly create a real understanding have been used by a huge majority of "financial professionals" to avoid their responsibility to be professional, which must include integrity and dealing with others in

GOOD FAITH. Functional and ethical communication must elicit mutual comprehension, not false conclusions.

There is a distinction to be made between conduct where words have been utilized to obfuscate rather than illuminate. Can you be professional and not ethical?

There is no way to understand or accept how so many self-professed "professionals" could have participated in allowing our financial world to get to the brink of such a large chasm of financial destruction. So we have no choice but to regard their unconscionable actions as the behavior of sociopathic, self-absorbed, infinitely greedy pigs.

How sensible was it to tear down the barriers erected against greed? What nomenclature applies to this incredible act of self-interested professional financial hit men? Deregulation – but not for the benefit of the American Dream, as Wall Street Godfathers and Republicans contended and as a large majority of Congress ratified. My nomenclature is Financial Darwinism, which means as David Satterfield pointed out - "survival of the richest." And this is transparent nomenclature because it elicits mutual comprehension.

The next chapter will illuminate the raison d'être for this chapter, to help you follow the inkblots in this chapter. And speaking of inkblots - should there be a Rorschach Test required as an entrance exam for Congress, especially Tea Party Republicans, and Wall Street? There are all kinds of government requirements for professional continuing education, why not an entrance exam for certain groups with no continuing education government mandates?

CHAPTER 15

THE INSIDIOUS USE AND ABUSE OF LANGUAGE BY ALLOWING IT TO SHAPE THOUGHT

Vocabulary is taught in all elementary schools through the sixth grade. So we have all been exposed to words, and dictionaries and spelling. But we have not customarily learned much about how language works. And we do not study the purpose or role of language unless we are exposed to relative linguistics in college. Most of us do not stop to think about whether what we hear or are told correlates with what we can see and actually observe, and we do not listen for what someone means. So there is a disconnect with reality; and this disconnect is taken advantage of to the Nth degree by those who want to control what others think or do not think. This is how Wall Street and lots of other salespeople get bad names - selling all kinds of stuff from investments to advice - by telling people what they want them to hear not what they ought to know or how something actually works.

1984 by Orwell comes to mind, or the recent election in Iran where the words proclaiming victory had little to do with the actual vote, especially if there were 3MM more votes than voters. It is simple to remember how Wall Street was so amazed by all the risk in the system, and the acceptance of collateralized complexities – collateralized by the substance of what was not a question. Investors wanted safety so it was created by the use of the word collateral, so the use of this word has shaped connotations of security.

Linguistics is the scientific study of language, and attempts to explain language and how it relates to thought in the mind. Benjamin Whorf was a pioneer in the study of linguistics who understood and postulated how language can be used to shape our thoughts. Whorf held that the purpose of language was to elicit thought, that language was a "vehicle for meaning." Unfortunately, too often language is used to shape thought because we do not think past the words we hear by allowing words to shape our thoughts.

Words alone are not thought or deaf mutes could not communicate. Communication which leads to mutual comprehension is the goal of language. When we do not utilize words as a tool to elicit thought (i.e. elicit thought) we are controlled by the motivations of the speaker or writer, as well as our emotions. Further, the lack of logic utilized in communication serves as a barrier to any attempt to achieve mutual comprehension. Because we do not study logic or its role in providing a path to understanding, it is important to be aware of the fact that logic is to language as breathing is to life.

So words are tools – not thought, and must be used with logic to achieve mutual comprehension in order to reason correctly. The study of logic is the study of the methods and principles used in distinguishing the correct from the incorrect. Philosophers have spent eons debating the functions of language and logic. By the mid- 20th century the complex uses of language were broken down into three basic functions: information, expressive and directive. The essential fallacy underlying the use of language is that effective communication which elicits mutual comprehension must be logical, and because words are only symbols to help us think there must be an awareness of the fallacies to avoid the trap of allowing words to replace reasoned thought. Truth and falsehood are the concern of the logician and apparently not on the radar for most investors, members of the financial universe or any media, or people who contrive financial innovation, economists, congress, rating agencies and voters – or the head of Iran. And that includes too many people, maybe even most of us. We need to demand more of ourselves to look past language designed to reinforce accepted homilies that have not been questioned.

I entered the insurance business in 1965 and spent years helping clients with succession planning in addition to being in the investment business specializing in Real Estate Private Placements. So I know a lot about insurance. The substance of an insurance contract is the promise to pay a stipulated sum in the future based on a specified event. For life insurance it would be death; and for general insurance or property and casualty -fire or a car accident. Insurance is based on receiving premiums which are a composite of: underwriting risk, expenses to maintain the stability and employees of the company, and to establish reserves and pay claims. Claim projections are the easiest for life insurance because mortality tables have been proven to be dependable unlike morbidity tables which are subject to all sorts of unforeseen events and contingencies. So insurance carriers that want to survive and maintain stability for policyholders to develop confidence in the promise to pay are concerned with being prudent and responsible.

To have said or implied that swaps or credit default swaps were insurance was absolutely fallacious. To have held out the notion that gigantic amounts of murky debt were either backed by other murky debt or collateralized should have triggered a barrage of questions from all concerned parties to have indentified the substance behind all the assurances that risk was reduced. But the fallacious use of language went unnoticed and unquestioned. If the piles and piles of leverage – which became the inverted pyramid, had been backed up by lucid, logically defensible reasoning then we would have known whether language was used for propaganda to sell worse-than-junk debt, or used to inform. But that was not the case, no one looked past the words.

There has been no logical proof offered that free markets are either self-correcting or rational. And there has been no logical proof offered that derivatives or any type of innovated financial product provide capital formation – except that derivative trading created a nauseating amount of excessive net worth for the innovators – at the expense of our economy. Supporters of financially innovated derivatives claimed it provided capital formation. However it became clear that it only created a housing bloat which created a need for more debt to fund more bloat, so the leverage became a self-fulfilling prophecy. And this should be regarded as a contrived scheme to have enough debt to sell to satisfy the demand Wall Street created for *secure debt instruments*. At best this is dialectic, which I will not attempt to explain, at worst this seems to constitute fraud.

The Chairman/Chairwoman of the SEC, in February of 2009, testified to Congress that 'innovation does produce capital formation," but no one, no one in Congrees asked how or why or what kind. Mary Schapiro, who has only worked for the government and who did not protect the markets from imploding (her stipulated duty) when she was the head of FINRA - did not explain. So **we accept illogical unsupported fictitious statements as fact based on words rather than requiring logically reasoned explanations.** And this is fallacious self-defeating behavior.

The acceptance of the fallacious has been a human failing from the beginning of recorded history, so a **credit default** swap seems to make sense on the surface, but when there was no Socratic debate swaps were allowed to exist, because historically we have not easily engaged in Socratic debate to find a higher level of truth. We do not examine assumptions because it might just take some effort so investors take the easy way out and just accept, like blind sheep, all the language concocted to make them feel warm and cozy.

In April of 2011, we remained mired in the unknown depths of quick-sand in a fundamental way due to the problems created by having accepted fallacious language which has also been a function of fallacious logic. Until the day in 2008 after it became clear that our economy was heading into a black hole of exploding debt no one questioned the propagandistic language and lack of substance behind too many financial products and too much financial behavior. **Deregulation was advanced as a positive good to get the** government off your back – when the substance of the propaganda really meant - get the government off Wall Street's back. And look what happened.

It is ludicrous that it is necessary to discuss how we do not have appropriate standards for the use of language, and have little understanding of the crucial function of logic as well as the limitations of words. However, if everyone had a better grasp or awareness of how words are only tools utilized to achieve thought, and when not used with logic then any thoughts created by the language become fallacious – the world would be a better place. And we might have avoided financial immolation. It is logical to reason that much of what has occurred to torpedo our economy and the lives of so many people trapped by dire financial circumstances would not have taken place if there had not been an acceptance of the fallacious use of language. Health care reform would also have been different (remember the death panels?) - think about how many things could be different.

It is wrong to intentionally misuse language to shape (create) the thought that you are protected from risk, when the substance is missing. It is fallacious – which sounds better than wrong? It is also a misrepresentation of facts – hence should be regarded as securities fraud, in my opinion and in the opinion of a prominent Cleveland securities lawyer. (Cleveland has almost as many attorneys as Chicago which may make Cleveland a strange place to live.) It is also unpleasant, even self-incriminating, to consider that too many of us have relied on words rather than questions of substance leading to an understanding of whether the mortgage we just signed made sense, or whether we knew we could not afford the house. It was wrong to accept the implausible essence of Madoff's consistently way too high, absolutely unrealistic, and *guaranteed* returns – especially without any plausible explanation. Madoff did tell my Yale, UVA law cousin who "invested" in 1985 that he could not share how he could guarantee 25% returns, because how he did this was "proprietary." The SEC must have accepted words over thoughts when their investigation of Madoff resulted in leaving him alone to continue his swindle.

To react to words rather than critical reflection to achieve a level of meaningful comprehension has become a severe and crippling problem. Where has our liberal arts education gone?

The following is a list of words used throughout this book with the real meanings mis- appropriated by all those who have either intentionally or unintentionally used them or passed them along to be used to camouflage substance or the lack of it as well as shape your thoughts: swaps, complex financial instruments, risk measurement tools, free market, deregulation, the market is rational, self-correcting, collateralized, backed, *too complex to explain*, derivatives, financial tools, innovation, triple A, protection from regulators, party philosophy, efficient market, professional, transparent, hedging, structured financial instruments, and the **most toxic word of all** *INNOVATIVE*, the **other most toxic word is** *SAFE.*

Innovation is typically thought of as something new which is positive, and used to describe creative people as innovators. Inventions like the automobile, the cotton gin, the airplane and computers were all innovative ideas which were real and positive. To innovate is to begin or introduce something new. But, as we equate innovation with something positive, no one stops to question whether Wall Street's use of the word means positive or negative. It is only possible to conclude that **innovation has been amazingly positive (profitable) for Wall Street and all the others involved with all the financial innovation – but a tragic negative meltdown of savings and jobs for our country and the world.**

When Wall Street uses the word innovation in a positive sense few have stopped to see past the word to what it really means and will mean if it is allowed to continue. (Which financial reform has blessed!) We need to listen for what someone is really saying when reality does not parallel the way the word is used. And Wall Street absolutely wants you to think their innovation is good.

If financial innovation has been toxic, then we need to question how much more financial innovation can this country or the world tolerate. The world was improved by innovators like Edison, Ford and the Wright Brothers. Alexander Graham Bell improved our ability to talk to each other without stringing tin cans. Madam Curie discovered Polonium and Radium which changed the way scientists regarded matter and energy; her discovery also led to x-rays which changed medicine. Albert Einstein's work is obviously considered innovative, and in 1999 Time named him the "Person of the Century." This is what most think innovation is about. So when Goldman and the rest of Wall Street argue for continuing their special brand of innovation are they not trading on what we normally associate with the intent of the word?

Does anyone want to be against innovation – even if there is "**tension between innovation and stability?**" **The tension that the CEO of Goldman referred to in his "remarks" was simply that Wall Street innovation destroys stability** - and this lack of stability resulting in a kind of depression has caused a shitload of tension. Tragic tension – i.e. economic suffering and displacement! Blankfein is a true financial professional.

It seems unnecessary to examine each word, but the insidious use of certain code-like words by Wall Street Banks and Rating Agencies has disingenuously permeated the language or nomenclature of our financial universe to willfully and intentionally create thoughts and impressions to support their activities in pursuit of unfettered greed. Keep in mind that financial investments are not real investments so they need to be described just like minimal art – minimalism would be nothing without the language used to describe it. Of course, a minimalist painting of an all black canvas in the Guggenheim (Ad Reinhart) can easily be seen visually to be possibly nothing. However, the world of the too complex to explain with AAA ratings appears to be safe if you don't care if you can't understand something which defies an explanation.

Perhaps Einstein's work was not altogether safe either because it was a critical innovation/discovery in physics in order for physicists to have made an atomic bomb. Wall Street's bomb was triple A leverage which it dropped like a nuke on the entire world. So it is crucial to stop and consider that safe is subjective and qualitative. American Heritage states that **safe means:** "1. Secure from danger, harm or evil. 2. Free from danger or injury, unhurt: *safe and sound.* 3. Free from risk; sure: *a safe bet.*"

Minimalism is subjective – go to MOMA and think how its collection could be described with calculus, or how you would quantify its qualitative essence in your own mind. Subjective means: ... "Particular to a given person ... existing only in the mind: illusory ... Relating to the real nature of something: essential." So Risk is what you think constitutes risk in your own mind, because it is open to your opinion, or your value judgment of its real nature. When risk is mathematically measured and further is assigned a AAA rating by an entity that is assumed to be unbiased and objective taking certain subjective factors into consideration as well as financial factors which must include leverage and the ability to repay all the debt – **the rating is used to create an impression of safety.** So a good rating shapes our thoughts, (but should not replace our own judgment.)

However, the contrivers of the innovation used the reputation of raters (whether based on substance or not) to get investors to think the innovation was safe and this was accepted by everyone who did not question why they did not understand how the financial product actually worked. No one really questioned – not even Alan Greenspan who has admitted in Public that he did not really understand. I did not hear the questions - and I listened.

We do not question the use of the word free, so when freedom is part of any consideration it must be good. Freedom to be a Social or Financial Darwinist – go for it, it's the American way. We support free markets, freedom of expression, freedom to lie unless it is under oath, freedom to use propaganda to market toxic amounts of debt, and then the freedom to continue to resume paying huge bonuses, (now called income when you paid TARP back with funds from the FDIC.) A good example of the use of the word free is how we applied it to the wrong war in Iraq. In this country and in other major countries there has been freedom to become swindlers, because there has been no intervention until after the financial massacre became manifestly apparent – even to a majority of economists who claimed in December of 2007 that we were not yet in a recession. Now the word recession is the chosen word for our dire straights – because if we called what we are now experiencing a depression there would be even less confidence, so we cling to a safer sounding word. Strange how recession suddenly sounds better   in 2011 than it did at the beginning of 2008? Recessions are easier to recover from than Depressions.

Beauty and Safety are in the eyes of the beholder. Some people parachute out of a plane, as my daughter did in Europe and my wife almost had a stroke in Cleveland when our daughter informed us that it was the "most exhilarating experience of my life." I only choked.

I choked when I heard that lousy debt was being backed up by more debt. The moment I heard the expression *Mortgaged Backed Bonds* I knew something was wrong because how do you back up mystery debt with more mystery debt? I understand a letter of credit or a CD or something that is tangible collateral, but the collateral must be explained, and proof (or disclosure) should back up the contention that the mystery debt has been collateralized, until it is demonstrated (or proven) that the collateral makes sense or does not. I never heard a sensible explanation that I could understand, so I decided (realized) that all the innovative stuff was BS contrived for fees rather than safe enough to invest in.

I have spent years attempting to get past words, to transcend the mere utterance of words to pure thought. James Joyce wrote an essay about epiphanies and the goal of his entire book "*Finnegan's Wake*" was to provide epiphanies to transcend mere words to elicit thought. Try to even read it out

169

loud – I experienced an epiphany from the first sentence, which was also the last sentence, so I named my 2nd and 3rd sailboat riverrun to signify the timelessness and constant flow of a "circuitous" river. At least if you try to read *Finnegan* you will not feel bad about confessing you do not understand it – which is what investors should do when any investment cannot be explained to provide a clear understanding. Actually, for all I know, *Finnegan's Wake* may be a description of a too complex to explain financial product.

This book, I confess, is the book of a former existential, self-confessed Joycian. So some parts of this book may be too philosophical for some readers. However, if there is no search for truth then we are bound to get swindled over and over; because **Financial Darwinism is like herpes – it does not go away.** At this juncture, because our financial world has tanked and continues to be in the doldrums (sailing without any wind) for so many of our fellow human beings here and around the world - it is critical to analyze all significant causal factors. Only then will it be possible to be committed to a pragmatic evaluation to arrive at solutions to fix the present and reach conclusions required to avoid future meltdowns.

One conclusion to make from this disaster must be that - we have participated in allowing dysfunctional language to shape our thoughts rather than using it to help us think. We have trusted in and followed safe harbor words without reasoning. So we must further conclude that our educational system is a primary culprit because it has failed to explain the purpose of language which is to elicit thought and how to avoid using or allowing language to shape thought. If high schools taught how language is used to create propaganda and relate this, not just to Hitler's Goebbels, but to a plethora of other examples – we might listen for whether something makes sense. Instead, it is only important to study a grammatically correct sentence according to rigid rules in a book written by a judgmental grammarian. If we required just one course in logic in high school or college, we could recognize propaganda before succumbing to its fallacious message.

We know propaganda techniques are not new, so they are not innovative. But they are subversive because they disingenuously erode the fabric of the truth. If we are open to consider the how the acceptance of the fallacious use of language, which includes the acceptance of illogical reasoning, and accept that this acceptance is in reality a posture toward ignorance – then we have embarked on a new path toward enlightenment.

I have learned through my own tragic and awful human judgments the need to be on a path to enlightenment, which can only be seen retrospectively. Because this is a diligent treatise, I have shared with you why we are also personally responsible for being swindled, as well as why we need to change paths and how to start by searching for and reject that which does not make sense. I have learned it is not possible to learn from the past until you accept what has been dysfunctional in order to remove it to go forward. That we are dysfunctional communicators - although everyone agrees on the importance of communicating and may think they are doing it effectively - must be analyzed and accepted to be on a new path toward logic and reason. The true age of enlightenment has not begun yet, because it must start with letting go of rigid ideas from the past which put too much faith in words at the expense of pure thought.

A lot of the words singled out for discussion in this chapter and other chapters make sense in the proper context. However, when they are used to describe and characterize substance that is either not there or infinitely different from what has been explained, then a false realty has been created.

The realty of today was denied at the end of 2007 by almost every economist and media person. So many of these self-important people heard only the words and did not engage in reason with logic in order to get past the nomenclature of code words to understanding. So the rotten essence under the surface of things escaped critical scrutiny, and words were used to dismiss anyone who went against the popular concepts of *free markets* and *deregulation to get the government off your back*. The ruse words or phrases were too ingrained from decades of repetition – free, rational, self-correcting, safe, and diversified; as well as the validity of slogans like - mathematical risk measurement and risk reduction tools. Of course, many of us are afraid of complicated math and are reluctant to criticize what we can't explain and are generally unfamiliar with – but we cannot accept language or use language that allows confusion and lies to proliferate.

It is not surprising to consider how poorly we use language. We do not study language or logic - we study spelling and grammar. We study when Ponce de Leon went to Florida to find the Fountain of Youth (I don't remember the date of his discovery) and it is important to know the date Magellan first spied the Pacific Ocean. Too bad he did not buy property in Malibu. We place all the emphasis on form – not on substance or on the quality of thought – so there is tension between the superficial and the profound – as Goldman Sachs might contend. Form is what counts and so the goal of mutual comprehension may sound incomprehensible. To have jumped on the bandwagon of let's get in on the *good news* of safe mortgaged backed bonds and safe collateralized debt obligations people had to accept the words and not think about the lack of substance.

Thomas Wolfe wrote about "Masters of the Universe" in *Bonfire of the Vanities*, which has become an American classic novel about greed. In *Bonfire,* "masters of the universe" lived on "golden crumbs" from selling bonds. Today we know that innovated complexities have produced more crumbs for the Masters than most people can imagine, and a lot of bread is missing. Hopefully, there will be higher standards for language used to sell crumbs in the future. This would arm investors, Congress, regulators and voters with a clearer view of reality to see through all the propaganda. How ironic that Wall Street Godfathers use propaganda as skillfully as Goebbels. Goebbels' mission, as most of us know, was to get Germans to accept implausible glittering generalities, irrelevant conclusions and fallacious double talk to fix the blame for Germany's problems on one group of people who were not Arians. Wall Street's Masters of the Universe, although not totally Arian, have used similar propaganda methodology to extract all the gold they can from anyone gullible and ignorant enough to believe their propaganda.

That we have allowed the misuse of language to take advantage of us and skew reality is a crucial element of how we got swindled. And ignorance of how to use language to create real understanding is a major reason underlying how our political process has become so adversarial. So now is the time to accept as gospel that the way we allow language to shape irrational thoughts and attitudes is self defeating. If we want to stop history from happening again, and to proceed on a rational and stable path forward into an always unknown future we need to use language to promote clear mutual understanding. **One thing for certain, if we do not change the present - the future will not improve, and the future is tomorrow.**

CHAPTER 16

THE FINANCIAL MEDIA – REPORTERS OR SHILLS? OBJECTIVE MEDIA – A CASUALTY OF THE WAR!

T oday's media has become increasingly adversarial in its search for ratings in lieu of an objective search for the truth. So now there is a left and right, which too often do not recognize that port and starboard may be different sides, but on the same boat. The right calls the left - liberal partisans, while the right is overly zealous in promoting a political agenda usually based on the ethic of Financial Darwinism – "survival of the fittest." The left is not so united because it is more concerned with objectivity based on a concern for the public good and there is always disagreement on the left about priorities and what the best public good is. This concern for public good on the left is a condition that so-called conservatives do not suffer lightly.

The right and left are more transparent in our financial media where economics and money is their special domain. Financial Darwinism is clearly the core ethic of the left, just as "Survival of the fittest" was the core ethic of Social Darwinism and conservatives during the hay day of the robber barons.

The right and left is the product of all media except for network nightly news it seems. Balanced has replaced objective! However, when the cable political news on the left becomes strident in its objectivity it is always called partisan. It is not politically correct for members of the press on television to pin the liars to the wall so misinformation is allowed to remain in our public dialogue.

For example, Republicans love to point out that Obama's budget was so high that it would have increased the deficit so they refused to approve it. A little discussed fact was the additional funding earmarked for jobs to address the vast deferred maintenance festering nationally in infrastructure needs. Like 100-year old water pipes and sewers in New York City or the lack of appropriate barriers against the sea in New Orleans, all the aging bridges and a host of other fundamental needs that if addressed would create jobs. And jobs produce income and income taxes.

Broadcast journalists lead by CNBC, and print journalists, lead by the Wall Street Journal, have been **cheerleaders for team Financial Darwinism** as well as shills. CNBC and Fox people jump up and down with glee in the land of the greedy casino owners (or it is the land of the Jolly Green Giant piles of money) when the bell rings on Wall Street. And these financial gurus from their plateau of self-importance analyze why the market or markets went up or down (retrospectively of course) and fawn over the mumblings of each CEO interviewed – no matter how self-serving the point of view expressed. Almost never do these incredibly savvy, oracle-like market analyzers enter into a Socratic debate to arrive at a clearer view of the truth.

Acceptance of the self-absorbed mumblings from deep within the vast wealth of the most important promoters of unfettered greed is the rule. I remember (do you?) hearing Ken Lay tell someone on CNBC that Enron was planning to control the world market in water – the response from the duly impressed interviewer seemed like – wow, let me kiss your feet. All the Wall Street propagandistic ruses discussed in this book are accepted and passed on like a fundamentalist read of the Bible old or new, or the Koran. And the repetitive use of ruses by what are supposed to be objective members of the Fourth Estate contributes to skewed and irrational public opinion.

A prime example of propaganda is the ruse used to create irrational public opinion based on the fallacious contention that *deregulation will get the government off your back.* The fact of this deceit is that Financial

Darwinism is the root cause of our financial malaise and **deregulation was used to get the government off the backs of the greediest and most self-interested** – like Goldman Sachs. Just ask an ordinary man on the street who considers himself to belong to the party of Republicans, and he will confirm his belief in deregulation, not knowing that Glass-Steagall protected him with a barrier against greed.

Our antagonistic political process and irresponsible politicians helps the media foster inaccurate public opinion. Inaccurate public opinion is often a reaction born out of a reasonable mistrust of our government's ability to get it right. The majority of our zealot free marketers in financial broadcast media certainly did not get the repeal of Glass right due to their core belief in Financial Darwinism and abiding mistrust in government. Only eight members of the senate knew enough or remained above the tentacles of lobbyists to have voted against repealing Glass-Steagall.

Senator Byron Dorgan of North Dakota, one of the eight, was visionary when he strongly pointed out in 1999 that within 10 years; "...we will look back and say we should not have done this but we did because we forgot the lessons of the past, and that which was true in the 1930's is true in 2010." Senator Paul Wellstone of Minnesota said that Congress had "seemed determined to unlearn lessons from our past mistakes." The New York Times business news reported this on November 5, 1999.

Larry Kudlow, a CNBC darling of the right, has remained rigidly steadfast in his self- absorbed belief that the repeal of Glass-Steagall is equated with unfettered individual (American) freedom. His objectivity does extend to an acknowledgment of all the empirical evidence which proves that Senator Dorgan, along with Senators Wellstone, Boxer, Feingold, Bryan, Harkin, Mikulski, and Shelby were right ten years ago. They should have been the only ones on the 2010 committee to fix the regulators and the regulations. I don't think any of them were ever partners in Goldman. However if you are not an economist, you are not eligible to qualify as a financial expert like Larry Kudlow PhD, Economics, or like Phil Graham PhD. Integrity and judgment are not part of any PhD or even prerequisites!

Kudlow's favorite senator who astutely voted for tearing down barriers against greed (along with 91 other genius senators), was Judd Gregg, who did not want to be a census taker. Kudlow on his blog shared his objective reporter's reasoning skills by reporting in 2009, or noting that Gregg – "has more backbone than anyone in politics"....and is a; "tax cutter, budget-cutter, deficit-cutter, and a debt-cutter." I guess Kudlow forgot to take into account or analyze the lack of debt Clinton bequeathed when he left office. **Kudlow the economist with so many others, has apparently not noticed that as taxes went down for the last 30 years, so did jobs.** And he has steadfastly neglected to observe that the deficit was created by Republicans and everyone who voted/votes to remain in Afghanistan as well as maintain an Army in Germany and Japan.

Members of the media, whether print or broadcast, are considered members of the Fourth Estate. Fourth Estate is the term originally given to newspapers who served as the watchdog over the power of government and the abuses that seem to naturally flow from power – remember it is held that power corrupts.

The media is supposed to be objective in its role of creating informed public opinion; and is protected by the 1st amendment as well as by not (usually) having to reveal its source of news in fulfilling this critical role. So, in the past, the Fourth Estate has functioned as part of the system of checks and balances to preserve our democracy - which is why our founding fathers established the three branches of government. The term "Fourth Estate" was coined by Edmund Burke an 18th century British politician who noted that there were three Estates in Parliament, but the reporter's gallery contained a "Fourth Estate more important than all the others." The rationale behind protecting the Fourth Estate is that Democracy needs honest information, and open information to survive.

Consider what Bernstein and Woodward did for Democracy when they reported on the Watergate break-in along with the cover-up, and what their source did to help save the country from a paranoid abuse of power. Retrospectively Nixon seems far better than some of the ideologues who followed him. Never forget how Edward R. Murrow had the guts and concern for preserving freedom of speech as well as Democracy itself when he exposed Senator Joseph McCarthy by using McCarthy's own words and actions to illustrate his systemic and poisonous impact on our society. Murrow's television show *See It Now* saved our country from the plague called McCarthyism. And Arthur Miller's play *The Crucible* captured the tragedy of McCarthyism. I wonder who will write a play about the tragedy of tearing down the barriers to greed.

Not long ago too much media power concentrated into the hands of a single owner was considered bad for Democracy. So a chain of newspapers could not own a chain of television stations. There would have been an outcry over too much concentration of media power, and it would not have been allowed. Television stations could have their license revoked if their independence was questionable, notwithstanding their major network affiliation.

The Federal Communications Commission had established rules which protected the public from dissemination of information from the personal slants of just a few owners. Massive media conglomerates like the kind owned by Rupert Murdoch, were not allowed not long ago – too much concentration of power! And now the world knows that Murdoch has no ethics from what clearly has taken place in England, yet he still owns a vast network of media outlets in the US, which spew forth whatever is necessary to achieve the largest audience or readership. Murdock owns the Wall Street Journal and Fox Views which are among the other far less than objective news sources he knows nothing about, according to his unsworn testimony to the British Parliamentary Committee investigating how his news organizations tapped so many cell phones and even interfered with an ability to know where a young girl was in the throes of being killed.

Again, the ability to compile an aggregate of interlocking interests was viewed as dangerous to our democracy. But somehow Financial Darwinists gained control of the FCC and the danger was unleashed - like the breaking and entry of that famous box which supposedly belonged to Pandora. News and media conglomerates are so powerful today that even the greats like Edward R. Murrow or Walter Cronkite would have had their hands tied by the personal agendas of the too powerful owners. Keith Olberman was fired MSNBC for being too vehemently objective! But MSNBC continues the tradition with Lawrence O'Donnell's, Last Word.

Publishing suffers from similar problems, for example McGraw–Hill owns S & P. (Try to get a publisher for a book which calls for a Special Prosecutor to investigate a rating agency gone terribly awry when it owns one of the major culprits.)

Today there is a complexity of abilities to influence and slant public opinion. In addition to newspapers, (which are dying a slow death for a variety of reasons – a major one being the desire to avoid reading anything more than a sound-bite or a tweet) we have hoards of cable news stations. The cable networks are owned by a few people who want to bend reality to reflect their personal agendas without regard for objectivity. There is paucity of cable news that still cares about objectivity. And then there is the vast world of the Ethernet, where everyone is entitled to a blog no matter how ignorant. Sometimes strange stuff comes out of your radio - I think there is someone called Rush Windbag inside some radios spewing forth totally bizarre stuff aimed at his audience of zealot fundamental hypocrites who prefer the shelter of ignorance above all else.

Public opinion is up for grabs without a vigilant FCC or a concern for finding objective information leading to a rational understanding of reality. It is now more important to be politically correct than to be honest and open, which used to be regarded as "forthright." Ranting is OK on the air as long as there is enough of an audience to attract advertisers with their personal agendas to support the overpaid host and the media which offers the *ranter* the platform to emotionally appeal to ignorance and prejudice, (always in the name of freedom and the flag.) Try listening to G. Beck and wonder why he has not been institutionalized. Or is much of cable a loony bin. There should be bars in front of some faces to add a semblance of reality.

It is important to revisit the proscribed role for the Fourth Estate - to understand the responsibilities incumbent upon the media to protect the public from the abuse of power, and the abuse of the truth by objectively creating informed public opinion. It is the Fourth Estate's responsibility to objectively create informed public opinion to protect the public good!

Regrettably, our media has misplaced its mandate for objectivity. To lose one's way is a reflection of human imperfection. However, our media's imperfections are way out of balance considering that "fair and balanced" in many circles has replaced objective reality. Today there is a new ethic which mandates that our media must furnish a public platform for those who would still argue that the earth is flat or that the history of man and our planet dates back 6,000 years - when dinosaurs and man scavenged together for food and survival?

Most of the 2011 leading Republic Presidential candidates for the 2012 election believe in creationism – which is functionally ignorant. And for the 2008 Presidential Debates the media did not indulge in any appropriate Socratic debate with the creationist idiots. They sat politely on the sidelines, in a shroud of political correctness! They did not vigorously defend facts and self-evident truths provided by hundreds of years of scientific discoveries.

Let's not be judgmental about lying about nuclear weapons of mass destruction not ever being in Iraq. Should the media not condemn the non-acceptance of a non-partisan exhaustive study of how our government made up reasons to attack Iraq?

I wonder what Walter Cronkite would have reported about the events leading up to the call for war. Walter Cronkite went to Vietnam in 1965 and observed that war was "unwinnable." And when he returned to Vietnam in 1968 he concluded, on the air, that Vietnam was "hopeless" and that we needed to get out.

The conclusion Cronkite shared on the air with his fellow Americans caused President Lyndon Johnson to reassess his view of the war as well as a majority of the rest of the country. Johnson was desolate about the fact the he had lost Cronkite and therefore the support of the country. War protests then transcended the early group of those against the War to a mainstream desire to get out of Vietnam. Johnson did not run for office again. Johnson, like so many other Americans, trusted Cronkite's integrity, objectivity, judgment and passionate concern for the welfare of the US, and so believed in Walter Cronkite's conclusion.

This was a moment of truth for the war and the public outcry over our participation finally led to our kicking and screaming exit. This is the backdrop for how the Fourth Estate is supposed to function.

Because our country is suffering from Born Again Social Darwinism transformed into Financial Darwinism, major news anchors and the best of cable news ought to know that "free markets self-correct" is not fact but totally fictitious. They need to know that free means Laissez-faire, leave us alone. They need to identify the lies behind the slanted financial reporting that created the irrational public opinion which fostered the rampant acceleration of Financial Darwinism.

If the Fourth Estate had done its job, the re-emergence of Social Darwinism in the form of Financial Darwinism would not have snowballed from the end of 70s into the devastating avalanche it has become.

Major network anchors stood up to the line when reporting Hurricane Katrina. Brian Williams and Sheppard Smith (who seems out of place on Fox) clearly were objectively outraged by our government's incompetent and uncompassionate response. Katie Couric and Charles Gibson did not retreat from relentless and fair questions to Sarah Palin which revealed her lack of preparedness to be a Vice President – let alone the President or anything but a shining symbol of ignorance for the T Partiers. And I still remember Dan Rather yelling – "This is Dan Rather, kicking and screaming" being carried from the floor of the 1968 Democratic National Convention. Rather relentlessly pursued Bush 1 about Iran Contra. Ted Koppel went after the truth for decades and 60 Minutes is still at it protecting the public. But our financial media, with few exceptions, has refrained from the responsibility and obligation to be objective in creating informed public opinion.

NBC has CNBC replete with Kudlow. And to balance CNBCs bastion of Free and Rational Market unfettered Laissez-faire Capitalism, NBC has provided MSNBC which is concerned with relative political objective reality – with object reporters like Mathews, Ed, Rachel and Lawrence O'Donnell. So this is fair and balanced? Objective political reporting is considered a liberal bias by those who prefer the shelter of their own well defined boundaries of ignorance.

Financial broadcast reporting on CNBC is considered the "word." Ignorance is not confined to any specific political party – however, the religion based on a **rigid** belief in free and unregulated markets, as practiced by CNBC media gurus, is usually Republican. Democrats may not believe in this religion, however, they are usually not up for religious wars, which does not excuse the 38 democrats who voted to deregulate greed when Graham-Leach-Bliley was passed and not vetoed by Clinton, (but he was a lame duck?). Did the media report this event as a return to Laissez-faire pre-Great Depression economics?

Many members of Congress may just not have enough financial experience, and although they are not poor, it is more likely an issue of judgment and what side of the war against the American Dream they have joined - the ultra rich Financial Darwinists or Abe Lincoln's *the for the people*? Can we expect our media to be objective when Congress does not ask the right questions or expect to make sense?

It is important to consider that members of the media who are not experienced with financial considerations typically listen in awe to financial guests and even when an utterance obviously makes no sense do not follow up with simple questions like – how can you say or think that, or just WHY? They lap up ludicrous stuff like hungry puppies. There are no pointed questions, so propaganda and ignorance flourish.

Hosts without financial experience or insight have allowed too many interviewees explain innovative financial products as *too complex to explain* – and accepted this outrageous statement. To accept this as a legitimate response or reason is to give a fallacious (as well as probably fraudulent) excuse a platform to exist, and this response became acceptable with repetition. At least the MSNBC host of the House of Cards, in 2009, a two-hour grotesque oversimplification of how we got swindled, asked Alan Greenspan to explain the complexities. And Greenspan admitted that he "honestly did not understand them." Wow – isn't that an admission of guilt??

This admission of wretched regulatory malfeasance swept through the back halls of the beltway Senate Office Buildings like the news of 9/11, or like the news that Reagan was a closet Republican when he registered as a Democrat to be elected head of the actors union. My source said it moved through the buildings like Montezuma's Revenge! (Where were these people when Congress interviewed Greenspan?)

I will not burden you with my conclusions about each member of CNBC's financial programs. Some of the most blatantly slanted, even in the middle of 2009 surrounded by financial carnage, steadfastly clung to their fervent belief in the tenets of Financial Darwinism.

The most overtly outrageous of the 2009 clingers (who are still clinging) was Larry Kudlow, who was thoughtful enough to have posted his true thoughts on his blog to help me make my following points with great authority.

Kudlow is a heavily credentialed supply-side free market "economist," who became a member of the Fourth Estate. Although his spiritual leaders, Milton (Nobel) Friedman, and Laffler (who claimed to have invented the Trickle Down Theory) have been proven wrong by all known empirical realities, and their ideas have been relegated to the dump where infected ideas go and should by now be properly subject to ridicule – Kudlow continues to spew forth like the Don Quixote of Financial Darwinism defending the Freedom to lust for greed in a totally unrestricted way.

Kudlow formerly shared a show with Cramer. Cramer, who seems more concerned with seeing himself as objective, may have been too flexible in his views to have shared a show with a total raving ideologue. Kudlow knows a lot about the economics he believes in, but not much about what he doesn't know, and is so one dimensional that he is able to confound objective reality for ordinary fans who do not understand that he is one of the leading cheerleaders for all the Swindlers.

Perhaps his recovering addictions and conversion from Judaism to Catholicism has given him a religious zealot's relationship with the financial Darwinism core ethic of survival of the richest. So Kudlow has an unquestioning belief that trickle down can really work – if given enough time. If given much more time Chicago School trickle down economics would have taken more savings from regular investors and from lots of millionaires to have been converted to the pockets of the ultra rich. And in 2011 with Republicans again touting free-market, self-correcting rational market, self-absorbed greedy babble, the philosophy of Financial Darwinim lives on.

Kudlow's lack of objectivity, as supported by CNBC, allows him to specialize in interviewing reactionary members of the far right, whose self-serving pronouncements sound like Moses inscribing commandments directly on some mountain top. On October 1, 2008 Senator Cobern said, "The root of the problem (the looming meltdown) is political greed in

Congress." He should know. Kudlow responded, "it is time to restore the principles of limited government and free markets that made this country great." Right let's go directly back to survival of the fittest! (As someone who attended USN OCS in 1964, I would have thought Democracy and the concern for individual freedom is what makes this country great – which includes freedom for Kudlow to regurgitate slanted misinformation as gospel,) My question at the end of this book is – great for whom? For everyone at Goldman, for the essential executives at all the failed banks like Citi and AIG and Merrill - or for millions of Americans without jobs and the millions more whose retirement plans have gone up in a cloud of greed. Here are some additional choice **Kudlow truisms directly from his own blog:**

October 27, 2008 – **"I wonder if our free-market capitalist system doesn't really need a nice big failure to reassert its bona fides."**

October 2, 2008 – **"Palin is an energy expert." Let's verify that with members of the McCain campaign.**

July 24, 2008 – **"...media reports painted a pessimistic picture of today's release on existing home sales. But inside the report was an awful lot of good news; in fact, may be the tiniest beginnings of a recovery."** ..."It's a pity the mainstream media keeps searching for more and more pessimism. The reality is a possible upturn in the housing trend, and the very least we are getting a bottom." (The great value of a free market economist's prediction in full frontal view.)

Not long ago anyone who contended that we were on a shaky, egregious-ly leveraged road to disaster was derided and ridiculed by our financial media. Instead of any attempt to disprove the truth, as Plato advised, those who asserted the financial truth were attacked. Peter Schiff, who I believe is fundamentally wrong about his Financial Darwinist beliefs, was completely correct when he asserted our economy was on a certain path to ruin. His interview from December 2007 was on the internet, and conducted at a time when most economists could not conclude that even a small recession was in progress. The most advanced economists were still promoting the myth - the self-correcting free market myth. Logic would term this as Argumentum ad Hominem – ask your lawyer.

Our financial broadcast media uses language to shape thought, and propaganda at the highest level. Stop to think about the conflicts. Is there a conflict to cheer for greed? Who owns the stations and what is their political persuasion and posture toward finding some interest in the common good? Do the owners believe in the fairness of transfer payments, or do they begrudge their fellow Americans social security or a modicum of health insurance?

Is it not an objective good to be for humanity and the public good? Or is this merely too far left? What about the lack of valuing families who are in deep financial quicksand – by the family value Republicans, who are Jesus quoters? Where are the vehement Socratic questions from the main stream media today? They seem to be confined to MSNBC cable and Keith on Al Gore's network. There are a few newspapers left that care about objectivity, but not at the some level as twenty years ago. Perhaps from too much political correctness, or is it just the concentration of power.

Not wanting to share is Financial Darwinism, and wanting to share is not socialism, but humanity.

Lack of objectivity and selfish personal slants in the financial media should be regarded as aiding and abetting the Swindlers. In reality this ought to be identified as a propaganda arm for the ultra rich in their war against the rest of us. And it is worse and more insidious than just a difference in

Philosophy. It is worse than a shill who is a plant to reinforce a slanted self-interested point of view.

If Walter Cronkite or Edward R. Murrow were members of the CNBC team, or the Wall Street Journal, or the deteriorating CNN team today reporting would be either be diametrically different or they would not be allowed on the air because it is not politically correct to be against the hand that feeds. And today there is an enormous concentration of media power in the hands of a few. Edward R. Murrow saved the country from McCarthy and all the mechanically operative spineless citizens who allowed his poison to infect our society. Although, in the aftermath of Murrow's timeless lesson in courage to stand up for truth CBS faltered and Murrow had to leave.

Networks who allow shills and cheerleaders for unfettered greed are responsible for trashing the ethics of the Fourth Estate. They are responsible for not creating objective informed public opinion. Giving a national platform to anyone who rearranges reality by pulling a few facts out of context to make an infinitely slanted point is providing credibility to the wrong side of reality.

There is a well-defined history of the reality of self-serving unbridled Greedy self-interest. Greed brought the government in to Pittsburgh to kill striking workers for Andrew Carnegie. And now, our financial media is too often imbedded in a philosophy that is apparently only for the good of the few which is set in opposition to "for the people." This is what the core philosophy of Financial Darwinism done to our economy and the people trapped in a society of financial immolation.

How many members of our financial media have you heard cry out against the bigness of the Trojan Mega Banks? How many have vehemently and passionately railed against the repeal of the barriers against greed? Who has blamed the tear-down of the barriers well ahead of Freddie and Fannie, and who has called for the rebuilding of firewalls before new regulations can be presumed to be functional? Where is the drive to appoint a Special

Prosecutor to investigate at the upper levels of the Banks responsible for all the malfeasance for fraud? And where has the media been in relentlessly pursuing the context of the truth regarding how anyone can sell an innovative financial product that is – *too complex to explain* – without breaking the law?

CHAPTER **17**

MALFEASANCE – THE OMISSION
OF SIGNIFICANT INFORMATION
CONSTITUTES FRAUD

T o understand the iceberg of malfeasance behind how the Swindlers operated so freely -

it is necessary to summarily revisit an oversimplified snapshot of what happened. First remember that financial markets were providing risk capital to play or fund a shell game.

A normal shell game consists of three shells with one tiny pea which is moved around under one of three shells and then the player bets on their ability to guess which shell the pea is under. The game our financial institutions played was similar except there were 30 to 40 shells with one tiny pea; and this tiny pea was expected to offer a cash return on all the bets which were placed on the shells with the fundamental assumption being that there was no need to find the pea. And this game had terrible odds against guessing right. Far worse than the "Carney" game.

Further, to attract lots of players **the money bet on 40 shells containing one pea was collateralized or backed up to assure the players that if the money bet on the shell game did not work out that the bet would be replaced.**

However, when the tiny peas turned up missing, or became microscopic, and the shells cracked wide open – suddenly it became apparent there was no funding to back up or return the money bet. So trillions and trillions of dollars went down the tubes in spite of t so many representations that all the

CDOs and CMOs had been collateralized or backed up. And again, this encouraged, and enabled investors to conclude their bets were guaranteed, or at least that the risk was lowered. And then investors were provided AAA ratings to further back up the thought of measured low risk.

This chapter must be redundant, because this is a specific call for investigation, and everyone needs to understand the substance of the insidious nature of the Swindle to get mad enough, based on material substance, to petition Congress to do something to protect the public good for the future of our children by properly identifying and prosecuting leading culprits. It is time again for a sea change in how our Congress does business to return to: "of the people, by the people and for the people." There is a war, and this is the time for Americans to rise up and accept the challenge to be great in the name of Democracy and humanity – which are the values and precepts the United States was founded on. It is time to unite with the single purpose of taking our country back from the creationists, from the survival of the richest warriors, and from those who judge everyone but themselves.

Implicit in all the representations (misrepresentations) that risk had been mitigated by – quantifying it (with mathematical risk measurement tools); by collateralizing it (with collateral of no material substance); and by rating agencies granting a AAA seal of approval (without any back up justification) – is the logical conclusion that this process was permeated with deceit. The purpose of the deceit was to sell huge amounts of innovated (*too complex to explain*) financially engineered products securitized to generate a monstrous velocity of transactions from which to produce a stupendous amount of fees. So the fundamental intent of the deceit was to obtain gluttonous amounts of money, to increase profits to pay out, 747-sized bonuses.

Swindled is defined: "to cheat through trick, or device or false statements with the intent to acquire money; to obtain money by fraud or deceit." **The definition of Swindled is essential** to the substance of the premise of this book and must be specifically understood to embrace a clear view of transparent motivations which caused the realities of financial chaos and human suffering that we now must address – and that too many of us, in the US and around the world, must find a way to merely survive.

Further, it is equally imperative to stipulate the meaning of Malfeasance, along with the other definitions that follow, for readers who have not spent their careers in a financial business and possibly more important for those who have. Because if you are aware of the fiduciary obligation the recommender of an investment has to their client, which should be kept in mind when either making a recommendation or giving advice then you understand the significance of Malfeasance.

American Heritage, my favorite guide for word meaning to achieve mutual comprehension, simply defines **Malfeasance** as, **"Misconduct or wrong-doing." Omission** is also simple, **"The act of omitting, to fail to include or leave out."** And implicit in the use of the word "act" is the thought of intent. **Fraud** is, **"A deception deliberately practiced in order to secure unfair or unlawful gain." Significant** is, **"Having or likely to have a major effect." Disclosure** is, **"the act or process of revealing;"** for example it would have been adequate disclosure, from a securities standpoint, to have explained that the collateral backing up the subprime debt mortgage bonds has no substance, no liquidity, no equity, it is nothing more than unfunded promise based on unrealistic and totally optimistic metrics which assume housing prices will constantly trend up.

Because my opinions and contentions, (based on my research and forty years of experience in the securities business) in this chapter are likely to sound contentious to those who are in denial or just plain avoiding the truth it is necessary to have defined the "terms of endearment," before proceeding to Socraticly discuss and fully appreciate why **swindlers should be held accountable with the application of commensurate consequences.** Also, it is important to be critically objective in the use of specific language to eliminate misunderstandings and not mischaracterize the history of what has occurred.

If these terms are simple to understand, as well as supported by a preponderance of legal precedent and case history, then - **why did the people in charge of protecting financial markets and investors not intervene well before the collapse?** There are reasons already stated in this book so I will, for a change, not resort to even more redundancy; however, this is a critical and crucial question.

The mandates for regulatory supervision and authority are peppered with the word intervene, so intervention must be considered a regulatory tool and responsibility. Does intervene mean before financial hari-kari is committed and our economy and citizens are bound by the destruction of their assets and jobs? Or does it mean to wait long enough until, retrospectively, everything becomes clear – like in the case of Madoff. Of course, the SEC can be proud that their prosecution resulted in a conviction of 150 years, however, what about intervention? Who is investigating the SEC and others who should have pursued him into the middle of the unmistakable stench of his implausible lies twenty years ago? Where is the special prosecutor authorized by Congress when you really need one?

After all, we know Congress is prepared to spend tons of money on special prosecutors, even when it seemed on the surface that nothing was really wrong except that President Clinton lost $100,000 on a real estate partnership. Why - because certain members of Congress were out to lynch him. Now the entire economy has been decimated by Greed and unemployment has increased to over 10% with no discernable end in site – it only seems fair to ferret out the culprits.

Culprits are not confined to the SEC. The SEC did overlook its own rules, maybe because it has historically been run by former Wall Street Godfathers or bureaucrats who really do not understand the investment world, as they have been too busy administering compliance with form versus substance. The SEC did not concern itself with the lack of disclosure and the omission of significant information, which was a part of all the financially engineered complexities. The special prosecutor could start by reviewing the Private Placement Memorandums, which securities must have in order to be sold by anyone involved with the CDOs, CMOs, Swaps and Derivatives. To have sold any of the innovative financial products a PPM had to have been given to each and any investor, including counterparties first. So there is a way to search for malfeasance and how the SEC did not get functionally involved with intervention when it should have.

The Fed also did nothing to monitor risk to the banking system as it allowed BHCs to be so intimately involved with CMOs – which Alan Greenspan admitted to not understanding fully. I remember that he was Chairman of the Fed. I wonder if Geithner can explain the stuff no one admits to understanding. (**Do not forget IM-2210-1.** *Communications with the Public About Collateralized Mortgage Obligations (CMOs) ... are complex securities and require full, fair and clear disclosure in order to be understood by the investor,* see chapter 8.) CMOs were overloaded with leverage and too much leverage means banks had too little capital; and that should have signaled that something was amiss. If something was amiss – it was time for intervention.

This fact can be investigated to determine if there was fraud or malfeasance but there should be accountability and consequences. And only for the Americans who trusted representations from Wall Street and Banks, and then wound up paying an unheard of price for their misplaced trust. **It was a critical violation of IM-2210-1 to have sold CMOs and to have had anything to do with something that was and still is** *too complex to explain,* hence to understand. **This is a fundamental reason why I am vehement.** Greenspan still does not understand. The breaking of this rule helped break the banks and the investors and our economy – so there should be a profound level of scrutiny and accountability – not just a TARP bailout for the *alleged* wrong-doers!!!! Hopefully you are beginning to understand why I have beat the too complex excuse into the ground over and over – because it is one of the worst things I have heard in 40 years of being concerned for truth in the wonderful world of investing. **AND WE ALL DESERVE TO BE VEHEMENT.**

If there were PPMs and they were given to investors by Wall Street and the Banks then it should be easy to decide if there was an adequate disclosure of the risks and if there was significant information that was not disclosed. Disclosure for example; that it is not logical to measure risk with math because risk is subjective, therefore not subject to being quantified. Further, there are laws which govern whether it is possible to make an offer to sell any security that cannot be fully explained and therefore understood by the buyer.

Can you imagine that you are approached by someone in the investment business to buy a security and you are informed, it is disclosed, that the security, the financial product is too complex to explain – but that you still may want to proceed at your own risk. Another good example would be to disclose that the AAA rating was given by a rating agency because Wall Street and Banks paid huge fees to get good ratings. Because if the ratings were not good enough to portray safety at the highest level it would adversely affect the rating agency's revenue. And have a dampening effect on the entire market which specialized in selling as much bad debt as could be created. Another good thing to have disclosed would have been that what you are being asked to invest in is too complex to understand. And that is why it will not be fully explained – hey, even our Chairman of the Fed does not understand – so it's OK if you don't. (**Are you mad enough? This is what has happened – it sounds too crazy to be true, but unfortunately it is.**)

If Swaps and all kinds of Derivatives are traded and sold then clearly a PPM should also be required. So how could there have been appropriate disclosure considering that there must have been the omission of tons of significant information. Adequate disclosure would have been to disclose that there was no material collateral to back up anything, and that swaps had no material substance.

This is a **warning** label that would have been spectacularly appropriate – *DO NOT THINK A SWAP IS INSURANCE OR OFFERS ANY MATERIAL SUBSTANCE TO BACK UP YOUR WORSE THAN JUNK BOND DEBT – FUTHER THE AAA RATING IS TO BE DISREGARD AS IT IS A MARKETING SCHEME.*

How about another warning – *THERE IS NO EMPIRICAL DATA IN SUPPORT OF THE EFFICACY OF THE MODERN PORTFOLIO THEORY, IN PARTICULAR DIVERSIFICATION.* Retrospectively, it is crystal clear that diversification has been an abysmal failure; which I specifically addressed in my last book published 20 years ago. (see appendix I)

So if all these financial products were innovated to create a velocity of trades for fees; and if the real lack of substance was not disclosed; and if this significant information was omitted; and further if these financial products of systemic poison were contrived – it is logical, and rational, and just makes sense to conclude this stuff was willfully and intentionally marketed to create profits for Wall Street and Banks. Obviously, without any regard for the impact of all this stuff on the markets, investors, counterparties – or on our fellow Americans. So now we are at 9+% unemployment, but actually closer to 18% real. Jobs are imploding in the public sector with negligible growth in the private sector – which is not a recovery. (The remission seems to be over.)

Suddenly the velocity of fees was illuminated by the New York Times on their front page Friday, July 24, 2009. The headline was - **"TRADERS PROFIT WITH COMPUTERS SET AT HIGH SPEED."** So the Times revealed **a dirty little secret called high-frequency trading**, which allowed computers to execute orders on high speed computers which are 30 milliseconds ahead of other trades based on inside information given by the electronic exchanges as a quick millisecond preview of forthcoming orders. (The Times described this as, "an early glance at how others are trading, and this information is going directly via the electronic exchanges powerful computers to a handful of high frequency traders super powerful computers with "powerful algorithms" which process the inside information in time to beat the slower traders.)

This is a function of yet another failure by the SEC to anticipate what could go wrong when in 1998 it authorized electronic exchanges to compete (ostensibly) with market place exchanges like the NYSE. This offers some insight as to why the average daily volume on exchanges is up 164% since 2005. The SEC is studying this. But all of the prominent security attorneys I have spoken with consider the controlling substance to be akin to inside information – not just front running. And the continuing pattern of the dissemination of advance information makes this form of inside information worse. This is the meat of a special prosecutor appointed by the U.S. Attorney General.

The people who lead all these important financial firms along with the leaders of the rating agencies should be investigated in order to determine what Security and Banking laws have not been adhered to, or have been overlooked, or possibly violated. There must be lessons taught just like the lesson that Madoff represents. There must be a search for fraud along with the backbone to find culpability based on the Truth of what has happened. There ought to be accountability and consequences. I am not suggesting that I know who should legally be called a Swindler. I just know that it feels like we have been swindled because there have been so many professional misrepresentations. And my fellow Americans and all the counterparties who invested without demanding to know why, as well as all the Americans who thought they could buy a house with nothing down, even without enough income to remain current on a mortgage are also responsible.

There is enough blame to go around. Is it greedy to pay an exorbitant price for a house based on the motivation that it can be flipped for a substantial profit in a short time? Is this not also contributory negligence? The giant demand for CDOs and CMOs could not have been satisfied if so many had not foolishly rushed headlong into unaffordable debt. Maybe they were all gullible and naïve, but is it irresponsible to get taken advantage so badly? Is it honest for so many mortgage brokers, who are totally unregulated and probably uneducated, to have placed so many mortgages just because they got paid to satisfy the insatiable appetites of so many lenders to participate in the hurricane of so many fees flying about?

There is a complexity of malfeasance and Congress has abdicated its obligation to have continued to maintain the firewalls which served as a barrier to man's personality problem of giving into greed rather than controlling it. Maybe murder is a human tendency judging from all the wars over economics and religion, judging from all the chaos and killings for no reason – but we know that murder is wrong and we along with society do attempt to control it. Maybe the truly greedy who want more than they can ever spend or need must have a barrier to get their own personality problems under control for reasons which have now become obvious and tangible again – only sixty years after we came out of the Great Depression.

If we are a "Nation of Laws," as so many politicians claim in public when they are trying to look good – then we owe it to our laws to investigate anyone and any entity who may have violated SEC and Banking laws and rules. We owe it to ourselves to logically and accurately determine if what has happened constitutes fraud, and if a special prosecutor finds there has been fraud then we need to have the integrity and strength of character to prosecute anyone responsible for wrong-doing.

Now is the time to tell banking lobbyists to go to hell, because that is where they have placed so many Americans financially! Congress needs to stop seeking the approval of Mega Bank Holding Companies and Wall Street and just decide what is right without a concern for what they think because they all need to be investigated and it is transparent that they only care about what they think and how much money they can make. Unbridled self-interest is the underlying ethic, which is fully justified by a burning belief in Financial Darwinism – and this does not have to be disclosed or debated.

Is Congress guilty of malfeasance if it pays any attention to the self-absorbed lobbyists who fight tooth and nail for the self-serving and totally self-interested who became ultra rich on the backs of their fellow Americans and their counterparties? American taxpayers bailed out Financial Darwinists based on the plan of a former Secretary of the Treasury who was a former CEO of Goldman Sachs and prince of peace in his own right. What is going on?

Don't we have the right to expect consequences for those who caused so much pain? Where is the "Rule of Law" that our Congressional leaders love to refer to?

It is time to call for a Special Prosecutor to head an investigation of the facts which led to being on the brink of financial destruction, or in abject ruins, for so many millions of our fellow Americans.

Investigation is required to conclude there has been fraud. It is not appropriately legal to reach final conclusions from the outside looking in. However, from the abundance of empirical evidence, and after 40 years inside the securities business - I smell deceit, wrong-doing and broken regulations which are broken laws - what about you? It is time to apply the Rule of Law even to Born Again Social Darwinists if it fits! Creationists believe the world was created in six days six thousand years ago – and Financial Darwinists believe the world was created for them to create vast riches - no matter how, because of their fervently religious belief in the survival of the richest ethic.

Again, keep in mind that Swindlers do not care about victims, so we do not need to sympathize with a prince of peace who falls from grace as a result of his own deceit - like Madoff.

CHAPTER 18

EXECUTIVE COMPENSATION, REASONABLE OR DISGUSTING: TAX LAWS PROMOTE BONUSES NOT DIVIDENDS; NO ENFORCEMENT OF IRS SEC. 162(M)

T he growth of Executive Compensation has been unstoppable since the mid 60s and for the past ten years has accelerated like a mushroom shaped cloud. Forty years ago the average compensation for a CEO was 25-30 times the average wage level of the CEO's corporation. By 1980, it was up to forty times. Today it is not unusual for it to be five hundred times. The average workers pay, measured in terms of real dollars has essentially not increased for twenty-five years and is actually lower in buying power than thirty years ago.

Yet Congress could not figure how to "increase" the minimum wage for nineteen years. It is worse than alarming to note that not since 1929 have so few people controlled so much of the wealth. And Michelle Bachmann who wants to be your President, supported by T Party survival of the fittest pawns, wants to "get rid of the minimum wage – to create jobs!"

Congress feigned confusion, in 2009, over how top public company executives could take so much in income. A definition of income from the IRS, based on our tax code, would include all forms of remuneration: fees, bonuses, stock options, deferred compensation and retirement benefits, green parachutes, life insurance, health benefit plans which cost in excess of $40,000, the imputed value of having a plane for personal travel, cars, drivers, and clubs. Congressional confusion is especially bewildering as so many of the companies that fund obscene compensation lost billions and billions of dollars for their companies and at a formidable cost to American taxpayers. There is a long list – including the always blue chip General Electric, the downtrodden GM and Chrysler, AIG, Citigroup, Lehman, Bear Stearns, Morgan Stanley, (National City, my ex bank – and probably your own bank), all the other BHCs including a plethora of other financial institutions and publically held companies.

What if Republicans had torpedoed GM and Chrysler when they did not believe in funding them? (Takes you back to survival of the fittest – doesn't it!) How many more jobs would have gone down the drain?

Bank of America and its high profile acquisition of the failed, but storied, Merrill Lynch were singled out for media scrutiny when soon after the beginning of 2009 it became public knowledge that the failed Merrill was set on paying out bonuses in excess of $12 Billion. This was unusually disgusting when clearly the only money Merrill had was from TARP. And Congress wrung its hands over what to do about this because the public was tossing their cookies at Congress. Congress was going to pass a new tax on the ludicrous $12 Billion and on other outrageous bonuses when it already had IRS code in place to handle just such a piggish event!

Let's keep in mind that Christopher Cox, who was Chairman of the SEC at that time was a Harvard Law grad who had been an editor of the Harvard Law review. Certainly Cox had the intellect and the background to have argued the ridiculous Merrill compensation contract was not enforceable. Cox could have reached this conclusion based on the **sales and corporate practices of Merrill** leading up to their demise - which must have **violated regulations referred to in earlier chapters, as well as numerous regs not mentioned.** Merrill's "irreplaceable traders," traders who specialized in sub-prime derivatives and how to flip all the egregious risk to generate volcanic fees at the expense of their customers and the markets; who were led by their brilliant CEO, could have had their contracts invalidated for breaking the Merrill Bank and so many of their customers!

Merrill, at that moment in history, had a long and well-documented track record of caring only about fees without regard for ethics or investors. Merrill was involved with Enron and helped it park/hide debt to keep it off their balance sheet, along with JP Morgan Chase and Citigroup. Merrill was charged with conspiracy to commit wire fraud, falsifying books and records, and perjury. A number of Merrill executives were convicted in the Enron debacle. **Merrill paid Orange County $460MM in 1994 when Orange County had to declare bankruptcy, primarily because of a "bad mix of interest-rate derivatives."** Merrill was involved with ImClone, not a good story either. Merrill was also a leading proponent of privatizing social security which Austin Goolsbee, a leading economist, estimated would have resulted in $400 billion to $1 trillion of brokerage fees. Clearly if this Republican plan had been approved it would also have cost social security recipients a huge percentage of their retirement benefits. Privatizing was only for Financial Darwinists. Merrill, in 2007, was accused of failing to disclose pertinent information concerning its collateralized debt obligations, or CDOs, mortgaged backed securities in a shareholder derivative lawsuit; and when Merrill CEO Stanley O'Neal left in October of 2007 he took an exit package with him of reportedly $161MM at a time when Merrill had lost over $10 billion for the two proceeding quarters.

Yet the Merrill billions of dollars in bonuses had to be honored under contract law?

No one, including our Secretary of the Treasury T. Geihtner, could determine how to tell Merrill to stuff the $3.6 billion of unreasonable compensation, year end 2008 bonuses, paid for out of taxpayer dollars, at a time when Merrill was a sunken ship wrecked by the weight of having lost all of its capital plus another $40 billion. Of course it would have been impossible for CEO John Thain to understand not honoring a Merrill contract considering he had just spent $1mm to redecorate his office. Nauseating?

It is clear to anyone with an ounce of sense that *unreasonable compensation* was the primary motivational factor in getting swindled. By mid 2009 there was a growing consensus, even in Congress, that compensation must be based on results which can only be measured retrospectively. The results - the enormous compensation, were primarily a function of creating and incessantly flipping a 9.9 earthquake of risk. And the tidal waves continue – pounding into housing and jobs, and shattered lives of all the victims.

Friday, July 31, 2009, Floyd Norris, business Editor of The New York Times Business Day observed that, "...there is **plenty of evidence that no one who counted – traders, chief executives or regulators – understood the risks that were being taken.**" Norris based his absurd contention on a new study by Rene Stulz, originally from Switzerland, a finance professor at Ohio State with bloated credentials, along with Rudiger Fahlenbrach of the Swiss Federal Institute of Technology. Norris said, "...the new study shows that banks run by chief executives with a lot of stock were, if anything, likely to do worse than other banks in the crises." The study concluded that, "Bank CEO incentives cannot be blamed for the credit crises or, for the performance of the banks." Stulz said, **"A plausible explanation for these findings is the CEOs focused on the interests of their shareholders** (bizarre!) in the build-up to the crisis and took actions that they believed the market would welcome."

Norris' unfounded contention must have been a function of being blinded by his respect for the backgrounds of Stulz and Fahlenbrach. Possibly, Norris just did not believe so many other articles run in the Times which provided nothing but empirical evidence to the contrary of the Swiss', very *neutral* conclusions. So two prominent Swiss financial oracles reached a nut job conclusion based on their zealous belief in Financial Darwinism and faith in their own arrogance. And Norris accepted their bizarre and slanted, "study," contention - because CEOs lost money on stock received as compensation. Norris also accepted the lie from the Godfathers that they did not understand the level of risk. (Norris has written numbers of exemplary articles, but should have known better.)

It is insane to think that – the contrivers did not understand the risk of 40-1 leverage collateralized by their own misrepresentations? This is called GREED; and the Swiss have customarily been on the side of Greed and other forms of inhuman behavior because they are so perfectly neutral. Historically the Swiss have not been neutral about being for dictators, cheaters and the ultra rich, or hoarding Nazi Gold!

It is so simple to see how we have "deregulated greed and devalued ethics" (e. henry schoenberger) when you consider the negative impact of and attempts to justify swine compensation.

Certainly we can trust the Swiss, especially after reading *Nazi Gold*, and considering how UBS assisted ultra rich American taxpayers with bogus tax shelters to evade taxes, and paid the IRS a settlement of $780MM. Additionally, in 2010, the **IRS** sued UBS for the names of 52,000 account holders as a part of an **investigation of tax evasion which the Swiss vowed to resist** and fought, because their neutrality was under attack. There ought to be, by now, a heightened awareness of Switzerland's role in international secrecy either for money laundering or tax evasion. It is also instructive to remember that for a multitude of decades Switzerland has been the planet's repository for holding cash out of the light of day for any character in the world who has stolen money from its own citizens as numerous dictators have done. And we should never forget how Swiss banks fought to keep the gold in their vaults extracted from the mouths of all the Jews exterminated in Hitler's gas chambers (see the book *Nazi Gold*.) Germany has spent decades trying to make amends, the Swiss have not changed it seems.

(In September of 2011, UBS is once again in trouble for 2 billion dollars of fraud.)

Contrary to the unsupportable and absolutely ludicrous thought from Stulz that CEOs are focused on the interests of shareholders – these are the

CEOs, **whose** "leadership" (**greed**) caused so many huge financial problems for our country and millions of people in dire financial straits. And these same bank CEOs are still at it, still using FDIC billions and billions for egregiously leveraged proprietary trading to rake in record amounts of compensation. Does it make sense to think that too many took too much risk to make too make – is this not self-evident?

There is a section of the Internal Revenue Service code – Sec. 162 (m) which specifically addresses unreasonable compensation for top executives of publicly held companies by limiting the deduction for remuneration paid only to what the service defines as a "covered" employee to $1 Million per year. This would not apply to the thousands of top traders and bankers; for example, of the nine largest financial firms that in 2008 the year of the collapse, and into 2009 received more than $1MM each, even at Citigroup and Bank of America. So was it logical to accept that if a bank lost billions the CEOs justified this compensation because it was paid to retain their most important people. Clearly, paying out TARP dollars to not lose the morally bankrupt money makers was not in the interests of shareholders of worthless National City Bank stock or the United States taxpayers who bailed them out. I wonder what Stulz would say about this, probably – it's important for the integrity of the financial markets, because we would be lost without all these people who did not, and do not understand the size of the risk of crazy leverage backed up by worse-than-junk bond debt.

I know the following information and discussion will not be warm and cozy reading, but it is necessary to expose the lies, misrepresentations and misunderstandings circulated at the time we were told by an ex Goldman CEO, and Secretary of the Treasury under Bush that if we did not bail out the billionaire bankers and their counterparties with TARP we were doomed. And we were also told there was nothing that could be done about existing "contracts" to compensate the pigs who were directly culpable is creating a financial holocaust. Further, because the underlying core ethic is "survival of the richest," always keep in mind unreasonable compensation is one of the key issues.

Sec.162(m) limits corporate deductions paid to certain executives to $1mm. These limits apply only to publicly held corporations and to compensation paid to covered employees. There are other applicable sections which further define how this section is applied, and neither you nor I want to become tax attorneys, but it is good to know that **Congress does have some existing IRS leverage to deal with swine pay. Think of the tax code as a swine-flu shot.**

Early in 2008, the IRS issued Revenue Rule 2008-13 which signaled the possibility of a change in the services position toward compensation that was not "qualified performance based compensation." As a result, compensation paid to "Covered Employees" in excess of $1MM would not produce a deduction for the public company paying the compensation. The ruling was met with a avalanche of responses from more than 90 law firms who contended the agency's position was incorrect. This ruling is within the meaning of 162(m) (2) for readers concerned with the basis of the ruling. It is of interest to know that the IRS is concerned, even if a Congress full of lawyers, does not know how to tell Merrill that compensation contracts based on potentially fraudulent sales tactics should not be enforceable. Unreasonable compensation is only subject to regulation for "Covered Employees;" and not for the traders or brokers or financial engineers who may have created and flipped all the innovative, hugely leveraged poison into our environment. Maybe the EPA should step in to protect our economic environment, no one else has!

Sec. 162(m)(3) defines a "Covered Employee" to include the CEO and four other highest compensated officers. There is an exception for performance based compensation. To qualify, compensation must satisfy a detailed set of rules, including being based on the achievement of specified pre-determined objective performance goals established by a compensation committee comprised of two outside directors. Everyone knows there is nothing more objective than an outside director. So corporate governance can easily navigate around this and has. I will not burden you with an in-depth discussion of the requirements of Sec.162(m)(4)(c) to be considered performance-based, but they are simply: *outside director - shareholder approval - certification by compensation committee performance goals were met prior to paying compensation.*

So what compensation committee would approve huge salaries and bonuses for executives of companies losing mega billions of dollars, like GM and Chrysler who are still alive because of American taxpayers? Did it make sense that traders of failed companies due to WILD AND CRAZY risks (as a function of wildly speculative volatile leverage approved by leading corporate officers) should have been paid gluttonous bonuses, or given huge severance packages by tanked companies like AIG and Citi, or Merrill?

In August of 2009, Andrew Hall Phibro trader who ran a huge profit center for Citi became the poster boy trader who profited from all the leverage provided by the failed bank. Outrage about too much contractual compensation was centered on Hall who was "owed" $100MM under a 'contract" from Citigroup. And Citi argued vehemently that Hall's contract was covered under contract law without regard for his toxic impact on the taxpayers who were asked to fund his contract. That contract argument makes sense only if your core belief is in "survival of the richest," and executive compensation has somehow faded into the background today – while the Financial Darwinists' fight to not raise the tax rate on incomes in excess of $1MM.

It is not that I am envious or that Americans are necessarily so – it is just that shareholders, investors, customers, and taxpayers are imbedded in or crawling in the ashes of too many financial companies that engaged in immolation which we underwrote by assuming their risk. And we, all of us, have bailed out the companies who have treated their customers, taxpayers and our society the worst.

In addition to Wall Street - are the oligopolistic health carriers who continue to generate disproportionate profits while denying claims, raising premiums through the roof and paying gigantic bonuses, and apparently not adding the profits to pooled claims reserves to either stabilize or lower premiums? I am unaware of United Health has taken its $28 billion from 2010 and used it to reduce premiums based on a huge injection of profits into reserves. That's where underwriting profits formerly went.

The financial deregulation, so many Americans wanted in order to get the government off their back - in reality got the government off the back of the ultra greedy Financial Darwinists so they could climb on all the backs they got the government off of! Free market no matter what means laissez-faire.

Americans who are being taken advantage of everyday by the deregulation still cling to the idea that Capitalism must be free from any government interference – even when the government must interfere at times to protect the public. Capitalism does not have to mean unbridled, unfettered self-interest. Capitalism can mean building better infrastructures in cities; it can mean building great buildings and public projects; it can mean better jet engines and turbines; better more innovative energy efficient planes; and creating new technology or better medicine or breakthrough drugs. It can mean a lot of things, but it should not mean free to fabricate financial innovation at the expense of our entire country. Welch made GE successful by building better products. Goldman made itself rich by building financial products too complex to explain. What if GE jet engines on all the Boeing plains we fly on blew up like all the financial products?

Congress was in a quandary in 2009, and still is trapped in the glare of ultra rich headlights, about disgusting compensation paid to people who so successfully manipulated financial markets and corporations for their own greedy ends. Americans have been betrayed and the betrayal continues. Profit is important and necessary to economic growth, and the ability to become a financial success is part of what has made our country great. Reward for individual excellence and innovation which creates something real is American, but it should not be American to take advantage by diverting capital from real investment into financial investment because the results of all the trading for fees has created unreasonable compensation of such piggish amounts which was unheard of only thirty years ago.

Real Estate developers have created real investments which produced jobs and skylines. The good ones and the great ones, with the help of their kind of financial engineers called architects and real engineers, helped create cities and museums and places to live. Profit does not have to be a dirty word. To amass fortunes by improving our culture and way of life is a positive good. America still has many corporations which have added to our society. Bill Gates and Warren Buffet amassed huge piles of money but not at the expense of shareholders or the economy. Both are examples of compensation which was earned the hard way – not by calling egregious leverage collateralized – when there was no collateral. However Congress chose to go after Microsoft and not Goldman - Microsoft was too big but not the Trojan Mega Bank Holding Companies! Gates did nothing toxic; it seems he only figured out a better way to grow a business than his competitors and his products have provided positive innovation that can be explained.

Although Gates and Buffet are at the top of the ultra rich, they are not part of the war against regular people, when they have pledged billions to help humanity and have expressed that they are for raising taxes for the top tax bracket. Everyone filthy rich is not filthy. And as Americans we can admire success, just not those who take advantage and take out their Greed with as much vehemence as possible.

There is a problem with the enforcement of unreasonable compensation standards because rigid rules do not always fit all large compensation. Compensation flowing from real innovation utilized to create real investment adds to the economy. Compensation flowing from purely financial investment diverts dollars away from the real into the pockets of the contrivers which adds to their net worth but has created nothing but a depression (which too many lying liar economists prefer to call a "Great Recession.") In the final analysis, the lying liars have pronounced the recession is over technically – but truthfully admit that recovery could take five or ten years, while some admit they don't know when. (Because based on Republicans being against everything as well as the idiotic support of some members of the middle class, who I refer to as pawns of the ultra rich – we are not united as Americans.)

Tax laws which have not allowed dividends paid to shareholders to be deducted by corporations has led to retained earnings to fund bonuses which caused stock prices to be based on future anticipated earnings. Regrettably, the **earnings never filter through (trickle down?) to shareholders so the stock market has become a casino to bet on earnings in lieu of a place to invest for cash on cash returns, dividends.** In the 60s and the 70s dividends were subject to a top tax bracket of 90%, so it is easy to see how this tax and the lack of deductibility discouraged the payment of dividends and encouraged an increase in top executive corporate compensation. Then - compensation specialists got into the game. Why? Because greedy executives decided to accelerate their idea of their own personal worth which was unrelated to profits, and all sorts of ways were devised to get around Sec. 162. There still is no mandate to return to price to dividend ratios to relate the value of corporate stock to an actual cash return to shareholders.

In the late 70s "trickle down" economics was born at the University of Chicago based on Milton Friedman's supply side, expansion of money theory which has now been disproven to all economists, except the hard core free market, Laissez-faire zealots – who have been shills for the street and their consultants. Friedman got a Nobel Prize and our country got Reagonomics.

On December 2, 1942, Enrico Fermi, in a hand ball court under University of Chicago's football field, achieved the first self-sustained nuclear chain reaction. Fermi already had a Nobel Prize in physics. By August 6, 1945, there was a mushroom shaped cloud over Hiroshima that rained destruction on Japanese civilians. This was followed within days by another bomb on Nagasaki. On August 15, 1945, Japan surrendered to the Allied forces which stopped WWII in the Pacific, so through the terrible rain of nuclear fallout a terrible part of the war stopped both for Americans and the Japanese.

It took almost 28 years before an economic holocaust (the Wall Street Flu) became a mushroom cloud hanging over the heads of too many people worldwide. So the University of Chicago has played a role in two distinctly different but violent events.

Self-sustained nuclear chain reactions at least produce electricity, but it looks like bad economic theory has also been self-sustaining. So-called Free Market - Supply Side economics led to the acceleration of compensation for the ultra rich, taxes on upper incomes were reduced and there was an enormous shift of wealth creation.

Now, it seems apparent from the context of "Reagonomics" and all of the deregulation which followed, (deregulation in the name of getting the government off the back of "Mainstreet") that this Financial Darwinistic economic theory resulted in a feeding frenzy by Wall Street which gobbled up the retirement plan assets of so many Americans and caused the implosion of banks and galloping unemployment.

The questions to answer now revolve around how to curb man's current propensity to contrive financial innovations designed to provide a feeding frenzy of fees and bonuses for greedy financial gluttons, at the expense of most of us. How can socially engineered tax laws (tax laws to produce social good) be used with wisdom and reason to curb all the unreasonable compensation, as well as be used to encourage real investment again? And how can Congress and the media get past all the misinformation, mistaken ideology and misunderstandings promulgated by zealot Financial Darwinists to reach a symbiotic agreement regarding the need to build a better, more stable financial world based on fairness and common sense? To establish a new dialogue of understanding there must be some emphasis on finding a modicum of self-interest in the common good without destroying our Capitalistic system which has been a positive, creative force for real investment and can be again.

CHAPTER 19

ESTABLISH ECONOMIC FAIRNESS AND STABILITY BY RISING UP AGAINST FINANCIAL DARWINISTS

There is a war against the middle and upper middle class. And this war must be acknowledged and recognized as Financial Darwinism, which David Satterfield noted in the foreword means, "Survival of the richest." Financial Darwinism is the core belief and driving ethic of the right in the US, and is a shared commonality in the world of the ultra rich around the globe.

There is an individual responsibility to listen for whether something makes sense. Our present society has abdicated their individual responsibility to listen for whether something makes sense by trusting in the supposed brains, and deemed professional standards of the infinitely greedy sociopaths with advanced degrees in physics, business and finance who have only been interested in their own needs and wants.

We have been swindled by having made an investor existential leap of faith into the presumption that risk can be quantitatively measured as well as reduced. And this faith-based acceptance of risk reduction contrived to pander to an investor's aversion to risk is a leading culprit along with all the others.

Faith in risk reduction due to the acceptance of Quantitative Risk Measurement by Financial Engineers opened the floodgates to getting ripped off by greedy, implausible investments in geometric leveraged 'instruments," to place bets on. Because Greed still rules, we continue to bet on the direction of indexes and derivatives and anything in the futures market.

215

We allowed banks to bet on insurance for the uninsurable, which never made sense, but it was justified with phony math. Although it clearly did not work, Wall Street Banks' array of financial engineers is still doing their thing. If AIG could have gotten away with it and made any money - it would have insured the outcome of a horserace, a rat f—k, a baseball game, and why not the probability of its own swaps being able to provide any semblance of insurance. Keep in mind, insurance is supposed to have reserves, and life insurance is the only insurance based on stable actuarial tables due to appropriate underwriting' and mortality tables which statistically have provided future predictability for well over 100 years. There are no other tables which offer equivalent statistical relevance.

Investor, Congressional and regulatory faith in risk reduction and acceptance of quantitative risk measurement was to accept a fundamental Wall Street ruse (LIE) – that our free market (Laissez-faire market) is self-correcting as a function of the rational market lie. And acceptance of the rational market fable enabled the greedy, heavily bonused Wall Streeters and Bankers to take advantage of investors as well as their own disciples. Acceptance of their own lies was, perhaps, a reason how so many so-called brilliant Wall Streeters and bankers allowed themselves to be duped by their phony excuse, by their own self-interested, unbridled greed.

All the self-proclaimed astonishment at all the "unseen risk" – which created the vast abyss of financial losses, clinically termed "toxic assets," was/is a vast lie. The hubris of the greediest, most self-absorbed, apparently narcissistic sociopathic financial rulers of the kingdom of Wall Street and Banks allowed them to join together to form a collusive wall of misrepresentations to culture personal wealth from their contrived and tote board-like markets. Possibly, like Andrew Carnegie, they thought it was their manifest destiny to become a member of the billionaire's club.

Billionaires, Multi Nationals, Global Banking Giants and wannabe billionaires organized important parties and gave money to charities, **and**

bought important art - and important politicians! They lobbied behind the scenes like mafia Godfathers to get their own way – and still do! Unlike mafia Godfathers, who it seems from movies, possibly killed for a reason (whether right or wrong,) financial Godfathers have killed our country's economy and assisted in killing the global economy laying waste to tens of millions of lives – which is Social Darwinism revisited as financial.

We know killing is wrong and we learned from history books that Social Darwinism was wrong. However, our financial Godfathers left their father's or grandfather's Depression psychosis behind as fast as they could repeal rules designed to protect future generations from the greedy, self-destructive excesses of their grandfather's generation. Do you remember that Dr. Phil (Graham) called US citizens "whiners." And he was one of the leading culprits having dreamed up Credit Default Swaps while he ushered the repeal of Glass-Steagal through Congress. Financial Godfathers never cease their maneuvers to maintain their kingdom at the expense of our treasury.

In 2009, Goldman sold its $13 Billion stake in rancid AIG "instruments" for a dollar on the dollar; $13 billion of new dollars for $13 billion of toxic dollars, because one of their former Godfathers was put in charge by a President named Bush and then aided and abetted by Congress, drove the cash to Goldman's safe-deposit box. So Goldman was bailed out for its collusion with AIG, as well as a number of other guilty firms who have also been enablers. Goldman drove the primary get away car by being more successful at selling more than the others and flipping faster.

If this is beginning to sound like a Shakespearian tragedy, let's hope the shelf life is not as lasting as Shakespeare's. Although I am not a wizard with a clear view of the future it seems that **until Congress and investors stop equating important credentials and the largest piles of money with reason and wisdom as well as continue to buy into the self-interested, greedy pronouncements of Wall Street Banks, we are doomed to repeat this** scenario. **We are doomed to a Social-Financial Darwinism culture. And past will remain prologue.**

Questions must be asked like:

- Would it not be better to regulate the **substance** of all the leveraged "financial products" Wall Street Banks are still allowed to sell? (Reform, humbug!)

- Is it really okay to sell swaps – is it okay to bet on swaps or leverage? (Not prudent no real justification!)

- Is it really possible to insure against the risk of geometric leverage? (Come on!)

- Are some risks uninsurable; like people with cancer that has metastasized, you can't get life insurance with cancer; and you can't get fire insurance when flames are crackling on your roof; physicians who take even the smallest amount of a drug for depression or stress cannot get disability insurance; pyromaniacs cannot get fire insurance; and houses built on Old Faithful would have a tough time getting volcano insurance. But AIG, along with so many others, insured crappy, geometrically leveraged debt - and Goldman along with all the other respected investment houses "never realized there was so much risk." (Depressing!)

- How can unmitigated leverage be insured – leverage so essentially egregious that even Wall Street could not sell it - unless it included bogus insurance? (Nuts!)

- And if there are insured uninsurable "financial instruments" issued, does not the lack of disclosure constitute fraud? Swaps without **meaningful reserves** are implicit misrepresentations; does not the omission of this significant information and lack of disclosure constitute fraud? What about the grave misrepresentation from financial engineers and everyone who participated in selling the idea that subjective risk can be measured quantitatively? Where are the investigations, all the jail sentences? (Yes!) Bernie Madoff is finally in jail, but 25 years late.

- Where have our regulators been? They were not merely asleep at the switch. They were enablers of the great velocity of illicit securities issued for fees. They allowed the vast amounts of profits to proliferate for a few at the expense of the markets they were supposed to protect! Where is the admission of abject failure? Do regulators not understand the substance and intent of the law and regs because they have chosen to focus on rules versus the substance of what Godfathers have contrived to look like low risk financial instruments to sell for fees rather than provide future financial viability for investors? Where did all the firewalls go? It is self evident that regulators were in the pocket of the *uber riche* who hired them as shills – as their consultants, speakers and writers of professional position papers.

- **Was high frequency computer trading not front trading – is the controlling substance not INSIDER TRADING? This has still not been finally corrected.**

- **Where have the tough follow-up questions been – from Congress, from the media, from the regulators, where? When the new regulators were among the culprits, what do you expect? Congress was there as well, interviewing Greenspan for reassurance!**

Why has Congress allowed regulators to promote the empty promise of diversification without question? And why has Congress participated in all the lies about how the SEC, FINRA, nee NASD, and Wall Street can possibly self-regulate their own self-interest let alone unbridled self-interested greed? It is self-evident in the aftermath of the Great Depression that Wall Street self-regulation did not work, does not work, and cannot work. To depend on the self-regulation of greed just does not make sense – just like it does not make sense to argue that the world is flat or the holocaust did not happen.

So there is a critical need to finally identify all the symbiotic factors which created the Great depression-Recession of 2008, to understand why we remain stuck in its continuing aftermath like a small boat caught up in the wake of the Titanic. There is a critical need to acknowledge the continuing human tragedy of enormous unemployment, no real job growth and foreclosures stemming from the deregulation of greed and the devaluation of ethics. There is a need to recognize the greed or delusions of homeowners who knew better than to buy unaffordable houses, and homeowners who could have been OK if they had not refinanced to buy things that they could not afford.

We must find the political will to rebuild barriers to greed and enforce regulations in place that do no allow the salting any of mine necessary to help create piggish fees and bonuses for survival of the richest practitioners. We need to correct a tax code that favors the ultra rich and recognize there is war against the American Dream.

And understand that this financial tragedy is a human tragedy for so many millions of our fellow Americans as well as fellow human beings across the planet who live in the shadows of quiet desperation.

We live in a country where Republicans think they subscribe to a specific Republican philosophy and Democrats have a philosophy too. But too few know enough about economics to have seen through Alan Greenspan's, Milton (*Croatian Bafflegab*) Friedmanomics, or Jack Kemp's early onset economics; early onset to forget about what led to the Great Depression.

Congress did not know, (feigned ignorance?) why rules and regulations, and the **Firewalls** were designed and constructed to prevent greed from taking over Banks and Wall Street again. They did not know because they were more concerned with money from lobbyists to get elected and stay elected. Prominent economists did not know because they were paid consultants of Wall Street. And no one connected the flow of so much money away from the middle class (and the upper middle) to the core ethic of Financial Darwinists? The most influential never connected the indefensible opinions of their financial experts, almost all from Wall Street or favored cousins of families, to all the money to be made from unrestricted free markets – just like prior to the Great Depression?

To successfully recover from so much financial innovation it is vital to recognize the motivation behind the "philosophy of Laissez-faire unfettered free markets, and acknowledge that markets cannot be self-regulating, because they are SELF-SERVING.

We need to realize that our Financial Godfathers willfully and intentionally contrived innovation to culture fees! They knew about all the egregious killer leverage but they did not care what havoc it had to cause! They told each other in interoffice emails that the stuff they were selling was "shit!" So never believe they were dumb enough to not know how much risk they sold for their own enrichment, and then flipped to get rid of the risk. They thought they could pass the risk off without getting haunted in return due to their self-inflated hubris; which is worse than stupid. BUT THEY GOT AWAY WITH IT!

Faith-based economics and faith-based investing has allowed the Evangelic-like leaders of Wall Street and Banks to have their way with the dollars of all their investors (stockholders are investors.) It sounds sort of biblical – so did the justification for Social Darwinism, which has morphed into Financial Darwinism. Keep in mind that Financial Darwinism is based on the financial ethic of survival of the fittest. And this practice has been at the expense of everyone else, because the "fittest" only care about their own self-interest. (Their saving grace may be that they have not used mustard gas.) However with the advent of the Republican Governors' collusion to destroy unions, led by the strong "leadership" of the Republican Governor of Wisconsin, Social Darwinism is not dead.

We need to establish a no-fly zone over Financial/Social Darwinism, which is what Glass Steagall and the 1956 Bank Holding Company did!

Books have been written about some of the individual factors which led to the gigantic meteor of imploding leveraged instruments which splattered like a moon-sized meteor into our global economy. However, because there are so many symbiotic culprits, who are intertwined, co-joined - even co-mingled - it is not possible to truly understand the context of what has been so wrong and continues to exist by just blaming: Wall Street Investment Bankers; or Banks; or Insurance Companies; or Freddie and Fannie; or Congress; or the Fed; or the SEC; or Financial Engineering; or the Modern Portfolio Theory; or investors searching for the promise of safety; or that risk can mathematically measured and identified, managed or reduced mathematically; or the abuse of language. (Whew!)

A micro understanding of the parts is fine; however, the macro overview this book provides is the only way to understand the interrelationships of the parts to functionally understand the brilliance, and insidious nature of the swindle. It is my intent that when you have finished reading you are left with more than a profound impression of how wrong this has been. Hopefully, you will be left with more than a sense of outrage. I hope you will have a burning intellectual desire in your guts for a new direction, a direction which will be more ethical, functional, lasting and just makes sense.

The past is prologue unless we learn from past mistakes – and the sum of the parts in this book equals the whole. And the whole adds up to a 30-Year War against the American Dream.

If I were in college today or just coming out, I would feel betrayed to find out that the Laissez-faire economics of the Chicago School is still taught by economists with PhDs. Shouldn't these PhDs know that Laissez-faire was clearly revealed in the aftermath of the Great Depression to have been wrong - to have been for the survival of the fittest. Today many professors, perhaps unwittingly, still teach economics that is only for the survival of the richest.

And this inability to critically rethink what was learned in error continues to enable the flow of fees for Wall Street and the ensuing political contributions from many corporations and the monopolistic health carriers. How can this make sense?

We have all heard a lot about the importance of investor confidence, but nothing about investor gullibility. There have been timeless dialogues devoted to analyzing market psychology - but not much about **how Wall Street has preyed on the psychological need of humanity to receive assurances that the insecure nature of investing is under control.** (Where's the sense?)

For the past 40 years that I have been in the securities business, regulators have required that new customers identify their "risk tolerance" as if low, medium, and high make sense. Media stock market shills talk about risk and "risk measurement tools," but never identify or raise the question of how can it be valid to measure risk quantitatively. Regulators have never questioned the egregious, fallacious substance, or lack of any logical basis, for quantifying risk. No one I know has questioned the generally accepted practice of assuaging man's deep-seated fear of the unknown through the use of strategic risk measurement contrivances (tools) which have become a self-propagating and integral part of our "free market," "free" enterprise system of self-delusion. **Clearly man can not be left entirely alone to deal with controlling his own greed.**

There exists a cult-like group of **Republicans** remaining in Congress who are **joined in lock step** to never acknowledge that "free" has been at a tragic, unaffordable price to the vast majority of their fellow Americans – including me. "The Free Market will correct itself" is only a redundant ruse promulgated by Wall Street Godfathers. If the tone of this book is redundant, it is because of the redundant nature of Financial Darwinism and redundancy is important to any learning process, especially if the message is different than what is commonly agreed upon – no matter how wrong.

223

If I am angry it could be because I wrote about what needed to be addressed twenty years ago in my first book; and I have watched it happen for the past twenty years. I know I am not alone, but it is borderline nutty to be a voice of reason (even for someone in Congress) in a sea of greed, backed up by the power of a mountain of wealth. And this current **Republican lock step extends to Health Care**, because nothing that makes sense for humanity makes sense to a huge majority of Republicans, so **making sense is stuck in gridlock.**

Deregulation free market lies have easily been extended to blocking an appropriate Health Care bill. Crazy objections like Republican members of the House and Senate calling a Single Payer approach a socialistic government takeover of health care to rally their base of tax cutters no matter what - when these Republicans all have government supported health care, making socialism OK for them. And the socialism lie was parroted by the masses who clamored to see Obama's birth certificate; as well as so many others who did not have a clue that the Republicans apparently only care about self-interest and care about avoiding and denying objective facts.

Many Democrats did not defend the health care bill that was passed so had reelection problems for attempting to appease the idiots who believed in the socialism crud. (Crud is stuff at the bottom of a cesspool.) Certain limited forms of socialism may just be for the public good like health insurance, and allocating some tax dollars for transfer payments, so some children can eat a "free" lunch at school.

Why are there so many idiots who have no awareness of any functional economics? And how can these idiots adhere to the self-evident lie that lowering taxes has provided jobs in the face of the reality that taxes have been more than cut in half since 1980 while millions of jobs vanished. Twenty million jobs were added during the Clinton years but to reason from lowered taxes rather than understand a number of other significant and controlling factors is to miss the forest for the trees. One answer is that our public education is in decline which must be recognized as part of the job problem.

Another part is the proliferation of idiots, who are fellow Americans who prefer their own unfounded opinions rather than objective analysis.

During the past thirty years CEO, compensation climbed from 40 times the average wage rate to the stratosphere – 400 to 1,000 times. So how dumb is it to live in a coma of ignorance to remain pawns who are duped by "survival of the richest" Republicans - who are fervently against raising the richest who earn over $250,000, or $400,000. How many T-Partiers make that much, yet they have signed a pledge to not raise taxes (revenue) no matter what.

Never have the duped or the infinitely self-interested acknowledged that it only makes sense to raise the rate (go back to the post-Bush rate, better, the Reagan rate which was much higher) for incomes in excess of $250,000. Why not at least eliminate subsidies for the richest companies that indulge in price gauging at the gas pump? And why not tax corporations that avoid taxes offshore or by not bringing their profits back into their own country? Remember this kind of Greedy self-interest is at the core of Financial Darwinism, a belief system that has permeated our existence, and has infected everything. Do you really think that allowing tax avoidance creates jobs; do you think that the most successful are motivated to retain earnings - or motivated to have provided jobs, or to replace workers with robotics? (Multiple choice?) If a company is domiciled in the US then why is it OK to not tax retained earnings held outside of the country? What about a public discussion about the impact of the macro wage level on jobs in our country?

What about the terrible price we have paid for deregulation to have freedom for Financial Darwinism to flourish? What about the terrible price we have paid to deregulate chemicals in food, and allow GMOs, hormones, anti-biotics, high fructose corn syrup to the point that 50% of us are obese and we cannot export our food to many countries?

Democrats have failed as well to identify deregulation as the unraveling of crucial laws specifically designed to protect the public good from the ravages of greed – ravages which were clearly evidenced in the last Great

Depression. Where was the liberal outrage over Credit Default Swaps from 1999-2000, or in all the ensuing years? Almost no one had the guts or vision to even warn Americans or the World of the inevitability of a massive, nuclear-like train wreck, a wreck caused by financial products and a total lack of any fiduciary responsibility by all the important people who sold contrived products rather than investments. Unfortunately we equate the ability to think with advanced degrees.

In 1990, my first book, *Invest for Success*, compared investing in financial investments with "financial masturbation." Masturbation is OK if you do not want to create anything real but if future viability is a goal, if you want to create something real in the future then financial masturbation is not a good approach. And all the reassurances in the world will not make something real if it is not based on substance, but contrived to be easily sold. The most substance in the last 20 years went into the pockets of all the contrivers, and no one said anything until the contrivances failed.

The psychology of the Market is to provide reassurances which are accomplished by the repetition of implausible numerological theories fabricated to prop up confidence to keep investors in the game.

The stock market is the real casino game in this country. Casinos in Las Vegas and Monaco are regulated. Why do you think there is a bell ringing at the opening every day with people clapping gleefully – because they are about to get fleeced or because "investors" are being offered a chance to get in on all the gold, like getting in on the "Good News" and rising into the heavens to be closer to god, just like Jesus did.

Our Financial Godfathers have risen as measured by their piles of wealth just like casinos have risen on the desert – as a testimony to all the losers and suckers. The difference is that you are not allowed to count cards in Vegas and there is an illusion you can count cards in the market.

Geniuses like Cramer told investors how to make money on Wall Street every day on cable. I am not slamming Cramer, who seemed concerned about his own remorse. However, he, like so many other members of our "savvy financial media – the CNBC gurus" did not focus their important intellect on leverage of 30 to 40 times the capital base of banks, or how brokerage houses use your stock, held in street name, as their own asset base. Brokerages call your money their asset while they keep all the profits as fees and bonuses.

What if the investment banks had retained some earnings? Merrill, even at the end in 2008, shoveled out billions in bonuses in 2009, while we/taxpayers' bailed out their greedy stupidity. The essential lack of truth about the Wall Street Casino is self-evident.

In the glare of daylight, a large number of our most successful Wall Street Godfathers and Bankers appear to be swindlers – not exactly like Madoff, but nevertheless – in their own way worse because they have Swindled hoards of their fellow Americans out of their retirement assets, college funds and their jobs. A swindle also takes place when financial "investments" are contrived to look like something they are not.

Consider it was not disclosed to the "sophisticated counterparties" that what they were advised to do was invest in *tranches* of lousy untenable loans, backed up AAA bogus ratings, or by more untenable debt or swaps which had no value. And the counterparties were bailed out too, although their greed allowed their sophisticated experience to be duped into believing the lies of the greediest. Why not have a new rule that currently reinvented Swaps must be audited and assigned value by an enrolled actuary, and rated (by whom?) before they are allowed to exist.

Until Congress provides meaningful rules with appropriate Firewalls (again) and the leadership to eliminate the bigness and resultant complexities that confound Regulators who may be brilliant economists, but who do not think clearly with an ingrained sense of fairness and ethics (like Paul Krugman) we will not be on a secure path to financial fairness.

Until Congress, Regulators and the Fourth Estate (members of the press and media) along with everyone in the US who has invested in any type of security - stocks, bonds, real estate or mortgage debt, or any type of derivative gets rid of the ideas that: it is possible to insure against or reduce risk with high-tech quantitative measurement tools; or that it is possible to "hedge risk" (what in the hell does that mean?) silly stuff – our country's financial future will not be positioned for long term rationality. Until raters care about protecting the public and there are new regulations with teeth to enforce this - ratings will be meaningless and will remain part of our Wall Street Godfathers' protection racket. Until Congress removes the god-given Free Market right to securitize (sell) unmitigated leverage and then bet on the future of crappy 30-1, or higher, leveraged debt while hurling derivatives into the stew in addition to anything else which the market can bet on to generate fees - we will remain lost.

When hedging makes sense used as a ruse to camouflage the true nature of the risk and lack of substance of all the "complex financial products" we remain lost.

Regulators must learn questions to ask to search for substance; and listen for whether arcane verbal behavior is merely professional jargon designed to sound financially well- educated to elicit market and investor acceptance, (like a Pavlovian response). Regulators must conclude that all verbal and written explanations of any security must provide meaningful understanding and insight, in excess of mere disclosure. This would be infinitely more functionally protective than disclosure to remove labiality for the issuer - which is the real purpose of disclosure in practice. Ask any attorney, because you will learn that attorneys are more concerned with their own liability – than their client's.

Regulation will not be fixed by tinkering with the regulators, or by establishing a "Super Regulator," or by merging regulators into a larger entity. Then you would have a MEGA REGULATOR which is akin to a

Bank Holding Company. The bigness that has done us in is just what BHCs want so regulators can be confused by coping with their bigness while striving to preserve their vast complexities. Bigness has become so complex that very few individuals who work at regulation have the capability or capacity to understand and deal with what they are charged with regulating.

Therefore, it ought to be painfully clear today, as it became clear in the 1930s, that BIGNESS and the fabricated-contrived, innovated financial products bigness spawned for fees must go. And in the Fall of 2011 banks are doing whatever possible to avoid regulation in the name of preserving "free market capitalism." Lobbyists are hard at work and 600 trillion dollars of derivatives are out there waiting to implode with the fury of Noah's mythical flood.

Firewalls must be built again (I know, redundant!); and it is time to say no to all the too complex to explain financial products. This is the most rational solution and the one solution that the Bank Holding Companies and Insurance Companies fear the most – because that will charge them with the responsibility to act responsibly and prudently, once more, and generate profits from the real rather than the contrived. Fees will be less, but who really needs to be worth $1 Billion or more? Should banks not be required to provide economic stability rather than exist to make as much money for their own purposes as possible?

Everyone has an individual responsibility to stop buying the idea that mathematical theories or financial tools (like diversification which has failed miserably) which hold out the promise of risk reduction or measurement can make sense. Regulators ought to know this but they are "heavily creden-tialed" and share the same professional, beyond common sense, nomencla-ture of their brethren who they are charged with the responsibility of regulating. Besides, how could a former COE of Goldman, like Paulson or Rubin, not buy the financial engineering acumen of his own former partners? The empty promises are now self-evident and it makes sense to consider how too many of us have invested with blind faith in tools and silly, mathematically incorrect theories. Too many invested with unquestioning belief.

The blind acceptance of, or faith in fallacious financial engineering theories and arcane nomenclature is a major perpetrator behind how Wall Street Godfathers and Banks were able to sell all the financially engineered "products" – innovation which must be perceived as crazy-obscene leverage. Our financial engineering schools and our acceptance of financial innovation has created nothing real except for what should be termed a Depression. Certainly our Great Recession is unlike any recession since *the Great Depression*, the title of J. K. Galbreath's book which apparently was not read in all the important Ivy League Masters programs for all the morally bankrupt "engineers." We should have learned from the Great Depression that more cash coupled with less debt equals less risk. And more speculation equals more risk and more volatility.

To go forward there must be recognition and acknowledgment of the substance of all the guilt and lack of remorse – not remorse about losing $1 Billion of your $2 Billion, as the founder of AIG expressed on MSNBC one morning in 2009. Congress, along with the rest of us, and all the agencies in charge of protecting the public good must start asking hard questions, and not only question all the lies – but yell at the liars. Comity has not produced any public good for over a decade.

The media could do a much better job of following up the superficial answers and outright implausible excuses as well as the lies, BECAUSE it has provided public platforms for the culprits to maintain they - "did not realize there was so much risk in the system," and that they really did not understand their own innovation? The Godfather Swindlers, along with the getaway car drivers, need to be investigated, and if found guilty charged with securities fraud and racketeering (or whatever our Attorney General thinks fits the crime) for critically damaging our financial system, millions of investors as well as the human fabric of our society. We need to remember **Swindlers do not care about their victims.**

From 40 years of personal experience licensed in the Securities Business, and with a principal's license, believe me the violations were crystal clear if regulators wanted to have enforced the substance of their own rules. A regulation has the force of law - so if a regulation is broken the law has been broken. There must be a return to value investing to create something of substance to invest in. We must reject and outlaw all the flimflam contrived schemes if we want to improve the present for us and the future for our children and their children.

No more unexplainable derivatives, no more complex financial products, and no more Swaps. (Keep in mind there are 600 TRILLION DOLLARS OF DERIVATIVES LOOMING OVER US!)

If any investment is too complex to explain – then it should not be allowed, which is simple to explain and easy to understand! No more blaming Wall Street Godfather's lobbying for the deregulation of rules designed to protect us from Financial Darwinists. All Congress has to do is just say no to survival of the richest. Does Congress use heroin because Afghanistan wants to improve its export business with the US as a trading partner?

We must recognize the existence of Financial Darwinism as the evil force that has infected our society much as Social Darwinism did one hundred years ago. And we must acknowledge the behavior spawned by their core ethic of survival of the richest has manifested its presence as thirty years of war against the fabric of the American Dream.

The tearing down of the middle class has cost our society over fifteen million jobs. And this is directly related to the consumer demand necessary to encourage big and small business, the private sector, to invest in an expansion of plant and equipment as well as services that will create the jobs necessary to meet increased demand. This, of course, also results in more taxable income which creates more government revenue to reduce the deficit. However at this time we are in a state of limbo because of the lack of understanding of basic economics and ignorance of the lessons that have been learned from the Great Depression by the Tea Party joined by numerous Republicans, members of the press and our fellow Americans who cannot reason or think past slogans.

We must be open to what we ought to have learned in the aftermath of the Great Depression. Most of us realize that sometimes it makes sense to borrow to invest if the payback is realistic. And now we know the private sector, which is ruled by the survival of the richest ethic entirely based on self-interest, has shown no interest in creating jobs without demand. It is clear the private sector will not invest. Because the private sector will not step up to the line in its absence, and by default only the Government will and can protect our economy by investing in the necessary repairs and improvements to public infrastructure deterioration. Only the government can step up to this line. Only the government will fund high speed train service - which could produce a profit, as it has elsewhere. Only the government is charged with the role and responsibility to protect the public.

The deficit is not the real issue today. Investment in our country is the real issue, and now is the time for politicians to acknowledge what is necessary and have the guts to fight to have their fellow Americans understand, notwithstanding all the waste, lobbying and self interest Congress has caved into to either get elected or remain in office. If Congress just says no to all the lobbyists there is a good chance that Americans may begin to trust again.

Leadership is to navigate successfully across the finish line. It does not mean sticking a small finger out into a light breeze to measure the wind to decide upon your tack, direction. Like sailing – it means steering a steady and rational tack to get across the finish line. It does not mean taking an opinion poll from all the boats without navigation instruments, and then embark in a direction to follow all sorts of sailboats going the wrong way in shallow water. To follow boats without a qualified captain or anyone on board who can read a chart, or a depth meter or even notice enormous icebergs is senseless. Yet that is what has been happening in Congress. The Tea Party and most Republicans are apparently clueless about the value of investing in a better direction and seem to prefer to remain in irons – which is sitting still in the middle of the ocean without a breath of wind, and refusing to turn on the engine to get to a better place, because they do not want to waste gas. We are in irons and the Government could turn on the engine and run long enough to go in a better direction.

It's time to make sense for a change. It is time to step out of this mess into the daylight to at least establish a mission – a new path to find some common sense and some self-interest in the common good. Thomas Jefferson said the role of government is to protect the public – where has it been?!

CHAPTERS FROM INVEST FOR SUCCESS, HOW TO AVOID GETTING RIPPED OFF BY REAL ESTATE PARTNERSHIPS, THE STOCK MARKET, AND DIVERSIFICATION RIVERRUN PRESS, 1989

A. The Modern Portfolio Theory of Investing A Posture Toward Ignorance (Chapter 3)

As long as there has been history, man has searched for some view of the future. The unknown can provide us with a crippling layer of uncertainty which, at times, interferes with reality available in the present.

Kings in the Middle Ages had Wizards. Wizards relied upon crystal balls and all sorts of low-tech tools (which at the time were perceived to be high tech) to forecast future events in order to avoid tragedy and doom. One of the primary jobs of all Wizards was to turn lead into goal in order to enrich the kingdom. This, retrospectively, was the most universal failure of all Wizards.

In modern times, man has been no less concerned with forecasting. Historians justify the study of history to better understand the present and to avoid, in the future, mistakes from the past. This concern is primarily a human and societal concern; and because this involves principles and ethics and group behavior, it may have more relevance than society seem willing to utilize.

Since the Industrial Revolution, and as we are no longer involved with a barter guild economy, man has become obsessed with economic future. As our daily struggle for survival has been replaced with a struggle for wealth, our concern for financial success has overshadowed most other basic needs.

Business cycles have become more important than fires, religious wars, or plagues. Some of the best minds of the 20th century have devoted their lives to the study of economics and finance. Economics is, certainly, more concerned with human needs and wants than finance. Finance, on the other hand, seems to approach life not even through rose colored glasses but through numbers; and numbers are high tech, so it is a neat past time.

People do not count, societal considerations are not an issue – all that matters is how to best culture money without regard for philosophical considerations. To culture money, we are willing to close down marginally profitable factories in small towns all over our country. Closing factories closes down lives. To culture money in the present we are willing to become the largest debtor nation in the history of the world, and to culture money we are now willing to view black mail as green.

In this kind of culture, it is understandable how The Modern Portfolio Theory of Investing (MPT) became acceptable. Doctors of Finance, who worship numbers above the needs of human beings, had a new high-tech approach to personal invesing, a high-tech tool that did not depend on common sense or wisdom but upon numbers and even provided computers with input. Although computers were sort of new, Doctors of Finace had a sense, from the beginning, of the need for input material in order to be able to look forward to printout.

The only difference between Doctors of Finance and Wizards is that Wizards used lead and crystal balls and Finance PhDs use numbers and computers. Wizards were specialists who turned lead into gold, and Finance Doctors turn numbers into gold. Ironically, often the reliance upon numbers turns gold into lead!

The Modern Portfolio Theory of Investing (MPT) rest upon the assumption that different types of securities do not move in sync; and when portfolio risk is measured by the standard deviations of combined returns, portfolio risk can be reduced without giving up returns.

MPT is based upon the primary assumption that different markets containing different types of securities will move relative to each other in an opposite direction; i.e., when stocks are up, gold is down. In other words, opposite relative movement translates into standard deviations. **THIS ASSUMPTION IS NOT TRUE BUT TOTALLY FALLACIOUS.**

The fallacy of the primary assumption is that the future contains and infinite number of variables, many driven by human emotions – so valid future predictability as a function of number-crunching variables known in the present is logically absurd, as the future contains in infinite number of unknowns which cannot be quantified.

If the primary postulate of a theory is not true or not logical, the proof, even if logical is irrelevant!

At the time MPT was postulated in 1952 by Harry Markowitz PhD Finance, it was criticized by other Finance PhDs (a mark of some integrity); but when the investment community became aware of the marketing potential offered by MPT, criticism dissipated. Consider the value of a theory which depended upon diversification and numbers rather than on experience, wisdom or common sense. MPT would allow any idiot to sound professional and provide constant product through the magic of diversifica-tion. A new, important money culture dish was available, and investment people were prepared to push investors in.

Prior to 1952, and after the Great Depression, financiers had argued that one should pot eggs into only a few baskets – but only at a time when everything that could be known was know about the basket, only at a time when the basket was cheap, and only at a time when there was great value in the basket but when this value was, generally, overlooked, not wanted, and definitely undervalued! Bernard Baruch postulated this "unnoticed value" approach to investing. Baruch even advised waiting with cash for a market to break significantly – to be able to then pounce upon unpopular but obvious values. There is a about Baruch that, prior to the crash of 1929 – his shoe shine boy had offered a hot stock tip to him. This event convinced him to get out of the stock market, prior to the crash, as rampant greed leads to bloated prices with no value as everyone jumps on greed's bandwagon! People would rather die than get left out.

In this book I argue against diversification and for value. Portfolio people talk about price to earning ratios – what about price to dividend ratios? Assumed relationships of standard deviations, price to earning ratios, and asset allocation considerations based on diversification, timing, and econometric models do not focus on or reveal real, current values or future real potential value. DO NOT EVER GET TRAPPED INTO THINKING DIVERSIFICATION WILL DO ANYTHING BUT AVERAGE RISK – DIVERSIFICATION DOES NOT REDUCE OR MINIMIZE RISK! Diversification only spreads risk by investing in variety!

Acceptance of numerical theories has become so widespread under the surface of things that passive investors do not question where recommendations come from or why they are valid. Presumed future potential values forecasted by numbers contrived to predict the future offer illusory reasons for recommendations. The people who make these recommendations, who are aware of and operating by MPT-driven recommendations, do not stop to think about the true nature of numbers. AS THERE IS AN INFINITE NUMBER OF VARIABLES IN THE FUTURE, THE PREDICTABILITY OF NUMBERS DECREASES AS VARIABLES BECOME REAL.

We live in a forward liking economy and do not introspectively view, in the present, the nearsighted approaches we manufacture to cope with future risk. Numbers can document past realities; but, unfortunately, man cannot yet reduce future risk with number-based formulas. The acceptance of number-based future forecasting encourages ignorance in the present. Your own planner, stock broker, securities registered representative, or CPA is, probably, using a "diversification model" to validate recommendations. This is what it could look like:

1. Average return
2. Standard deviation
3. Correlation coefficient
4. sharp ratio

Isn't this "super and professional!" There is also always something new within a model; so refinement is what occurs, rather than trying to justify the validity of this approach. Refinement is more professional than Socratic justification (which would be philosophical, and philosophical is out!).

WHY QUESTIONTHE APPROACH THAT FEEDS? Product is the name of the game – not value. There is no real concern for substance as numbers have replaced this concern. Anyway, how do you stuff value and substance into computers which do not provide common sense but regurgitate only information.

Risk/reward analysis models are easier to reproduce that judgment based upon wisdom flowing from experience and, perhaps, common sense. How many "experts" emphasizing "portfolio design and implementation" have made more real money for their clients than themselves? A theory which always offers an appealing investment is, at best, a self-serving tool for the server offering a short cut to planned ignorance.

Marketing-driven recommendations of variety are an excuse to have CONSTANT availability and a short cut to avoid spending time necessary to become properly informed. Think how functional it is to always have a different appealing product at a time when yesterday's product is suddenly unwanted in the harsh glow of unavoidable realities in the present. Recommendations of variety have been at the expense of passive investors for the benefit of the recommender. It seems most of the people in this process, on both sides, have not noticed.

In the past, I bought the MPT approach. Why not, everyone with more experience and better credentials did. Bank trust investment officers, mutual fund portfolio managers, really almost everyone now uses MPT with variations. People brag about outperforming averages – can you imagine, they did better than the average of buying one of everything – what tremendous justification.

I bet people at the source, the wealthiest people, know diversification is bull, horse or chicken poop! They do not green mail the averages. Why do mailers only pick our one company or target at a time? Black mail works best when you know something no one else does and concentrate your knowledge.

The Modern Portfolio Theory along with it best friend diversification, depends on the unknown and the unknowing.

The best way for passive investors to side step this fabricated, unrealistic approach to the future is to concentrate on what can be known. If you buy, in the present, the substance of tangible values and the substance of a future plan to enhance values, then the future will unfold in a more predictable way.

The underlying assumption of MPT is not valid, and the common sense and empirical proof is to be found in the consistently inconsistent results of the past. Passive investors have been exploited by MPT – as numbers are easier to prove for than wisdom. **Wisdom cannot be number-crunched.**

MPT is the product of a market society, perhaps, in its last stages in the US – if we do not reject the security of ignorance. We now produce less real products, so we consume the products of other nations and are a debtor nation. We have a new more important product – than a real product – it is called service. I have heard that Cleveland, where I live, is now headed toward a service economy. I heard three years ago that Indianapolis had made the transition to a service economy. I know everyone opens clusters of fast food stores and fast car buying stores. Everything has been speeded up except speed limits.

We live in a high consumption, semi-low industrialized economy and have given away – for free – our technology. We have progressed to this point with the thought that the market mechanism fulfills prevailing social purposes best (**only if the consumer is rational and informed**). Central, macro planning has never really caught on, as it is perceived to interfere with our Lone Ranger Mentality. Multinational corporations may ultimately provide peace; but stable culture dishes for money are often overturned by raw, unreasonable emotions – look at Beirut. Stop and think because all of this influences the way we act or do not act as uninformed consumers, uninformed voters, and as uninformed investors. Ignorance is bliss – but also a leading cause of failure.

Before finishing this chapter, think about where we put our capacity for reason and why we choose to not question the theories which govern our daily lives. Where has the Socratic Method gone? (Maybe someone stuck it in a micro wave and it will not pop!)

MPT is a prime example of how we have turned our backs on reason to embrace simplistic "voodoo" investment practices. Perhaps as our economy, societal structure and the nature of life have become increasingly more complex we have turned toward oversimplification to protect ourselves from the insecurity of facing the complex and the unknown. We have turned to things we can control, or do not have to control, like computers and McDonald's hamburgers. McDonald's helps us to avoid the decision as to what belongs on a burger – and computers need input to give us output – simple.

Investing can be made simple with a "diversified asset allocation model." All you need to do is buy enough products to achieve numerical diversification – so your portfolio can be "properly positioned."

Wizards are not dead; they live on and on. In wizard fashion, they have transformed themselves from people wearing gaily colored long gowns and turbans into professors wearing black flat topped hats and long black robes.

Modern Wizards have PhD's, computers, numbers and formulas which protect them from failure by standard deviations and diversification – unfortunately, modern Wizards also protect themselves from reality by ignorance.

B. The Stock Market: Financial Investment Versus Real Investment (Chapter 4)

The stock market formerly was a place where savings were invested in corporate growth. We have lived, for some time, in a forward-looking economy, where personal savings have been invested to participate in the growth of corporate values. Corporations typically retained earnings to generate future growth, and all of this growth took 5 to 10 years to be realized.

The process works when investment is real rather that financial. Real investment produces improved, more productive, and more innovative plant and equipment which leads to increased GNP. Real is different that financial, because financial investment may only be reflected by a larger or lower net worth which is not translated into economic growth.

If the stock market is a mechanism for issuing new securities, bonds, or stock, and if these new securities produce real investment, then our economy benefits. If the stock market becomes an arena of financial masturbation, then our economy suffers, as real investment is lost in the mad scramble to shuffle dollars.

We live in an investment-driven consumption-driven economy. Investments in corporate growth have become more financial than real. We have switched to consumption investments, and personal savings available for real investment are less.

The misdirection of savings occurred in the late 1920's when the stock market soared and "investors" gobbled stocks on margin (leverage) in order to be in the market while stock prices soared due to unbridled speculation.

I am not trying to become an economist, as I specifically decided in college to participate as a minor rather that a major. I do feel however, it is time to tale a common sense look at what is actually happening today, because without real investment we all lose.

Perhaps corporations have also lost their way and now are primarily concerned with financial investment, rather than real. Short-term profits are not the goal of real investment. Corporations who purchase other corporations and then liquidate profitable divisions are not creating productivity but destroying. Corporations who have not attempted to produce better future quality have lost their way – look at GM, steel, and others who have diversified rather than re-investing in that they knew or who just took earnings as giant bonuses at the expense of real investment and at the expense of shareholders who did not receive appropriate dividends.

Perhaps shareholders have lost their way because corporations have not really shared profits in a meaningful, consistent way. Real investment cannot occur when speculation is the rule. Stock options given to shareholder executives are financial (which may be okay) but often motivate executives to manipulate corporate earnings in the short term to improve stock prices rather than corporate productivity, quality, or future real value.

As the current bottom line has become all important, the future has been sacrificed. This is not a new observation, but it has not yet sunk in.

Perhaps the investment community is responsible, as well as investors and corporations. One thing for certain, the investment community profits from either financial or real investments; but if there is too much emphasis on real, there will not be as much to recommend; hence, incomes and profits for investment people and investment firms suffer. Because the investment community controls the direction of investments as the mechanism and conduit between savers to corporations, and from corporation to corporation, the motivation of fess geometrically outweighs the motivation of economic responsibility. Integrity toward real recommendations of value is displaced by the profit motive – so financial recommendations are fabricated by all sorts of investment theories, backed by The Modern Portfolio Theory of Investing, to induce investors to invest in variety rather than substance. Whether this is wrong or not is not the problem. The problem is how long can investors tolerate losing dollars in a GRATER, and how long can we survive as a world leader as the largest debtor nation of all time?

I have read that personal savings in the U.S, hovers, annually, around 5 percent, which is the lowest rate of savings of any major industrialized nation in the free world. I do not know how much of this percentage is turned into real investment, but I bet the ratio of real investment to financial investment is, now, heavily in favor of financial.

Is we lose so much of the real investment power of our savings to financial investment, maybe we should take a new look at how our stock market no longer serves the purpose for which it was created. Certainly, the stock market provides absolute uncertainty for investors who prefer financial to real investments, as financial investment will never affect the nexus of an investment in a positive way.

If we could find a way to redirect our savings from financial speculation back into real investment for long-term corporate growth and economic stability, we would not need to contrive a computer-driven, number-based reality to provide us with an excuse to invest in diversification.

We must find a way to get back to fundamentals. We must focus on the value of positive substance and begin to invest in corporations who refuse to pander to short-term, stock option driven price priorities and reserve our savings for real investment.

Real investment could be encouraged by dividend payments to share-holders and by the government making dividend payments deductible, at least for publicly-held corporations. Certainly there could be more thought given to disallowing financial manipulations that actively waste dollars necessary for real investment.

More real investment is what our country needs and, ironically, what passive investors need as well for predictability. Real investment is to be found in the substance of improved products, more productivity, and innovation. When this occurs, profits and corporate values, often, increase; and this could be reflected in higher dividends to push stock prices. As an investor, you must begin to reject financial over real investment for your own good as well as the good of corporate America! Certainly we are investing more for the good of investment firms than any other concerned entity or needy entity!

In the final analysis, we have tons of special interest but no common interest; and common interest, sometimes, might serve all the special interests better in the long run.

Passive investing with savings in real investments would not only be better for our economy in the long run but would provide ore substance for investors to depend on.

Investing in stock market gyrations to participate in deviations deemed to be standard, is deviant! Maybe it is time to focus more scrutiny on the chaos structured into investment theories which encourage participation rather than the production of long-term, positive substance leading to real success.

Some investment manager, specializing in "liquid investment" (that is to say stocks and bonds actively traded in a market), stipulate they are long-term investors. This is true is they invest primarily in "real" investments; but in practice it seems this reason is offered to elude judgment in the near term, as their portfolios, more often than not, concentrate on financial investments and diversification.

Do you think we can return to a position of economic world leadership as a service economy? Fast food, fast plumbing, and jiffy lubrication for the world? I do not want my children to live in a jar of Vaseline – do you!

HOW MUCH REAL SAVINGS CAN WE AFFORD TO LOSE TO FINANCIAL INVESTMENTS DISSIPATED BY MARKET VOLATILITY?

How much stronger is a country with real economic strength generated by industrial productivity, quality, and innovations? Will defense spending offset trade imbalance and deficit spending in the long term?

The stock market can be an important arena to generate real investment – but we have turned from the real and we have turned from positive substance, to the world of illogical, invalid, fabricated, number-based investment theories in order to average risk in an economy increasingly devoted to financial investing and service businesses!

Perhaps passive investors could lead a charge against the unreal, as passive investors are footing the bill by sacrificing their savings on an altar of financial investments motivated by short-term greed in lieu of long-term success.

Trading is the real name of the game, liquidity is more important that determining substance, and success for passive investors is as elusive as knowledge of the future is in the present.

Economists tell us we live in a forward-looking economy, but it is our responsibility to create something real in the present – to produce something real in the future to look forward to! We appear to have one foot in the looking glass – think about it – is Wonderland where we really want to be?

Investing as a shareholder can be more predictable if you invest in a corporation which practices real investing. Investing in the stock market, motivated by high-tech equations, is not likely to be less that a volatile financial experience.

Investing in real estate, also, must be real to participate in values. Over-building is not real without demand, so avoid partnerships which practice financial investing. (The next three sections will explain how to do this.)

Real investing is the best way to avoid Wonderland.

C. The Predictability of Substance Theory (PST) Should Replace the Modern Portfolio Theory (Chapter 26)

Books about real estate, stocks, precious metals, or just planning investing share a common goal which is the exploration of a specific path to achieve financial success even though many go to extremes to avoid it.

Although financial goals are similar, it is critical to keep in mind there is a distinction between INVESTING and SPECULATION. A clear perception of this distinction is obscured by words used to rationalize, excuse, or legitimized a path toward speculation in order to give the appearance of a logical and wise path toward investing designed to remove the taint of greed from our motivations for this pattern of business behavior.

Is an investment something which has more predictable substance than less – less risk; real cash returns; verifiable book values with low leverage, i.e. well capitalized; less subject to large swings in value; economics derived from cash returns and safety of principal?

It can be assumed when we commit capital or money in order to gain by purchasing property, securities, or bonds that we are investing. Furthermore, we may also assume that the act of investing presumes a judicious approach has been followed or why would we do it! When we FABRICATE an APPROACH designed to look wise which, in fact, is NOTHING but NUMEROLOGY and then choose to not recognize this fact (based upon all empirical data available), are we not also fabricating an excuse to speculate based upon a faulty, illogical reasoning process – not based upon substance, but upon numerology.

No matter how bad GRM's and CAP rates are, the Modern Portfolio Theory (MPT) is worse because of the pervasive, widespread use of insidious stereotyped words which have allowed us to pursue mad speculation in the name of logic and reason.

MPT has allowed us to escape reality and substance and avoid the responsibility (an inescapable thought) for avoiding greed in order to avoid self-destructive investment behavior. When we value future price to earning ratios over current price to dividend ratios, something smells speculative and greedy. Are blue chip stocks within a speculative market place really conservative? Is the Dow Index, which is a function of so-called blue chip stuff, conservative if it is subject to wild gyrations in value? Are not most professional sounding stock market jingoists nothing but "wolves in sheep's clothing" not by intent but by the acceptance of form (MPT) over substance? How critically introspective is this process when our major excuse for being an unpredictable speculative arena is to be able to become liquid, maybe, by selling at market in order to get whatever cash remains, and thereby, again be in control.

Liquidity has come to mean control in an unpredictable environment. If we avoid a path to find material substance in order to determine reality through a more concrete, bottom line view of an investment, we cannot make a commitment. Why should anyone be committed to an individual investment when it was only obtained to satisfy an orderly amount of variety relative to the bizarre idea of "standard deviations"? Concern for quantifying risk has superseded a concern for value! *Why not avoid risk by obtaining value?*

I am aware that some investors, whether or not they know this, invest in Betas rather than cash on cash returns. A debt to equity ratio, i.e. amount of leverage, can affect your pocketbook well before your Beta. Where's the value? (Many planners and brokers only recommend Betas and Alphas.)

Because most passive investing is to invest in an activity in which the investor is not an expert or in control of the success of the investment – *liquidity* is perceived as control merely because once the investment has been bought the only other personal choices that can impact on the original decision are to hold or sell. If an immediate ability to sell is either eliminated or moderated by the type of investment, we feel trapped. If the arena of our investment offers little or no predictability, then we do need the comfort of an immediate back door out.

It is amazing to me how logically, bright people reason illogically from a part to a whole - from the unpredictable to the predictable. It is necessary to be able to get out of unpredictable investments fast because we all know is: a Beta, that there is no dividend, i.e. no real return, a fairy tale, and that this investment offers diversification. Liquidity is essential to diversification because it gives us control to get out fast. If we invest in P/Es, Betas, Standard deviation, and not in cash on cash returns as a function of an asset which produces income for verifiable fundamental reasons; then we better be able to get out fast because we never know why we are there until we can see some movement – either up, down, or horizontal!

The most predictability the stock market offers is to be able to get liquid fast however on October 19, 1987, many investors could not even reach their brokers to get them out so they were locked in. I do not understand why so many investors reason from liquidity and the lack of liquidity in real estate to avoid investing in real estate which can offer the predictability of substance.

Maybe I should call this obvious observation **The Predictability of Substance Theory**, as "Dr." Harry M. Markowitz's work in 1952 became a part of The Modern Portfolio Theory (MPT) – finance people love initials. We all remember that Markowitz explained the advantages of combining securities that do not move in sync. Although Markowitz "demonstrated" that portfolio risk, measured by the standard deviations of returns, could be reduced without giving up returns, he has been strangely silent about the lack of positive results.

I am trying to demonstrate that under the surface of investor thought lurks a body of scholarly numerology designed to average risk, not improve results by searching for predictability.

My Predictability of Substance Theory (**PST**) holds that numbers are less important than value. Value is a function of capital, market position – i.e. location in real estate, management, and the fundamental ability of the activity or asset to produce income to investors and the ability of the activity or asset to grow in value through an ability to generate a larger income stream to investors, rather than depending upon an inflation multiplier.

Investing in the stock market can be a function of **PST** if the company has a real market, is well capitalized, underleveraged, has good management, and distributes a decent return to investors and has a long posture of integrity to investors. This is most unusual, just as a worthwhile real estate limited partnership is unusual – but this is what every investor needs more than the perceived ability to control through an immediate out which is then called liquidity!

Predictability is obtained through value, by investing in substance to achieve value, and by viewing value as cash on cash returns achieved by the investment.

Consider whether PST will provide better returns with less risk than **MPT**. (I am not only talking about stocks.)

Most real estate public programs have sold deviant portfolio variety rather than substance. Remember, Robert Stanger is an MPT guy. If you prefer numbers and neat graphs or quadrants over popcorn, then diversify your portfolio making certain you *always* have an *optimum* ability to become liquid for control.

This chapter is not, nor anything in this book, intended to be construed as a diatribe against investing in corporate America through the specious mechanism called the stock market. My fundamental contention is that it is not logical to use investment theories and language designed to offer protection from a speculative unpredictable universe and apply this to a different investment arena like real estate. It is not logical to reason a part to the whole.

If our tax laws allowed corporations to provide dividends to shareholders without a conduit of double taxation, then it would be more predictable to invest in a company willing to provide decent returns to shareholders for the use of their capital.

The Modern Portfolio theory may, because of variety, spread risk for people putting their after-tax savings or their pre-tax dollars from tax-qualified, deferred compensation plans (i.e. pension, profit sharing, Keogh, or IRA) into a speculative arena, but it really does not improve your chance for success; it really interferes.

If you really intend to be successful, then it is clearly more prudent to search for substance and predictability whether in real estate, stocks, bonds, options or cash.

As an active advisor in real estate partnerships, as a passive investor myself, I am wiling to wait for the predictability of substance over the excitement of Betas and Alphas. I prefer to expect rather than hope, or I hope to expect instead of hope to hope!

The Predictability of Substance Theory is simple: **if you search for substance and invest only in positive, tangible substance, then future value will be more predicable in the present.** Stop counting on numbers and start relying on substance.

D. The Predictability of Substance Theory - Greed Interferes with Substance and Predictability – (Chapter 28)

Have you ever stopped to think, "I really like that guy because he is so wonderfully greedy, what a great guy"! Probably you have not. What about a Nobel Prize for factoring greed into economic theory; it had to be stated by an economist and the first one to observe the obvious got a prize!

Do you ever stop to think marketing-driven real estate partnerships, stocks, and even bonds are marketed to appeal to either latent or overt greed and all the money that had to be saved and then lost evidences the response? Very few people want to think of their conduct as greedy – especially the most greedy. You know these people. They always recognize and accuse others first of their own primary motivation.

Many passive investors must be greedy as so many have willingly invested in so little substance. Perhaps underpaid regulators are most happy when the taxpayers, who fund their salaries, lose because they are envious of the product of someone else's abilities or desire to produce more.

Maybe economists should read more philosophy, which is closely linked to the so-called social sciences of psychology and sociology. They would be less certain about living in a sterile quadrant composed of numbers which are probably created to support self-fulfilling prophecies.

The emotional nature of man is manifestly apparent as evidenced by illogical, bizarre, inhuman behavior from the beginning of recorded history. The longest continuous war in history is still playing in Ireland. Everyone is on God's side, but greed and envy, which pits the haves (Protestants) against the have-nots (Catholics) are, conceivably, the true root of the cause.

Perhaps we are happier if we avoid recognizing the risk of greed by turning to numbers and diversification, which on the surface sound technical and professional.

I gambled my way through college by playing gin and bowling. I played poker in high school but I felt I could limit my risk better by becoming involved with activities of chance requiring a higher level of skill (so I switched to gin). I never played for more than I could afford to lose even though I averaged over 200 in bowling, and usually prevailed at "Hollywood."

In retrospect, I have customarily played in arenas offering good odds but I have also been a life long (from the age of 11) crapshooter in the stock market. I know greed because I have seen it across the card table, on the faces of "board rats," and in the mirror.

I carefully try to maintain some self-awareness of this common human frailty in order to avoid the unpredictable results flowing from greedy motivations. Fortunately, I have never hand much envy, so confronting greed and facing it down has been easier for me than for some. I do, however, know greed always interferes with predictability and consistency.

I gambled to support myself not to get rich or wiped out. I must have inherited some of my father's "depression psychosis."

My favorite dictionary defines greed as "rapacious desire for more than one needs or deserves, as of food, wealth, or power; avarice – greedy. 1. Excessively desirous acquiring or possessing something, especially in quantity; covetous (envy), avaricious. 2. Wanting to eat or drink more than one can consume; gluttony." It is also important to reconfirm the meaning of the word lie, "1. To present false information with the intention of deceiving. 2. To convey a false image or impression…"

It would seem that we have contrived all kinds of kinds of postures toward investments, toward relationships, and toward ourselves to protect us from reality which if acknowledged would cause us to be unhappy with ourselves. These postures have allowed us to proceed living with excuses in order to participate in behavior motivated by greed and envy based only upon self-interest.

The first deception begins with self-deception. If we want to believe that The Modern Portfolio Theory is a tool for improved performance, rather than an attempt to justify the greedy marketing hype, and investing in unpredictable, speculative investments then, that is a choice. If we stop this kind of approach, which is self-defeating, perhaps then, we can move toward more predictability by investing in cash on cash returns, which can flow more consistently from stocks as well as real estate partnerships. I really do not see how to make precious metals anything but speculative, other than as a store of value if they stop fluctuating widely!

As a financial planner 20 years ago and as an estate analyst, I thought most people were driven to invest by the need to replace earned income with unearned income for retirement or emergencies. Building a capital base slowly, but consistently, was the goal commonly espoused. I had not thought about greed too much.

Everyone has different needs and wants, and what I am discussing only pertains to how to achieve goals with results that are more predictable as a passive investor. Of course, my passive investors are not at all passive in their own occupations or businesses, but they need to be reminded that outside of their own activities, control is best achieved by obtaining a clear view of substance, which is not the concern of The Modern Portfolio Theory (MPT).

MPT interferes with a view of the lack of substance within the stock market. Perhaps greedy corporate officers have encouraged the double taxation of dividends because it allows them to escape sharing substance with "shareholders." Is it not interesting that these corporations can buy each other's stocks for dividends that are 85 percent tax free to them? Greed is the source of MPT and is a substitute for substance, just as maintaining the double taxation of dividends is an excuse for not sharing and not sharing is a form of greed.

I know many men involved with upper-level management in Fortune 500 companies. The majority of the individuals I know have integrity. Unfortunately, the stock market as it functions, along with envious members of the press, makes these business leaders look bad, along with Leveraged Buy Outs and Green Mail.

If the market is greedy, it has to be a function of the players, primarily the players who control the market. Because of MPT and its pervasive influences on language and because stereotyped words cause stereotyped thoughts, I must consider the impact of the stock market in a book mainly concerned with real estate. The greed flowing from the fundamental movers (wirehouses and investment bankers) in control of the stock market is so strong it insidiously influences the less greedy by obscuring reality using "professional" sounding verbal behavior.

I have been licensed in the securities business for 20 years and personally have invested in stocks for 35 years, so I do have a working overview. I read *How to Make Money in Wall Street*, by Louis Rukeyser, published by Doubleday in 1974. I thought at the time it was well written and of value. Fourteen years later, I have read Rukeyser again and still think it is a valuable, lucid statement of how to functionally deal with a maze. However, it does not address the underlying lack of substance or even consider a need for change. In 1974, sixteen years ago, who could have foreseen today's market chaos and lack of concern for investing in value?

Is it effective or correct to maintain a market structure for passive investors, which is based upon so much greed? As the market stands today, greed is the driving force rather than substance. Cash paid to shareholders in the form of dividends is substance, but investors in the market are investing in indexes and price fluctuations and are motivated by psychology and emotions emanating from the greedy who hope to have their stock prices move up for every reason in the world but the reason of substance which is reflected by dividends.

Greed in real estate partnerships is less obvious. It is also essentially uncontrolled by the National Association of Securities Dealers (NASD), state regulatory agencies, and the Securities Exchange Commission (SEC). Certainly public program corporate general partners are unfamiliar with the point of diminishing return theory when they raise $400 million for fees rather than because they can get a better price for properties.

Greed is a big area and is often obscured by design. Greed is a primary basis for the failure of many real estate partnerships. Greed is the basic cause of overbuilding. Banks joined the overbuilders in a lemming-like rush which has destroyed their asset base by lending well above legal limits of required asset to loan ratios.

If we could all focus more on the greed within ourselves and stop tolerating greedy structures designed to *have* appealing numbers rather than *produce* appealing results, then maybe many of these structures will stop.

You must stop eating numbers like a gourmand, but eat more substance like a gourmet. Sometimes financial gluttony pays off, but more often will not be cured by gulping terms.

Financial hot buttons are tumors of greed and if you want better results maybe see a dermatologist; personally, I prefer a psychiatrist. (Sometimes it would be better to talk to your family vet.)

Nothing is certain, but greed is a leading cause of the "Hot Button Syndrome" of investing. It is not possible to discuss a part of the investment world without considering the whole which includes some consideration of emotions and motivations. Greed is one of the fundamental ingredients of history and current events.

Perhaps, as man has become more aliened from society and relationships, he has turned inward to focus more on self; and greed is more a function of self than concern for others.

Remember, greed interferes with the pursuit of substance; hence predictability and consistent results will suffer.

All of us need to demand a change in the lack of concern for substance on the part of the investment community. We should demand this change from the source, from the issuers, from people who recommend, and from ourselves, the people who buy.

Greed is a fundamental problem. If we can get past this universal human failing, we certainly would have a more logical, less emotional investment arena, an arena more concerned with words like substance, prudence, and conservative. Conservative may be defined as "prudent, not showy, preservative." It does not have to be scorned by greedy speculators "resistant to change" in order to diffuse attempts to remove some of the obscured lies sold to and bought by passive investors.

Maybe it is not popular to consider naked greed or talk about prudence and substance. Boring, boring, boring – nothing compared to the wantonly capricious excitement of winning or losing money – but I am convinced that it is time to deal with closet greed and either throw some of it out or gift some of it to your favorite army, perhaps one called The Salvation. Perhaps you could obtain a deduction that would no longer result in tax savings, but at least a deduction which is a reduction in a negative would be something (as a debit reduction).

Remember the trite expression. "Live by the sword die by the sword." Everyone has a choice, but swords kill fast while greed eats you up alive!

APPENDIX II

LETTERS FROM 1989

E. HENRY SCHOENBERGER

CAPITAL FORMATION PLANNING & CONSULTING

December 4, 1989

Senator George Mitchell
176 Senate Russell Office Bldg.
Washington, DC 20510

RE: FINANCIAL DARWINISM

Dear George:

Enclosed is a copy of my book, which is the outgrowth of the early draft I
sent you a year and a half ago. Also enclosed is a copy of a book review
done by the business editor of The Miami Herald which was run nationally
by other members of the Knight-Ridder chain. As you may know, in the
trade book arena, to self-publish is to acquire instant negative esteem.
As the only single-book publisher/author to have achieved national
distribution with Barnes & Noble/B. Dalton and with national press, as
well, I may now (hopefully) be regarded as an entrepreneur who published a
diligent, worthwhile book rather than as a would-be author who wanted to
see his name in print.

Recently I became an NASD member firm. As a broker/dealer in a
self-regulating environment, I am too honest to not notice my environment
is run by self-servers who design rules which they then regulate to
preserve their own incomes rather than protect the savings of investors!
I have enclosed copies of letters sent to other government members and
wonder if it is not possible for the Democratic leadership to search for a
MACRO point of view to recognize that our securities and tax laws
encouraged real estate partnerships which created geometric overbuilding
in this country, overbuilding which drained the assets from
S & L's and which is yet draining assets from national banks as they
continue to fund overbuilding (along with LBO's). I know there are
terrible problems with this equation. The ultimate problem is all of us,
as taxpayers, have to support not only the lifestyles of unscrupulous
promoters of partnerships but also the lifestyles of the self-servers who
self regulate to preserve their own world at the expense of the rest of
the country. Perhaps this is done in the name of "free enterprise;" but
when the price of free enterprise becomes exorbitant to the citizens who
must support bankrupt banks, bankrupt real estate partnerships, LBO's,
green mail, and bankrupt values, maybe the price of "free enterprise"
becomes too great. There is a new drive to return to the days of Social
Darwinism -- let's call it FINANCIAL DARWINISM.

After so much time devoted to writing a critically introspective, diligent
book, I sincerely feel I have emerged with a clearer overview of what

Senator George Mitchell
December 4, 1989
Page 2

really is wrong. I am so frustrated and depressed with the lack of
fundamental understanding as exhibited by media reporting of the
superficial pronouncements of our legislators that I sincerely wonder if
anyone has achieved any understanding of how bad this equation really has
been and still continues to be. I do not hear senators or Congressmen
honestly and intelligently discussing the scope of the material substance,
of the interrelationships, of our financial problems. We seem to be
immersed with a plague of micro-minded, self-interested, self servers.

I believe you care and others care as well. However, crucial problems
continue to be either perceived as or dealt with as micro. Separate
committees are run by senators who have aides who do not seem to
coordinate their efforts or insights in order to come up with a cohesive
plan which takes into consideration all the various interrelated problems
in order to arrive at solutions which encompass a macro overview. There
is no compatible cooperation, only special interest. From my extensive
real estate experience, I can guess at how much worse S & L's real
problems are. I see a grotesque amount of overbuilding still continuing
-- all someone has to do is get off the beltway at Bethesda to clearly see
bizarre, excessive real estate supply and yet the national banks are
allowed to fund this kind of mentality because the S & L's are dead.
Insurance companies also seem to be hell-bent on committing immolation as
well, because no one wants to get left out.

How can Congress allow Drexel-Burnham to stay in business after they plead
guilty to 19 counts of fraud (admitted felons!). Where is the SEC, or is
$650,000,000 the perfect bribe? An ordinary citizen would have been in
jail for life. SIPC may have been necessary in the past, but it is no
longer a viable organization to protect any consumer. People in the know
are in total agreement with this thought. Not only do our securities laws
NOT PROTECT the consumer, but I think there are regulators who feel the
laws are only designed to regulate disclosure, fees, net capital
requirements, and preserve the trading mechanism of our stock market,
rather than protect the consumer. There is so little consumer protection
available. I know of no one who could argue effectively that consumers
are being materially protected by net capital requirements being raised or
by regulating registered investment advisors in a more stringent fashion.
No one seems to care about having higher standards for the substance of
ethical performance. We have devalued ethics and deregulated greed, and I
firmly believe unless we coordinate our efforts to clearly look at the
benefits to be derived from seeing some self interest in the common good,
we will all go down as individuals together in a hopeless mess of
geometric deficits and leverage. All these problems are NOT ONLY CONSUMER
ISSUES, but, at the core, issues which are ruining the financial
infrastructure of our country! I addressed these issues in 1986 -- and
remember I wrote enough letters to our elected representatives to say I
told them so.

Senator George Mitchell
December 4, 1989
Page 3

So what do we do? Continue to ignore substance and treat our systemic
financial cancer with an antiseptic -- and only when an open sore becomes
visually unpleasant?

I apologize if this letter is somewhat disjointed so have enclosed an
outline of interrelated problems. I am prepared to donate time if anyone
cares enough to hear a non-self-serving, honest overview of reality from
someone with enough experience to know and with too much integrity to
avoid the truth. As a member of the investment business and as a U. S.
citizen who cares about finding some self interest in the common good (I
am not a Socialist), I am for higher standards and more rational laws,
laws which would arm well-intentioned regulators with teeth to uphold
self-evident truths. We need to move from the micro into the macro --
before it is too late to do it by choice. It is time for all who care and
see to take a political stand for self-evident truths against
self-interested, micro-minded Financial Darwinists.

I look forward to hearing from you. Thank you for caring enough to give
up living in Maine full time and giving up an income in the private
sector, as well.

Best regards,

E. Henry Schoenberger

EHS:law

Enclosures

cc: Senator Llyod Bentsen
     Senator Christopher Dodd
     Senator John Glenn
     Senator Howard Metzenbaum

P. S. Certainly I am sleeping better knowing you are there watching
       over us in your present position -- especially considering the
       wisdom of our current vice president. But it is necessary for
       our best legislators to take the unpopular, abrasive stand of
       sharing the macro truth with those of us who avoid it!

E. HENRY SCHOENBERGER

CAPITAL FORMATION PLANNING & CONSULTING

SCHOENBERGER FINANCIAL LTD.
NASD MEMBER FIRM

REAL ESTATE INVESTMENTS

LIFE INSURANCE

ESTATE ANALYSIS

PERSONAL & CONFIDENTIAL

October 11, 1989

Jonathan G. Katz, Secretary
Securities and Exchange Commission
450 Fifth Street, NW
Washington, DC 20549

RE: File No S7-28-89

Dear Mr. Katz:

Although I am a Series 39 direct participation firm with a $5,000 minimum capital requirement, I read Release No. 34-27249 with great interest. I appreciate the thoroughness, level of insight, and understanding which went into the 87 page document which I read specifically in part and then skimmed through. I have been continuously licensed in the securities business under an NASD Series 1 since 1968 and was amazed to learn there are people who become principals in the securities business with no past experience. I was gratified to learn understanding and recognition has been given to the lack of need for raising capital requirements for broker/dealers who never receive a customer's check made payable to them and who never receive any negotiable instruments which could be transferred to their own account. I appreciate there may be some small broker/dealers who, occasionally, allow a client to make a check payable directly to their broker/dealership even though knowing it is totally improper; and raising capital requirements for small broker/dealers who do accept any customer funds allows the NASD a larger measure of control which I think is very appropriate.

I have enclosed a copy of a book I recently published which will shortly be distributed by Barnes & Noble/ B. Dalton along with Walden Books and Brentano's. My book has been called by some reviewers the most important book written in recent years for passive investors and their advisors, and I would hope the SEC does not stop with improving net capital requirements but continues to review additional ways to further protect the consumer.

I think it would be of infinite value to investors if disclosure requirements were improved to stop approving prospectus' which are designed to remove liability for the issuer rather than provide adequate and accurate information to an investor. I know about Rule 425; and I know if regulators begin to review for merit, it becomes a quagmire of value judgments. I do think there are ways to establish whether

Jonathan G. Katz
October 11, 1989
Page 2

information has been disclosed adequately and accurately; and when this does not happen, it should immediately become an act of fraud in the eyes of the SEC. The SEC ought to have enough teeth to protect individual investors who would bring a fraudulent act to their attention. Currently, it would cost an individual investor over $90,000 to bring an action against a sponsor in the wonderful legal arena entitled "fraud." I would hope the SEC could become more involved with consumer protection so the SEC could lead the fight for individuals who could prove fraud to the SEC!

Disclosure requirements could be meaningfully tightened up to eliminate:

1. Misleading track records -- for example, some track records are a function of appraisals which certainly have nothing to do with an actual sale in the past but are only an estimate made by one human being with the initials MAI after their name; and, as you may know, MAI stands for "Made As Instructed."

2. The majority of prospectus' are presentations of confused and misleading information presented in an illogical fashion, sometimes even with significant information buried in partnership papers.

3. There should be more rigid guidelines regarding the reality of fees rather than what a sponsor deems to be a fee; there should be stringent requirements regarding the use of numbers which have been tweaked to appeal rather than provide and projected numbers which have no relationship to either current operating results or any achievements in the past, should be disallowed. I would even be for, in the direct participation program area, requiring sponsors to furnish a prospective investor with specific and accurate information relating current operating results to past pro forma projections in existing deals. This would be far more protective than projections (or track records)!

As I have no way of knowing to whom I should address my observations regarding disclosure, I have incorporated them into the body of this letter. Perhaps if you read my book, you may conclude I am sincerely interested in improving things for consumers which would, at the same time, improve things for people in the securities business who are sincerely interested in their customers doing well.

I would like to again restate my admiration for the people in the division of market regulation who arrived at such a lucid proposal toward net capital requirements. I would also like to volunteer my time if anyone is interested in some additional insight into how to improve disclosure

Jonathan G. Katz
October 11, 1989
Page 3

requirements which would be easy to administer and which would not be a
function of individual value judgments. I have gained a lot of respect
for the individuals I have dealt with at the NASD in the process of
becoming a broker/dealer, and you have my vote to give them a higher level
of legislation designed to provide them with sharper teeth.

As a non-knee-jerk democrat, who is more of an independent than anything
else, I do believe trusting in responsible government carried out by
responsible individuals is sometimes the only decent solution available.

Best regards,

E. Henry Schoenberger

EHS:law

Enclosure

cc: Senator Christopher J. Dodd
       Senator John Heinz
       Larry D. Hayden, CFP

E. Henry Schoenberger

CAPITAL FORMATION PLANNING & CONSULTING

Schoenberger Financial Ltd.
NASD MEMBER FIRM

Real Estate Investments

Life Insurance

Estate Analysis

October 11, 1989

The Honorable Christopher J. Dodd
Chairman, Securities Subcommittee
United States Senate
Committee on Banking, Housing & Urban Affairs
Washington, DC 20510-6075

Dear Senator Dodd:

I have enclosed a copy of my book, INVEST FOR SUCCESS, to concretely indicate to you that as a registered principal in the securities business with an NASD member firm, I share your concern for protection of the public in the financial market system. I know you are in the process of attempting to further regulate investment advisors which I believe to be an exercise in futility, and very costly.

The best way to protect public consumers in our financial market system is to change some of the basic nature of the SEC, itself. I do not know if you are aware of Rule 425, but it provides a mandate for the SEC to have no responsibility for ascertaining the adequacy or accuracy of information contained in a prospectus nor does it make approval by the SEC a representation as to the merits of the investment itself. This, essentially, is the Rule 425 statement that must appear on the front page of every public program prospectus approved by the SEC in our country. The SEC must be given a higher mandate to protect rather than regulate!

Disclosure requirements are not nearly tight enough, specific enough, or extensive enough. The way in which track records are allowed to be presented in a misleading fashion, the way in which projected numbers are allowed to be freely waved around in front of an investor's nose without regard for the substance behind the projected numbers, the overconcern for fees versus value -- is the kiss of death for any investor trying to read a prospectus. This is an area that would be vastly more important and functional to correct rather than relying upon more regulation of RIA's. I think most of the direct participation programs in this country have been issued by sponsors in order to generate an income for themselves without regard for economics. Our tax laws, in the past, encouraged this kind of behavior with the exception of real estate structures which followed the substance and intent of socially engineered tax laws in 1981. (Unfortunately, Congress did not see fit to honor the tax law of 1981 and so did not honor the tax doctrine of "Grandfathering" which thereby helped cause the massive problems occurring in the banking community today, problems fueled by geometric overbuilding flowing from the 1981 Act -- Tax Law Churning in its purest state!)

29125 Chagrin Boulevard · Pepper Pike · Ohio 44122 · (216) 831-6368

Senator Dodd
October 11, 1989
Page 2

If the Senate is really interested in consumer protection, then give the
SEC the teeth it needs to allow an individual investor to complain to the
SEC itself about fraud and then allow the SEC to prosecute the sponsor who
furnishes fraudulent disclosure. As things stand currently, it would cost
an individual investor about $90,000 in legal bills to begin a fraud
complaint in civil court. Make it easier for an individual to bring an
action against a RIA. Why not establish consumer arbitration boards at
the regional NASD level with the power to recommend prosecution to the
SEC.

The Securities Exchange Acts of 1933 and 1934 badly need amendments
designed to tighten requirements to inflict pain for people who would
provide products rather than investments to the consuming public. Issuers
of "investment products" have tweaked numbers to appeal rather than
provide. We have allowed our stock market to go from an arena of real
investment (which was the original intent) to what is now, as Heilbroner
and Lester Thurow would term, an arena of financial investment. I call
the stock market a giant arena of financial masturbation, as we no longer
produce anything but now only manufacture fees based upon LBO's, rumors,
and unregulated greed. (I know there is more to it than this, but it
really is a terrible problem.)

I have enclosed a copy of a letter I sent to each member of the Senate
Finance Committee in 1986 and would like you to know the FBI tapped me in
1987 as a function of this letter -- I believe. I also provided some
extensive information to George Mitchell prior to TRA86, who was
interested in what I thought as we had met some years before at a
democratic meeting to support John Glenn for the Presidency. I am a card
carrying member of the ACLU, I am not a knee-jerk liberal, nor am I a
member of the republican party which seems to not care about people. In
my book I talk about how we need to find some self interest in the common
good, or I think our financial infrastructure will become increasingly
more shaky and corrupt. I talk about how we have deregulated greed and
how our Congress has become a group of "tax law churners."

I greatly appreciate how much (caring and honorable) members of the Senate
or Congress give up of their personal lives and income to become involved
with public service, but I think it is time for the best people there to
establish more of an overview (macro) and then try to fixate on real
problems. The way in which people recommend investments is a problem.
The best way to solve the problem is to attack the source of the
investments and how investments are produced to provide appeal rather than
economic results. I think it is time for those of us who care and those
of us have an ability to see to do more to eliminate malignant cancer and

Senator Dodd
October 11, 1989
Page 3

understand it enough to prevent it rather than primarily focus on more
medication to cope with it, after it has riddled our being. Our lack of
reason with regard to the lack of substance in our securities markets is
the cause not the lack of advice. Bad advice is only a symptom. Why not
get more involved with the fundamental substance of the real issues -- for
a change!

I would hope it is time to more appropriately focus on the regulation of
institutionalized greed. We cannot survive the geometric overbuilding of
our country, now funded by insurance companies and banks (as S & L's are
tapped out or dead). I do not see how our financial infrastructure can
survive the massive debt of LBO's and government spending (including all
the Social Security funds), not to mention the Third World. RIA's are
nothing to admire; but when Drexel continues and laws do not improve -- we
must be living in a bizarre joke from the theater of the absurd.

              Best regards,

              E. Henry Schoenberger

EHS:law

cc: Larry D. Hayden, CFP
    Senator John Heinz

P. S. You will also protect consumers (U. S. Citizens) better if you
     personally attempt to eliminate Tax Law Churning, etc. Why not
     reinstitute capital gains but eliminate the 5 percent surcharge
     on "middle incomes" and raise the top bracket to 33 or 35 percent!

FINANCIAL DARWINISM
1987 OUTLINE

I.   Contributory Negligence

- Deregulate greed (irresponsible legislative micro behavior)
- Deregulate stupidity

    Allow banks, S&Ls, and insurance companies to participate in too many businesses beyond the scope of their experience or expertise and run these special units with inexperienced, credentialed number-crunchers who live inside a computer

- Lost our way ethically and philosophically

    Green mail is deemed to be not black mail

    Program trading for the good of a firm at the expense of individual "shareholders"

- 1981 Tax Act (irresponsible legislative micro behavior)

    "Social Engineering" encouraging too much tax leverage in the form of "interest-free" loans of tax dollars – and tax-exempt bond financing

- Geometric overbuilding fueled by 2:1 real estate tax partnerships

    S&Ls, banks, and insurance companies fund geometric building

- Lack of regulatory controls
- Lack of Congressional macro concerns

I. Garn-St. Germain Depository Institutions Act of 1982 – HR 6267; Public Law 97-320: deregulated greed and stupidity. Has caused massive problems!

- Horrendous glut of new uneconomic construction
  Lack of tenants
  Lack of revenue
  Non-current bank loans, more and more of same
- No one ever says "No."
  Against "free enterprise" (which may be too costly to be regarded as free)

II. Securities laws provide no consumer protection:
- SEC basic concern to protect markets
- NASD only regulates to protect self-serving board of governors who are elected to self regulate
- State securities divisions (once again) have more concern for serving rules than investor protection of <u>material substance</u>
- As long as investment can be packaged to fit rules it's OK – no concern for positive substance. (Note: I can furnish lawmakers with meaningful parameters, which may be administered without creating the problem of non-objective personal slants.)

III. Security laws have failed – This is self evident:
- The 1933 and 1934 acts, along with SIPC, are not functional in today's complex morass of greed and self interest – with a total lack of concern for the common good

IV. Banking laws have failed, as they no longer functionally exist

V. Financial "Social Darwinism" is now the financial ethic:
- Schumpeter – maximize profits – period
- Survival of the fittest

- No sense of macro. Micro thinking has created the most vulnerable ex-premier economy in the history of man American quality has been shoved aside to improve short-term P/E ratios to push stock prices, like commodities; stocks are now a commodity, absurd and disastrous! **And CEO compensation/Greed the only thing that matters.**

VI. We are hopelessly now adrift in a sea of TOO MUCH LEVERAGE:

- Tax leverage from the past still destroying the present of millions of taxpayer citizen-investors
- Government spending leverage called "deficit spending"
- Third-world debt
- LBOs – unbridled corporate debt

  No macro awareness of reality

  State, county, and municipal debt

VII. Tax Reform Act 1986:

- Dishonored tax doctrine of "grandfathering" to protect honest taxpayers who responded with integrity to intent of 1981 "social engineered" tax incentives
- Established precedent that a tax law can now be an OUTRIGHT LIE
- Helped cause real estate collapse – limited partner defaults
- Created lowest tax bracket for highest income taxpayers
- Why not shift surcharge to above $170,000?
- Institute lower capital gain rates for taxable incomes below $250,000 phase out totally for those with earned taxable incomes above $250,000 (i.e. like tax credit phase outs)
- Try to remember capital gain rate helps small taxpayers by lessening double taxation on their invested savings (which were taxed prior to being saved). This was original reasoning.

VIII.   TAX LAW CHURNING
- Should be illegal; tax bills should remain unchanged for 5-10 year minimum
- Grossly irresponsible legislative myopia

IX. Taxpayer results (human disasters)
- Hundreds of billions of real estate either foreclosed or imminent - funded by partnerships, S&Ls, banks, and insurance companies (investors ultimately foot the bill)
- Investor losses staggering from RELPs (taxpayers foot this bill)
- Investor losses staggering from huge tax bills due IRS upon foreclosures which create a taxable event (taxpayers again)
- Investor (citizen/taxpayer) pays for:
  RELP losses
  Tax bills on foreclosures
  Taxes to fund S&L and bank failures
  Investors are taxpayers who must pay triple damages

Conclusion:

We now have a better skyline nationally, but more homeless sleeping in the streets below.

Legislators continue to blame everyone but their own irresponsible, special interest, functionally uninformed, micro mindsets

Even if our press did care enough, no one tells enough of the truth for the press to really understand; as their job has never been that of a tax, real estate, or business specialist.

Members of the Fourth Estate ought to be reminded they have no background or direct, functional, hands-on experience in order to know what has been not understood or left unspoken. And most members of

Congress should be reminded of this, as well. Keep in mind the American Heritage Dictionary defines lying as "the omission of significant information."

It is now time to establish total awareness of actual reality and move from micro thinking to macro to eliminate "Financial Darwinism."

We must attempt to philosophically search for a better, clearer view of reality. Begin a new search for truth by re-examining the mistakes of the past and the fabric of the present – if we want a real future.

We must regulate greed and stupidity. Replace "free enterprise" with ethical enterprise – and determine economic rewards for finding some self interest in the common good, or we will consume each other from within.

We must recognize we are now living with the ethic that "Financial Darwinism" is OK – just like Social Darwinism was OK at the turn of the 20th century.

CPA/CE 1987